THE FASTING GIRL

ALSO BY MICHELLE STACEY

Consumed:
Why Americans Love, Hate, and Fear Food

A TRUE VICTORIAN
MEDICAL MYSTERY

THE
FASTING
GIRL

Michelle Stacey

JEREMY P. TARCHER/PUTNAM
a member of Penguin Putnam Inc.
New York

Most Tarcher/Putnam books are available at special quantity discounts for bulk purchases for sales promotions, premiums, fund-raising, and educational needs. Special books or book excerpts also can be created to fit specific needs. For details, write Putnam Special Markets, 375 Hudson Street, New York, NY 10014.

Jeremy P. Tarcher/Putnam
a member of
Penguin Putnam Inc.
375 Hudson Street
New York, NY 10014
www.penguinputnam.com

Library of Congress Cataloging-in-Publication Data

Stacey, Michelle.
The fasting girl : a true Victorian medical mystery / Michelle Stacey.
p.   cm.
ISBN 1-58542-135-9
1. Fancher, Mary J., 1846–1916. 2. Eating disorders—Patients—Biography.
3. Compulsive behavior—Case studies. 4. Women—Mental health.
5. Anxiety in women. I. Title.
RC552.E18 S725   2002   2001052734
362.27—dc21

Printed in the United States of America
1   3   5   7   9   10   8   6   4   2

This book is printed on acid-free paper. ∞

Book design by Michelle McMillian

TO MY PARENTS

CONTENTS

THE
FASTING
GIRL

The Hunger Artist

One of the most curious experiments, from a physiological point of view, ever made in this City, is now in progress in Clarendon Hall, East Thirteenth-street.

—*The New York Times*, July 4, 1880

IN 1880, the curtain was about to rise on the age of neurosis. In that year, a new book titled *Neurasthenia* defined a condition of general malaise, attributed to the stresses of modern life, and laid the groundwork for our current understanding of common psychological maladies like anxiety and depression. At the same time, at Harvard, William James (a neurasthenic himself) had started writing his seminal *Principles of Psychology*—a task that would take more than a decade. In Vienna, Freud was completing his course of study at the university, which would award him an M.D. degree the following year. And in New York, in the dog days of August, an eccentric little man named Henry S. Tanner was writing a footnote to that incipient history of neurosis by making a spectacle of himself. The oddest aspect of his contribution was that it appeared at first glance to be not about the mind at all, but about the body and its mortal limits.

At seven-twenty a.m. on August 5, Dr. Tanner awoke from a fitful sleep and called for a glass of water—although he knew from experience what the result would be. After eagerly swallowing three ounces, approximately the amount in two shot glasses, Tanner was seized with a paroxysm of vomiting. Water alone was keeping him alive, but it was also, paradoxically, making him unbearably sick. He shortly thereafter fell back into light sleep, and slept until nine twenty-five a.m.

The details of one middle-aged man's digestive difficulties would normally have gone unremarked by anyone other than concerned family members, especially in the late Victorian era, when "dyspepsia"—an umbrella term for all manner of stomach troubles—was considered the inevitable wage of modern man's frenetic and mechanized lifestyle. But instead, a precise roster of Dr. Tanner's agonies appeared on the front page of the next day's *New York Times,* and included not only every episode of vomiting that followed, but every moment of nausea or reverie, and every mustard sponge-bath or alcohol-vapor bath administered in the hopes of relieving his symptoms. Many such details had appeared on or near the front page of the *Times* for several weeks already, with the narrative becoming daily more urgent.

The reason for this unusually personal and detailed coverage was itself quite out of the ordinary: Tanner, a temperance-boosting, unorthodox physician from Minneapolis, had undertaken to demonstrate for New York—and indeed for the entire country—the excruciating effects of starvation on a human being. August 5 was the thirty-eighth day that he had existed on nothing but water, and his body was exhibiting the extreme effects of such deprivation. He was listless and feeble, and like a newborn baby craved a nap every few hours, during which he lay in a huddled heap with knees drawn up. His stomach rejected almost every swallow of water, and when he vomited he ejected fragments of decomposed mucous membrane.

Not many people would freely choose to visit such ghastliness upon themselves. Tanner had ostensibly offered up his body in the name of science—but he displayed, as well, a strong sense of thoroughly modern media savvy. He did not squirrel himself away in a dim and private laboratory for the duration of his attempt to live forty days without food (an interestingly biblical length of time). Instead, Tanner rented Clarendon Hall, on East Thirteenth Street in Manhattan, a public meeting place, and sat down to his task in full view of visiting newspapermen, medical men, and hordes of average citizens eager to see a medically sanctioned sideshow. From the first days, his public display attracted the curious, who shelled out twenty-five cents (fifty in the later, even more dramatic, days of the fast) to view the suffering Tanner. Six days into the fast, the newspapers were already speculating on two key questions: Would he die? Would he go insane and become a raving lunatic? By the end of the first week, Tanner found the crowds overwhelming. When a Friday-night group of rowdy, cigar-chomping spectators pushed into the hall, perfuming the fetid, malarial July air with their bodily scents, Tanner was disgusted and sickened. His medical watchers imposed a new rule: Only reporters and physicians would be permitted into Tanner's inner sanctum.

But, as one reporter remarked, "the public, invited at first to visit him, now refuse[d] to keep away," and Tanner was by nature garrulous. His suffering made him restless, and he often couldn't resist strolling the hall, his attendants alongside, and indulging in lively discussions with members of his constantly changing audience. By the end of July, as he approached a full month without food, ticket totals were nearing $1,000 a day, and the ladies in particular were fascinated and full of sympathy for his agony. Various female admirers brought the short and (formerly) stout fifty-four-year-old physician bouquets of flowers and offered to serenade him with songs. Public figures—politicians, generals, famous physicians—paid their respects.

Dr. Tanner's remarkable fortitude may have been driven equally by scientific curiosity and a lust for publicity, but he claimed that its deepest motive was altruism. He said he wanted to support by his self-starvation the reputation of a woman who had lately become famed, whether willingly or not, for her own self-starvation. That woman, a bedridden, soft-spoken wraith named Mollie Fancher, had a year and a half before been the subject of sustained media attention that made Tanner's daily coverage look modest by comparison. It was the presence of Fancher, variously called the Brooklyn Enigma or the Brooklyn Fasting Girl—also variously called a miracle or a fraud—that shifted Tanner's experiment in starvation from the realm of the body to the realm of the mind, or the spirit. As he neared the end of his fast, a minister at Manhattan's Seventh Street Methodist Episcopal Church spoke of Tanner's efforts, and of his own profound regret "that so many members of the medical profession paid attention only to muscle and bone, and failed to recognize the existence of the invisible, spiritual, and eternal. . . . The forces in man are not wholly material. . . . We have a power in us that we don't understand."

Mollie Fancher claimed to be in touch with those forces and powers, and part of her claim rested on this: that, she said, she had lived without food, not for forty days like Tanner, but for twelve years (give or take the very occasional nibble of fruit or cracker). The fact that some highly respected citizens actually believed her was the impetus both for a fracas that encompassed many of the ambient late-Victorian ideas about mind and soul, faith and science, and for a fame that would virtually eclipse its human subject. Fancher was, in fact, one of those most intriguing of historical figures: one whose prominence is powerful but brief, and whose legacy lies not in what she herself accomplished but in what she ignited. This woman, whose name is unfamiliar today, who spent fifty years confined to her bed in the same unchanging bedchamber—while the Brooklyn streets around her home metamorphosed from unpaved paths to twentieth-century electric-lit cobbled avenues—became a lightning rod for some of the largest intellectual storms of the time. Food, its intake or its avoidance, was only the beginning.

CHAPTER ONE

The Accident

It is better to believe a little than too much.
—*The New York Times,* December 15, 1878

There is very little as a matter of fact, in the great domain of nature, that
we actually understand.
—Abram H. Dailey, *Mollie Fancher, the Brooklyn Enigma,* 1894

ON JUNE 8, 1865, eighteen-year-old Mollie Fancher went shopping in Brooklyn, New York. Two months short of her nineteenth birthday, she was tall, well made, willowy, with light wavy hair and an oval face. Her features were regular, and a photograph made around this time shows eyes with a serious, direct gaze. Mollie was active and energetic, and on this day she took brisk, hearty steps along the bustling sidewalks of Fulton Street—named for the forward-thinking Robert Fulton, who in 1814 had established the first ferry service linking Brooklyn and Manhattan. Her arms were full of packages; her thoughts lingered on an impending journey to Boston, and on her recent engagement to a respectable young man, John Taylor. She was, at that moment, all that mid-Victorian convention could require of a teenage girl.

But on this hot, oppressive June day, amid the chaos of dust and horse traffic and noise that was Brooklyn—then still independent of New York City, and the third-largest city in the United States—Mollie's regular progress along the path of middle-class Victorian propriety was about to come to a halt. That path had, in the sophisticated yet also oddly provincial milieu of Brooklyn society, its accepted stations: graduation from the select Brooklyn Heights Seminary for girls; attendance at the Brooklyn Yacht Club regattas and various strawberry festivals and musical performances that enlivened summer days and evenings; marriage to a suitable young man; the bearing of several children; the grace of middle age. Mollie had already experienced interruptions in this progress, including the early loss of her mother and a horseback accident at fifteen, but now she was back on stride. When that stride was next broken, it would be permanently, and in a way that not only would change her life, but would affect the lives of hundreds, even thousands, of people she would never meet.

Mollie boarded a streetcar, a trolley-like vehicle pulled along railroad tracks by a team of horses. Most of the old horsecars, which would be replaced by electric streetcars in Brooklyn beginning in 1892, traveled, at their swiftest, at a speed of only six miles per hour over the stone-paved thoroughfares. Even so, they could on occasion be lethal. That very day, June 8, *The Brooklyn Daily Eagle* had published an irate letter to the editor of the newspaper under the heading "Dangers of Railroad Travel." In it the writer, signing himself a "sorely bruised Sufferer," described his misadventures on a DeKalb Avenue car: He "managed to get a foothold on the rear platform" of a very full car, but when the vehicle rounded a corner at top speed, he "without any warning was suddenly landed in the street, to the detriment of his body, clothing, etc., and his watch thrown out of his pocket." The driver did not even stop the car after this unnamed "Sufferer" landed on the paving stones. And a week later, the *Eagle* reported that a young girl named Henrietta Cook had died of injuries received when she was run over by a streetcar. Again, the driver of the car did not stop after the accident.

Mollie Fancher climbed aboard one of these rollicking vehicles, laden with her packages, the lower half of her body encased in the full,

A view of Fulton Street in Brooklyn in the mid–nineteenth century, looking southeast from the ferry landing. Until the Brooklyn Bridge opened in 1883, the Fulton Street Ferry, begun in 1814, was the city's primary link with Manhattan; the bustling boulevard, the oldest street in Brooklyn, was the city's most popular business district. Mollie Fancher went shopping here on what would be the last day of her life as a normal, healthy Victorian schoolgirl. (THE MUSEUM OF THE CITY OF NEW YORK)

cumbrous crinoline that was the cross borne by every fashionable lady of the Civil War era. When she was ready to descend to the street at her stop, she signaled the conductor. He rang the bell, the car was halted, and Mollie stepped from the rear platform to the pavement. The conductor rang the bell again for the car to move forward, turned away, and walked into the interior of the car. But Mollie had not fully descended, and she was thrown to the ground by the sudden movement of the car. Worse, her crinoline skirt caught in an iron hook at the back of the car, so that instead of simply being dashed to the paving stones she was then dragged over them.

For nearly a block Mollie was pulled behind the horse-drawn streetcar, her body turning around and around as her skirt twisted into a rope. She lost consciousness, as horrified onlookers shouted to the driver to stop. Finally his attention was gained, and Mollie's battered body came to rest. She was disengaged from the hook and carried into the nearest shop—a butcher's. "It was long before she could be removed to her home," wrote Abram Dailey in his biography, *Mollie Fancher, the Brooklyn Enigma,* published in 1894. Eventually, friends conveyed her to her house, at 160 Gates Avenue, and to the distressed care of her family. She would never leave that house alive again.

In that manner, the Fulton Street car fulfilled its destiny as an agent of careless destruction, and Mollie Fancher began to fulfill hers as a challenge to Victorian thought and belief. She kept the twisted rope of a skirt to the end of her days, a poor rotting symbol of her cataclysm.

In the later nineteenth century, modern urban existence was plagued by risks not altogether unlike those of today, despite that era's apparently slower and less alienated lifestyle. Danger, disease, random violent crime, plain bad luck—the newspapers of Mollie's youth are full of gruesome tales; only in some details is the passage of more than one hundred years discernible. In the Brooklyn of 1865, workmen fell from ladders, scaffolding, and riggings at the Navy Yard and at building construction sites, breaking arms, legs, necks, dying sometimes on the spot, sometimes later at the hospital. A surprising number of people were injured or killed by lightning. Heartbroken young people, men and women alike, committed suicide by arsenic poisoning or other means. Innocent citizens were burned by vitriol thrown on them by persons unknown to them—a puzzling, random crime that enjoyed a brief popularity. Horses did all kinds of damage: pulling wagons over people, especially children; throwing riders to the pavement, often to their deaths. For June 5 through 11, 1865, the week of Mollie Fancher's accident, Brooklyn city records list mortality from cholera, consumption (tuberculosis), typhoid, apoplexy, scarlet fever, premature birth, stillbirth, croup, bowel inflammation, and several other ailments and accidents, for a total of 109 deaths. It was merely a piece of luck that Mollie was not in that number, her death reduced to a three-sentence paragraph in the "City News and Gossip" column of the *Eagle* (perhaps below "Arrest of a Burglar" and above "Killed by Lightning": "Schoolgirl in Fatal Horsecar Fall").

What marks the difference between these nineteenth-century ills and today's is scale and intensity: twenty-first-century threats are bigger, faster, often deadlier. We are killed not by six-mile-per-hour horses but by seventy-mile-per-hour cars; not scalded by the random terror of vitriol but incinerated, by the thousands, in a massive act of high-rise, airborne, international terrorism. Victorians were beginning to get a hint of a new world, and that awareness gave misfortunes like Mollie's a peculiar resonance. Disease, heartbreak, accidents of childbirth—those were familiar dangers, age-old threats to health and happiness. It was the newfangled perils that frightened Mollie's fellow Brooklynites most; such perils produced a special brand of fear that was only beginning to be labeled or understood. Today we might call it generalized anxiety: a sense of dread, or worry, often brought on by an overload of demands on our abilities and our time, or by an underlying apprehension of our capacity for self-destruction.

The psychologist Rollo May argued at mid–twentieth century that the roots of the modern "age of anxiety" (as W. H. Auden christened it in his 1947 Pulitzer Prize–winning poem) were planted one hundred years before, in the world that Mollie Fancher knew. "In the nineteenth century," May wrote in *The Meaning of Anxiety,* "we can observe on a broad scale the occurrence of fissures in the unity of modern culture which underlie much of our contemporary anxiety. . . . The rapidly increasing mastery over physical nature was accompanied by widespread and profound changes in the structure of human society." Those overarching structural shifts were accompanied by rapid-fire transformations in the routines of daily life, especially for people living in cities—transformations that accelerated throughout the second half of the nineteenth century.

Consider just a short list of earth-shattering Victorian innovations, beginning with the patenting of the electric telegraph by Samuel Morse in 1837 (the Western Union company would complete a transcontinental telegraph line in 1861, putting the eastern and western coasts of the United States in instant communication for the first time). Chief among the intellectual challenges that followed was the publication of *On the Origin of Species* by Charles Darwin in 1859; the work struck at the foundations of human belief in an all-powerful and benevolent deity who single-handedly created the world in the not-too-distant past, replacing that comforting vision with an unforgiving picture of brutal interspecies conflict and a godless, near-random universe. (To Victorians, the most insulting idea contained therein, of course, was the notion that noble man had actually descended from the ape.) In 1876, Alexander Graham Bell patented the telephone, and three years later Thomas Edison brought forth the lightbulb—both auguring monumental shifts in the way people spoke, read, lived. A few years earlier, in 1869, the American transcontinental railroad was completed, transforming an arduous, months-long journey into a jaunt of seven days, coast to coast. Even travel within a single building changed, with the installation of the first passenger elevator in a New York store in 1852. How could one help being nervous in this mind-expanding universe, in which the emerging world threatened to change unrecognizably in the course of a generation? How could one avoid ambient fear of all the noise and speed and light and steam? Humans had never been exposed to such phenomena; they had not yet learned to tolerate them.

In *Nothing Like It in the World,* his study of the building of the transcontinental railroad, the historian Stephen Ambrose points out that a person born before 1829 came into a world in which President Andrew Jackson traveled no faster than had Julius Caesar, "a world in which no thought or information could be transmitted any faster than in Alexander the Great's time." Ambrose argues that of any people in history, before or since, the Americans who lived through the second half of the nineteenth century experienced the greatest, most fundamental changes: electricity, telephone, telegraph, railroad. "The locomotive was the first great triumph over time and space," he writes. Those two properties are the central means for how humans experience reality; to conquer them was almost inconceivable.

Today, we understand that change inevitably brings stress. In the mid–nineteenth century, all that people knew was that they sometimes distrusted and feared these new gifts, which were also sometimes monstrosities. And while inventions like the telephone and electric light were challenging and exciting to the mind, innovations like the railroad and even the elevator demanded an actual physical involvement, a tangible demonstration of trust. When that trust was betrayed, the mind sometimes rebelled. Some nineteenth-century physicians diagnosed a new condition, "elevator sickness," believed to be caused by the effects of high speed on internal organs. Another commonly diagnosed illness, "railway neurosis," was a broader concept based on the same basic premise: the collapse of the human body—and with it the mind—when it confronted the physical reality of technology.

Freud diagnosed railway neurosis in himself in the 1890s as an anxiety or fear experienced simply from proximity to trains (self-attributed in his case, in classic Freudian fashion, to a childhood incident in which he thought he saw his mother naked while on an overnight train trip). Already for a decade or two before his description, railway neurosis had been a common medical and social phenomenon. Often it was triggered by a shock or trauma experienced on a train, and law books of the 1880s are full of suits brought against railroad companies for all manner of alleged injuries that led to fear and disability. Chief among the complaints were "railway spine" and "railway brain," in which neurological defects would appear; lawyers wrangled over whether the symptoms were genuine or faked.

In 1890 a young Kentucky woman named Mary Minogue sued Louisville Southern Rail Road, claiming that an accident on its line had caused a case of railway spine. Her lawyer argued that the impact of the collision had thrown Miss Minogue from her seat to the floor of the railway car, and that she had sustained external bruises and a great shock to her nervous system. None of her bones was broken, but after the accident she had been troubled with partial paralysis, or an insensibility in one leg from the knee down. Doctors who testified agreed that the railroad should pay Minogue damages, "since this was clearly a case of the railway spine."

Lawsuits were not limited to trains alone, or even to physical injury alone: horsecars and emotional trauma were considered equally potent. In Rochester, New York, Anne Mitchell brought suit against Rochester Railway for an incident in which she was preparing to alight from a train. As she stepped down, a horsecar was coming down the street. The team of horses rushing toward her turned at the last moment, and by the time they could be stopped, she stood right between the horses' heads. Mitchell testified that fear caused by the galloping horses made her faint and resulted in a miscarriage and subsequent illness.

It's easy to imagine that the very speed that railroad trains could reach might induce fear and anxiety in a species that had never traveled faster than a horse could run or trot; to see the landscape shooting by must have seemed like going to the moon. When one added to that the symbolism trains conveyed—the increased speed of everyday life, the personal demands of keeping pace with other denizens in a fast-growing city—even horsecars, loaded with that new breed, commuters, became threatening. Accidents were not uncommon; news stories about passengers thrown from cars or run over by them abounded. *The Brooklyn Daily Times* described in harrowing detail an

1866 incident in which a Greenwood horsecar was hit by a passenger car on the Jamaica Rail Road.

"The horse-car was badly crushed, and forced down the street at a fearful rate," wrote the reporter. "It was perfectly unmanageable, and intense excitement was created among the hundreds of people on that street. The passengers were terribly frightened." The story goes on, in cinematic style, with information supplied by a man who had been on the car that was rammed: "When the small car reached the corner of Fifth and Flatbush avenues, several persons, including two or three ladies, with a child, a poodle dog, two canaries in cages, two big carpet bags, and a man, got in; and several gentlemen subsequently took passage. At the Henry Street crossing someone called out, 'For God's sake look out for yourselves!' At the same time there were great shouting and screaming, both in and out of the car, and the harsh rumbling of a heavy car. On turning to see what was the difficulty, the passengers in the small car saw one of the large and heavy Jamaica passenger cars within a few feet, coming down with frightful velocity. The next instant it struck the small car, crushing in the rear platform, iron-work, brake, and top; smashing the wood into splinters, and glass into small pieces, and tearing the iron into fragments. Some of the passengers were thrown on the floor of the car, and the concussion hurled nearly all of them backwards." Although no one was killed, many were bruised, and several of the women on board fainted.

Another local paper, *The Brooklyn Daily Union,* described a horse-car accident later in the year that strongly evokes Mollie Fancher's disastrous encounter. In a brief entitled "Street Car Accident—Narrow Escape from Death," a reporter told how a servant, Catherine Powers, barely escaped being run over by a streetcar in front of her employer's residence. While crossing the street, holding a child by the hand, Powers tried to avoid an approaching horsecar and instead ran under the feet of a team of horses pulling another car in the opposite direction. The woman was knocked down and severely bruised by the horses' hooves. Her clothing was caught in the forward brake of the car, and she was dragged for some distance, receiving severe bruises and suffering a scalp abrasion. In Powers's case being dragged probably saved her life, because the brake kept her from being pulled directly under the wheels of the car. The child, meanwhile, was thrown to the pavement by the collision and badly bruised. Woman and child both survived, and no blame was attached to the driver.

Not only were horsecars and railways frightening and dangerous, but riders quickly discovered that mass transit could be noxious as well. In newspaper editorials and letters to the editor in the 1860s, writers sounded a modern note, familiar to New York straphangers of later eras. In "The Infelicities of Local Travel," an editorial published in *The Brooklyn Daily Times* in the mid-1860s, the writer praised and damned the new technology. Street railroads had undoubtedly contributed to the growth and prosperity of Brooklyn, he observed, yet there was still plenty of room for fault-finding. "On most of the lines of city railway, accommodations are totally inadequate, the cars are inconvenient, dirty, badly ventilated, and always overcrowded. The consequence is the great discomfort of all who use them. Is there no way to remedy these defects, and make the public accommodation accord with the interests of the companies?"

An inventive feature-writer for the *New York Herald* (anonymous, as was usually the case in nineteenth-century newspapers) in December 1878 contributed a long front-page story that gives the flavor of traveling on yet another innovation on the rapid-transit scene, the elevated railroad. In a lighthearted piece, "Rapid Transit: Serio-Comic Aspect of Elevated Railroad Travelling on the East Side / Crowded Trains and Irate Passengers / Merchants and Clerks Fighting Their Way to Hot Dinners," the writer first set the scene in its history-making context: "The establishment of the elevated railways has given rise to scenes of a novel and striking character—scenes that would make even Rip Van Winkle himself open very wide his sleepy eyes at the changes that have come over this city. When the *Herald* urged the building of these roads many people declared they would never pay and that people would never ride upon them. Now, when they have been running only a few months, it is already found that they are inadequate to meet the requirements of public travel."

The most remarkable scenes of overcrowding, this writer went on, occurred between five and seven in the evening, when the cheaper, five-cent fare prevailed. The wildest venues during these hours were the downtown stations of the East Side road in Manhattan, where there was as yet only one narrow stairway from the first landing up to the platform. When a crowded train arrived from uptown, the disgorged passengers would rush down the stairs—or they would have rushed down, had they not been wedged between the masses of passengers, many of them with bundles under their arms, who were trying at the same time to fight their way up to catch the same train. "The ticket agents' arms fairly ache from the frantic manner in which they have to throw the five-cent tickets through their little windows. And still the people come—black masses of hurrying, bustling men, scurrying home from business, with a stray woman or child in their midst, whose courage in venturing into such a dense, struggling multitude must be admired."

But the hardest part was yet to come. Once the hungry businessman, anxious for his dinner, had pushed his way through the obstructing arms and elbows and safely climbed up to the platform, he still had to get himself onto a train. The platform was long and narrow, placed between two tracks, and crowded with hundreds of people straggling from one end of the platform to the other. The questions uppermost in everybody's mind were: Where, precisely, will the train stop? Where shall I stand to be nearest one of the platform gates? Everyone knew that the cars filled up rapidly, and people who were not close enough to the gates would be left behind. As the minutes passed, the jostling and struggling and even fighting intensified for the best places—those,

Elevated trains—like this one shown passing the Manhattan offices of Harper's Weekly *in 1878—were an astounding addition to late-Victorian life. Even those that ran on the ground caused so much anxiety in people that a disease was named to categorize it: railway neurosis. In this engraving, horse traffic below and train rails above emphasize the nerve-wracking clash of old and new.*
(THE MUSEUM OF THE CITY OF NEW YORK)

the reporter explained, "nearest the edge of the platform, where the opportunities for tumbling down upon the track are excellent, but are coolly disregarded by the eager passengers."

Then perhaps a train would come, but it would be going only as far as Grand Central Depot; this news would be received with a general groan of disappointment by the crowd, most of whom were going farther north. Five or ten minutes might pass before a through train arrived—and often that train would be full and would rattle by nonchalantly without deigning to stop, while someone on the platform spied a cubic inch of space as it passed, and cried out, "It's a damned shame! There was plenty of room in there!"

By the time the desperate crowd got its chance at the next train, there was such a wild onset on the gates, and such a wedge of human bodies, that at first nobody could enter. The train, the reporter concluded, "is packed like a box of sardines and, by dint of hard fighting, the conductors and brakemen succeed in shutting the gates, while some enterprising passenger, who refuses to be left behind, tries to climb over them, and succeeds in being taken along, because to push him back now, when the signal has just been sounded, would endanger his life. Off goes the train, and the weary 200 passengers who have been left behind gnash their teeth."

These were scenes of complete novelty, and despite the writer's light tone, they were also scenes of daily social stress made even more stressful by the element of unfamiliarity. When one was faced with the real prospect of being accidentally flung on the tracks in front of an oncoming elevated train by the weight of the crowd, developing a fear of trains was not unreasonable. The forces, the very machinery, of rampant civilization could seem fearful unto themselves, exerting as they did an unrelenting pressure to change, adapt, learn new skills (such as how to squeeze oneself brazenly into a commuter train simply to get home for dinner). Railway spine or railway brain, writes one historian, "stands forth as the classical Victorian neurosis, that is, a psychocultural illness in which the human psyche collided with the changing nineteenth-century environment and gave birth to an epidemiclike neurotic illness whose form and severity are rooted in the Victorian era."

Mollie Fancher's horsecar misadventure, albeit occurring at six miles per hour rather than sixty, eventually produced symptoms reminiscent of railway spine—paralysis, mysterious neurological reactions, anesthesia (loss of feeling), among others. But even before she evinced what looks in retrospect like a "classical Victorian neurosis," Mollie had already endured, in the previous year and a half, two other misfortunes peculiar to her time and place in middle-class society. The first—dyspepsia—was so closely identified with the mid-to-late-Victorian era that some physicians and philosophers of the day took the ailment to be a physical commentary on the stresses of the age. Just as ulcers were seen in the 1950s as a response to the buttoned-down, gray-flannel-suit anxieties of the time, dyspepsia was understood by many Victorians to be the result of an involuntary roiling and twisting of the inner organs in the face of the accelerated, steam-belching pace of nineteenth-century American life.

Strictly defined, dyspepsia was a kind of glorified indigestion, but as its reputation grew, so did its range—and its moral implications. It came to symbolize modern man's abuse of his body and nerves in pursuit of pleasure and self-advancement. One of the early adherents of this point of view was Sylvester Graham, a minister and health reformer whose greatest legacy to the world is the graham cracker. Graham believed in simplicity; and his regimen of whole grains, fruits, and vegetables, and avoidance of meats and fats, bears a striking resemblance to today's recommended healthful diet. Gluttony, Graham felt, was the result of too much civilization: spices, rich cooking, overavailability of delicacies. "Gluttony and not starvation is the greatest of all causes of evil," he wrote in 1838. "Excessive alimentation is the greatest dietetic error in the United States—and probably in the whole civilized world."

Graham was joined in his suspicion of dietary indulgence by John Harvey Kellogg, founder of an extremely trendy Battle Creek, Michigan, sanatorium (his family's legacy to the world: Kellogg's cornflakes), who held that "the perversions of our modern civilization . . . are responsible for the multitudinous maladies and degeneracies which yearly multiply in number and gravity." As a result, humans were becoming "neurotic, daft, dyspepsic, and degenerate." Kellogg's remedy: natural foods, no meat or sugar, no stimulants (coffee, tea, alcohol), and a water cure that included numerous enemas.

By the 1870s, a diagnosis of dyspepsia could explain a large assortment of ills, from constipation to melancholy. Doctors were divided on how to treat the ailment, and ads for the (distinctly unscientific) medicinal treatment of dyspepsia proliferated in popular newspapers and journals. One such advertisement, for Hoofland's German Bitters, the Great Strengthening Tonic, lists under the heading "Dyspepsia, and Diseases Resulting from Disorders of the Liver and Digestive Organs" an astounding number of symptoms, including but not limited to: "Constipation, Inward Piles, Acidity of the Stomach, Nausea, Heartburn, Disgust for food, Fulness or Weight in the Stomach, Sinking or Fluttering at the Pit of the Stomach, Swimming of the Head, Hurried and Difficult Breathing, Fluttering at the Heart, Choking or Suffocating Sensations when in a Lying Posture, Dimness of Vision, or Webs Before the Sight, Pain in the Side, Back, Chest, Limbs, etc., Sudden Flashes of Heat, Burning in the flesh, Constant Imaginings of Evil, and Great Depression of Spirits." Such an array of symptoms would, in this modern age of psychopharmacology, likely prompt a prescription for an antianxiety or antidepressant agent rather than an antacid tablet—or at the very minimum the suggestion of a round of psychotherapy or biofeedback.

George Beard, a physician who became known as "the father of neurasthenia" in the 1880s for his descriptions of Victorian neurosis, considered dyspepsia the first step in what he called the Evolution of Nervousness. In his 1881 book *American Nervousness,* Beard drew a "tree of nervous illness" that progressed from nervous dyspepsia through sick-headache, sleeplessness, and hysteria, to nervous exhaustion (neurasthenia), inebriety, epilepsy, and ultimately, at the top of the tree, insanity. All of this disruption and distress, he insisted, could be traced to the stresses inherent in attempting to conquer space and time. "American nervousness," he wrote, "is the product of American civilization." Beard singled out five elements of modern life that were most culpable: steam power, the periodical press, the telegraph, the sciences, and the mental activity of women. Not that any of these should necessarily be discouraged (although he may have had his doubts about the mental activity of women), but they put new demands on the body and mind.

In women, whether they were particularly mentally active or not, dyspepsia had a special meaning. Young women (young ladies, anyway) were not expected to have hearty appetites; to do so was to be indelicate or masculine. Some level of dyspepsia in an adolescent female—picky eating, stomach pains, loss of appetite—was almost the norm. A popular health manual published in 1873 described this fashionable dyspepsia: "To dine heartily would carry with it an extreme air of vulgarity: hence, the less a young lady takes at table, the higher her preparation for refinements that are appreciated among those who think more of a fine form than of intellectual accomplishments. Light soups, rich cakes, choice fruits, and tea always, is held to be the dietary range of an exquisite woman. . . . Food most approved, and that which carries with it the endorsement of maneuvering mothers, anxiously looking forward to the establishment of their children in commanding social positions, even if the intended husband is a baboon, is a slice of dry toast, weak black tea, and an occasional teaspoonful of sweetmeats."

The manual made much of dyspepsia as "the disease of comfortable circumstances" and "that bane of pecuniary independence," and in fact it was clearly associated with the rapidly expanding middle class. "Those poor men and women," the author pointed out, "who rarely gratify their palates with rich preparations which greet the uncertain appetites of the rich, are exempt from their peculiar sufferings." Bourgeois mothers who had no necessity of physical labor could lavish their concern on fragile daughters who were never hungry, or who were taken ill by eating, while congratulating themselves on possessing pure and delicate girls. Appetite, after all, implied a carnality and a coarseness that was unacceptable in a respectable Victorian female.

Mollie Fancher's diagnosis of nervous indigestion came at the age of seventeen, as she was close to completing her studies of mathematics, music, Latin, French, and English literature at Brooklyn Heights Seminary. Her enrollment at that institution is an indication of her family's comfortable spot on the ladder of upper-middle-class Brooklyn society. An article in *The Brooklyn Daily Eagle* in June 1866 described that year's commencement ceremony, two years after Mollie's attendance at the school, as taking place "in the presence of a suffocatingly crowded and fashionable audience." Interestingly, in the face of the intellectual subjects pursued by the all-female student body, the section of the commencement address by the Reverend Mr. Thurston quoted in the *Eagle* pertained to a woman's place in the home. "The first place of an educated woman's usefulness is the kitchen," the reverend boomed. "This is woman's grand domain, her rightful sovereignty," regardless of her education. "We are prone to worship brain," he went on, "and many are forcing youthful minds to a hot-house growth, and, of course, to a weak and early decay."

Here is George Beard's worrisome mental activity of women, and in fact Beard would excoriate the educational practices of young ladies in *American Nervousness*. He cited a survey of current methods of schooling, especially for girls, conducted by a doctor in New York. The survey, he wrote, showed that "nearly everything about the conduct of the schools was wrong, unphysiological and unpsychological, and that they were conducted so as to make very sad and sorrowing the lives of those who were forced to attend them. . . . The routine of the schools was such as would have been devised by some evil one who wished to take vengeance on the race and the nation. Scarcely anything taught that needs to be taught, almost everything that ought not to be taught, and which girls ought not to know, everything pushed in an unscientific and distressing manner; nature violated at every step; endless reciting and lecturing and striving to be first; such are the female schools in America at this hour."

Mollie Fancher at sixteen, before the first of her mysterious ailments. Soon after this picture was made, Mollie began to suffer fainting spells and a nervous stomach that rejected most foods.
(FROM *MOLLIE FANCHER, THE BROOKLYN ENIGMA*)

Whether Beard's perceived "sad[ness] and sorrowing" or the Reverend Mr. Thurston's "weak and early decay" was feared to be overtaking Mollie in the spring of 1864 as she neared her graduation, it seemed that something was starting to go wrong. Thirty years later her biographer described the teenage Mollie as ambitious, rightly proud of her scholarly talents and of her high standing in her class. Those same attributes were described differently by an *Eagle* reporter in 1866, in the first article to be published about her case. "Up to the time that her nervous system gave way," the reporter wrote, "she was deemed a bright student, and stood deservedly high in one of the Montague street schools. Her books were her delight; like many another she neglected all for them, and would arise late in the morning in consequence of weakness, hasten away to school without a breakfast, fearful of being tardy, and then at evening, in her anxiety to learn her lessons, again neglect a meal for which she felt little inclination. In this manner her vitality gradually ebbed until she seemed too frail to carry the assortment of text books with which city pupils load themselves in going to and from school." Her situation, the reporter editorialized, was "an illustration of the condition of the nervous prostration to which a young person, previously healthy, may be brought. . . . It will be read with melancholy interest by all and should be particularly heeded by those to whom are confided the education of our youth of both sexes as well as parents, who allow the intellectual faculties in their children to be stimulated to an unhealthy action, and thus render them liable to all the sufferings now experienced by the young lady whose case is here partially described."

The reporter noted that Mollie's case perfectly exemplified the assault on nerves by the pace and demands of modern life—Beard's American Nervousness, coming more than a decade before Beard published his concept: "It has been held by many medical men that the remarkable vigor which characterizes the present century is a result of the preponderance of nervous energy in the races that people the earth. Where the driving, go-aheadativeness of Yankee energy and thrift is found, there is found an anatomic element known as nerves. Upon these all high pressure people build and work, and in this country they are 'run' at various rapidity, until 'Nervines,' 'Soothing Syrups,' 'Laudanum Troches,' etc., become indispensible [sic] to about half the population. It has long seemed the especial province of Americans to abuse their nerves from the cradle to the grave. . . . Over-worked and over-stimulated, the nerves are full of short-lived vigor, just the thing for a short raid as flying artillery, but utterly failing when the heavy work of bombardment is demanded." When they did inevitably fail, the result was dyspepsia, "attacks" of weakness, or even complete collapse.

What was perceived by teachers and family members as Mollie's failing health evidenced itself mainly as indigestion: her stomach rejected most kinds of food, she had "wasted away and become weak," and she was the subject of frequent fainting spells (not uncommon among Victorian women). She also had headaches and occasional coughing spells. These symptoms alarmed those around her, and it was finally agreed among her teachers and family that she be kept home from school in the hopes of restoring her health. That change proved the catalyst for the physical disasters that would transform her life.

The underlying causes—the wasting away, the nervous stomach, the weakness—may have been a sign that the emotional strains of Mollie's early life were finally asserting themselves. For her childhood had indeed been stressful, in a way that was all too common among families of the nineteenth century and before. She had experienced a great deal of personal loss in her young life. Mollie was born Mary Jane Fancher, in Attleboro, Massachusetts, on August 16, 1846, a healthy first child to Elizabeth Crosby and James Edwin Fancher, then twenty and twenty-six years old, respectively. (Mollie's death certificate and Dailey's biography give her birth year as 1848, but other records, including census reports and family genealogies, indicate 1846, which corresponds logically to the birth years of the four siblings who followed her.) Mollie was joined by a brother, William, in February 1848, when she was a year and a half old, and a sister, Georgiana, two years later. Sometime during this period the family moved to Brooklyn, settling first on Washington Avenue.

Then came Mollie's sixth year. In August 1851, the month that Mollie turned five, eighteen-month-old Georgiana died, of hydrocephalitis. Six months later another sister, Elizabeth, was born. Four months after that, in June, little William died at age four, of a heart ailment. Four children had been born to Mollie's mother by age twenty-six, and two had died. Not as stillbirths or newborns, when at least the process of bonding and the beginnings of love might be stillborn as well, but as toddlers and beyond: walking, talking personalities who had become full members of the family.

Mollie's family had plenty of company in their loss: as much as forty percent of the overall death rate in the United States in the nineteenth century represented deaths of children under five. But that prevalence didn't ease the agony of losing a child. Nineteenth-century mothers may actually have suffered more, or at least more guiltily, than mothers in previous generations. Colonial parents, inhabiting an even more uncertain, and undoubtedly a more religious, world, were more likely to interpret infant or toddler death as a sign of God's will—and therefore as something completely out of their personal control. Colonial households were also larger, and child-rearing often cooperative among friends and relatives, so that mothers tended to have less intensely close relationships with their children in their first few years.

That system gave way to much more secluded and nuclear households in the nineteenth century, in which middle-class Victorian mothers were encouraged to preside as the primary emotional and physical caretakers of their families. They began to see themselves as responsible for any illness or injury to their children—children with whom they were forming bonds far more intimate than had been the norm in the past. Women's diaries tell part of the story. When colonial mothers wrote about their young children, they tended to list physical milestones like teething and walking but to say little about the children's personalities or how they looked or behaved. Often a name was not mentioned until the child was at least a toddler, as if the mother was unwilling to attach fully until the child had a greater chance of survival. A woman who bore twelve children between 1760 and 1782, eight of whom died in infancy, described one of the deaths this way: "Sept. 5, 1767. I was brought to bed about 2 o'clock AM of a daughter. Sept. 6. The Child Baptized Mary. Sept. 7. The Baby very well till ten o'clock in the evening and then taken with fits. Sept. 8. It died about 8 o'clock in the morning. Sept. 10. Was buried."

In contrast, Victorian mothers took to recording their interactions with their children in affectionate detail from birth on, calling them "birdie" and "pet" and other nicknames and describing them as little people full of personality—sometimes in the second person, as if they expected their children someday to read over the entries about themselves. One diarist in 1848 wrote of her daughter's first steps: "At 14 months and 6 days old, you rose from your chair with great deliberation and walked across the nursery. . . . You seemed neither pleased nor surprised."

These rich mother-child relationships brought with them a terrible price, however, if the child became ill or died. For Fanny Longfellow, wife of the poet Henry Wadsworth Longfellow, her daughter Fanny's sudden death at age eighteen months was, according to one historian, "a tragedy from which [she] never recovered . . . the central event in [her] life." The loss of little Fanny not only plunged her mother into a profound depression, but also altered her relationship with her other children. She wrote in her diary that "I seem to have lost all interest in the future and can enjoy my children only from hour to hour"; she was in the grip of a constant fear of their loss. When her son Erny had pleurisy at the same time another daughter was being born, she felt "as if a great stone were hurled back upon my heart from which I had just been relieved. I have never been without anxiety for him but now it will be increased tenfold."

If Elizabeth Fancher kept a diary, it has not been preserved; but the double loss of daughter and son within a year of each other must have brought heartbreak and much fear to the Fancher home. Elizabeth Fancher may well have become seriously depressed, unable to express much love to her two remaining daughters, or perhaps seized with anxiety that they too would be taken away. The birth of another boy, James, in March 1854, almost two years after William's death, may have helped ease some of the pain of both parents (and of Mollie, who was old enough to remember and miss her younger siblings).

But a year later, precisely on Elizabeth's third birthday, came the most powerful loss any child can experience. Elizabeth Crosby Fancher died, at twenty-nine, of a slow, wasting illness whose identity is obscured forever in lost files of death certificates. Mollie was eight and a half. "The mother-child bond is so primal," writes Hope Edelman in her 1994 book *Motherless Daughters,* "that we equate its severing with a child's emotional death." Americans of the mid–nineteenth century did not yet have the psychological language for such devastation, but its toll was just as great. "The loss of a parent during childhood is one of the most stressful life-cycle events an individual can face," Edelman observes, and many children deal with that stress by burying it, denying it, only to have it surface in their adult lives—as it may have for Mollie. We have no record of what life was like in the house on Gates Avenue, of what form the children's grief took, of how the bereaved husband managed his sadness. Nowhere is it written how or where he met the woman who would become his next wife. But the story that can be discerned through the raw facts and dates of census reports and city street directories is sad enough, a story of loss upon loss.

James Fancher, Mollie's father, was remarried fourteen months to the day after the death of his first wife, to a woman named Mary Westfall. It's clear that he did not marry so quickly in order to provide a new mother for his young children, because within a year of the marriage, in 1857, he was no longer living with Mollie, Elizabeth, and baby James. James Fancher, Sr., and Mary were living in Springfield, New York, where she was to give birth to James's second family of eight children (four of whom died in childhood). His first family remained in the Brooklyn house, where they were raised by their maiden aunt Susan Crosby, in the nineteenth-century equivalent of a single-parent family. By age ten Mollie had, effectively, lost both parents—although she had gained a relationship that, by all reports, was a powerful and loving one, with her aunt Susan.

Abram Dailey, who knew Mollie in her later life and based his biography of her on her words and those of Susan Crosby (who kept a detailed diary of her niece's misadventures and maladies from age eighteen on), hinted at Mollie's troubled past without providing any specifics. Mollie's mother, he wrote, seemed during her fatal illness "to look out into the future and discern shadows over the life of her eldest daughter, who was always her favorite child." The source of his anecdotes is unclear, but he related that "she called to her side her sister, Miss [Susan] Crosby, then a young and accomplished lady, and confided to her her forebodings regarding her much beloved Mollie. Speaking of Elizabeth she said, '[she] will be able to take care of herself. But Mollie, I can see, is a child of sorrow, and will need your care, and I want you should make me one promise, and that is, if anything shall happen to her, that you will look after and care for her as your own daughter."

When Mollie's sorrow manifested itself as exhaustion and loss of appetite—if that was indeed the source of her ill health—Aunt Susan consulted the family physician. A general practitioner was the first line of attack for what was considered a nervous ailment, as Mollie's was, for the simple reason that nervousness meant something different to Victorians from what it means to modern doctors and patients. The word *nervous* has been in the English language for more than six centuries, and for most of that time it has referred to a physical state, not a mental one.

The exhaustive *Oxford English Dictionary,* which specializes in word histories and lists meanings in chronological order as they change over time, runs through eight full definitions of *nervous* before it reaches the one we know today: that is, "suffering from disorder of the nerves; also, excitable, easily agitated, timid." The eight meanings that precede are mostly focused on sinews, muscles, tendons, or the nervous system. The few that are metaphorical are opposite in meaning from modern nervousness: "vigorous, powerful, forcible; free from weakness and diffuseness." A literary example from 1828 reads: "Mr. Lockhart's own writing is generally so good, so clear, direct and nervous." In contrast, the 1993 *Random House Dictionary of the English Language* offers as its first definition: "highly excitable; unnaturally or acutely uneasy or apprehensive"; the last definition given is "vigorous or spirited," which is noted as archaic.

Until late in the nineteenth century, nerves were still thought of almost solely as physical units that provided strength to the body, and that transmitted physical messages from one part of the body to another, rather than as a metaphor for anxiety. When the *Brooklyn Daily Eagle* reporter who wrote about Mollie's case criticized Americans' abuse of their nerves, he referred not to emotional stress but to physical overuse; the phrase "nervous ailment" implied a problem with nerve function that should be treated with physical therapies. Even when mental states or emotions appeared to be involved, it was assumed that the cause, and the cure, lay exclusively in the body.

The therapy proposed by Mollie's physician to treat her dyspepsia and weakness, however, proved even more damaging than her nerve problems. It led directly to the second physical misfortune of Mollie's young life. There were at the time essentially two contradictory approaches to treating nervous ailments, especially those affecting women: complete rest, and exercise. The "rest cure"—an intuitive response to fatigue or sick stomach—had existed in some form for centuries, but it would flower into a virtual cult of invalidism in the late-Victorian era.

Elizabeth Barrett Browning provides a prototype from earlier in the century. She, like Mollie, developed mysterious symptoms during adolescence—at age fourteen, in 1820. They began with a pain in the head, which traveled to her ribs, then to her back and stomach. Her family was wealthy enough to send her to doctor after doctor, none of whom found anything organic (although she was treated for spinal disease). She was never well again. Her lungs were weak, and would sometimes hemorrhage; she had attacks of coughing and struggling for breath; she lacked appetite and was frail and delicate. She lived most of her life on a couch, although marriage to Robert Browning roused her enough occasionally to approximate a normal life in middle age.

The rest cure became known as such a few decades later, as a result of the work of Silas Weir Mitchell, a prominent physician in Philadelphia after the Civil War. Mitchell was in charge of neurological injuries during the war, and in peacetime his fashionable practice became populated with women who were tired, worn down, and nervous. He happened upon a successful formula with one patient, a Mrs. G., who at his insistence went to a secluded spot in the country and stayed in bed for six weeks. Sequestered with three people—a masseuse, a nurse, and the doctor—spoonfed, given hours in which to chatter with the doctor at her side (the first talking cure?), Mrs. G. returned a changed, renewed woman. Mitchell's program eventually became a popular manual, *Fat and Blood: And How to Make Them* (he stressed overfeeding of milk and fats to strengthen the blood), published in 1877.

The physician George Beard was conflicted about how best to treat overstretched nerves. For young men he often advocated productive and satisfying work as an antidote to weakness and neurasthenia. Paradoxically, he felt that although too much brainwork might use up the supply of nerve energy, pursuing the right kind of work, the right outlet, might revitalize and replenish that supply. Beard was also a fan of using mild electric shocks to restore nerve sufferers, on the theory that they would supply the body's natural electricity that had been depleted by stress.

But at other times and in other contexts, especially for women, Beard advocated a step down from what he saw as the frantic activity of the average nineteenth-century American. "The gospel of work must make way for the gospel of rest," he wrote in *American Nervousness.* "The children of the past generation were forced, driven, stimulated to work, and in forms most repulsive, the philosophy being, that utility is proportioned to pain. . . . Our children must be driven from study and all toil, and in many instances coaxed, petted, and hired to be idle; we must drive them away from schools as our fathers drove them towards the schools."

Many clinicians, however, believed that the cure for nerves or weakness, especially for women, lay not in inactivity but in activity that was vigorous and physical, taking the sufferer's awareness away from her fretting mind and strengthening her body. In November 1866, *The Brooklyn Daily Union* editorialized about the need for physical education programs for girls, claiming that "no fact is more obvious than the decline of the health and vigor of American girls." Some of "our wisest and best men and women," the writer commented, "have witnessed with growing concern and alarm this debilitating tendency of American girls and women, and are casting about for some means of averting consequences so calamitous." Their solution: physical training in the form of gymnastics and calisthenics, which Brooklyn's schools for girls were urged to provide. "Until public instruction shall embrace bodily as well as mental training, feminine feebleness and ill-health will be the rule, not the exception," the editorial concluded.

Alice James, sister to Henry and William, and a quintessential neurasthenic, tried the exercise remedy (among many others) specifically to treat her nervous condition. She was around the same age as Mollie Fancher, and like her lived in a large East Coast city, in her case Boston. Also like Mollie, Alice began in her teens to have what she called "nervous crises": fatigue, excitability, fainting fits, headaches. Various nervous troubles were almost a family tradition among the Jameses, but while Henry and William managed to produce great bodies of creative work between attacks of depression and anxiety, Alice devoted her life to her illnesses.

For help with her symptoms, Alice went with her aunt to New York in 1866 to spend months being treated by Charles Fayette Taylor, a doctor who promoted a "movement cure." Taylor, like Beard, felt that neurasthenics suffered from an imbalance in the body's energy bank; he believed that the nerves drew too much of the available energy to themselves, leaving the rest of the body depleted. The movement cure aimed to reverse the energy flow, from the nerves to the body, using special exercises, stretching, and massage techniques. There was a mental or emotional side to Taylor's cure as well: he prescribed an avoidance of any stimulation of the mind. Intellectual overstimulation, he felt, had caused the problem in the first place—at least in women.

Because women tended to be more emotional than men, Taylor wrote in 1879, they couldn't handle the intensity of rigorous thought without tipping the energy balance. "While education in men makes them self-controlling, steady, deliberate, calculating, thinking out every problem, the intellectual being the preponderating force, the so-called 'higher education' for women seems to produce the contrary effect on them. . . . While men are calmed, women are excited by the education they receive." Education, Taylor determined, so heightened women's inherent emotional weakness that in its wake "the woman of our modern civilization becomes the bundle of nerves which she is— almost incapable of reasoning under the tyranny of paramount emotions." Alice James, coming as she did from a fiercely intellectual family, did her best to curb her active mind and develop her body. But as with every other cure she tried in her lifelong struggle with nervous collapse—and there weren't many that she missed in her pursuit of health—its results were short-lived.

When Mollie Fancher's health began to fail, her physician showed himself to be a believer in the more active cure. He prescribed a course of healthy outdoor exercise, and in particular suggested horseback riding for a young woman of Mollie's active disposition. After lessons at a Brooklyn Heights riding academy, she became known as a skillful, even adventurous rider about the roughly paved streets and dusty back roads of Brooklyn. One day in the spring of 1864 a family friend offered her the occasional use of a horse he had recently purchased for his own daughter. Mollie eagerly agreed, and began to ride the horse around the city, supposing him safe for a female rider. He turned out to be nothing of the kind.

Startled by the fluttering of her dress, the horse suddenly broke into a wild run, plunging among the vehicles in the crowded streets with no heed to Mollie's efforts to rein him in—through Classon and Flushing avenues, alongside the Navy Yard, to Clinton Avenue and finally Fulton Street. Unexpectedly, he slowed and then stopped in front of a wooden house he seemed to find familiar. He pushed open the gate with one of his forefeet, then proceeded slowly up to the porch and tapped on the floor with his hoof. The house belonged to his previous owner, who opened the door and looked as astonished as Mollie had been to find herself astride a horse on someone's porch. The man explained to Mollie that he was the former owner, and that the animal had been taught tricks that were unusual for a horse—including opening gates. The man then gave her a warning: the horse had never been ridden by a lady, and was, in his opinion, quite unsafe for her use.

What happened next was a measure of Mollie's intrepid, perhaps risk-taking character. She continued to ride the horse, day after day. On one occasion he bolted and again ran heedless for his stall at the stables, with Mollie clinging to his back. "Miss Fancher could not halt him," Abram Dailey wrote, "and seeing she was likely to be swept from her saddle by the lintel of the door-way, she prostrated herself on his back and escaped injury." Still she went back for more. Until May 10, when her luck ran out. On this ride, when she was five blocks from home, she accidentally dropped the reins.

Before she could regain them the horse plunged forward, then kicked his heels high in the air. Mollie was flung to the pavement. Her head struck the curbstone and her side landed full-weight on the rough stone pavement. Two ribs were broken and she was knocked unconscious, although her heavy hat protected her skull from serious injury. Her foot remained caught in the stirrup as she lay motionless on the street, but strangely, Dailey noted, "as if satisfied with what he had succeeded in doing, her horse stood until some one released her foot, when he galloped away to the stable." Mollie was carried by strangers to a nearby house until her aunt and her physician could be summoned.

Mollie Fancher's recovery from this catastrophe was slow and uncertain. She had the misfortune of being injured in an era in which doctoring was still largely a matter of guesswork, and bed rest the default prescription. Without X-ray machines and other diagnostic devices, physicians could only speculate as to what was causing the swelling in her left side (they finally decided it was not an abscess but irritation of the flesh from the broken ribs) and the occasional hemorrhages from her right lung. In addition, she was plagued by continuing headaches, coughs, and fainting spells—the symptoms that had brought her to horseback riding in the first place, and that were worsened after the accident.

These symptoms gave rise to fears of consumption, as tuberculosis was then called, which was at epidemic proportions, and the leading cause of death in the country. Mollie's primary physician prescribed a long recuperative visit to friends in Cornwall, on the Hudson River, as soon as she was able to move around. She remained there several months, and returned to Brooklyn in September 1864. Mollie seemed to rally, her aunt Susan wrote in her diary, "and was quite smart during the Fall and Winter, and up to June, 1865." Somewhere in that period Mollie was engaged to John H. Taylor, according to Dailey a respectable young gentleman of good social standing.

Aunt Susan was also engaged at that time. Abram Dailey related Susan Crosby's romantic history in terms worthy of a Victorian melodrama. She was first engaged at sixteen, to a wealthy planter from Mobile, Alabama. The date was set, her trousseau was readied, and her fiancé boarded a ship to sail to Brooklyn. When the ship arrived he was dead of yellow fever. Heartbroken, Susan Crosby afterward took on the child-rearing responsibilities left to her by her dying sister, and the years went by. By 1865, when she was forty, she had for some time been receiving the attentions of a gentleman whose affection she returned, and she promised him her hand in marriage.

What happened in June of that year, when Mollie Fancher stepped off the Fulton Street horsecar, changed everything. Dailey's contention is that as Mollie's infirmity progressed, Susan Crosby weighed the promise she had made to her sister to care for her orphaned children, especially Mollie, against her commitment to marry, and felt the greater duty toward the former. She did not want to bring such a burden into the marriage, and also did not want to leave Mollie to the care of others. Daily left it to his readers to conjecture "how deep was the disappointment, and how strong the sense of honor of this noble lady, in deciding the question, which she did for herself, without the influence of anything but her own sense of duty." One has to wonder how strong the tie with the gentleman really was, that it could not permit Susan Crosby to combine both duties in one household.

It is unclear when Susan's engagement, and eventually Mollie's, were called off. The extent of Mollie's injuries was not immediately obvious, and after the first shock of the horsecar accident, Mollie's doctors were guardedly optimistic. She spent six weeks confined to her bed, but then began to hobble around her bedroom, clinging to chair backs and tables. Such progress, however, soon appeared illusory. Various aches and pains intensified, mystifying and frightening Mollie and her family. Something was wrong with her left side: the muscles of her left leg contracted until she could hardly reach her heel to the floor, and when she tried to put weight on that side she felt pain in her spine.

Then Mollie's left arm began to fail, sometimes dropping helplessly to her side. Her eyesight, which had bothered her after the fall from the horse, continued to worsen. By early winter, another symptom from that accident reappeared: Mollie's lungs began to hemorrhage. Aunt Susan, in despair, called in a team of four top physicians, all specialists in lung diseases, to consider her case. The four met in December at Mollie's home to examine their patient. Their prognosis was not favorable; it was discouraging in the extreme. Miss Fancher, they feared, would not survive the winter.

What followed is a tale of medical mystery, ignorance, even infamy, more appropriate to the Middle Ages than to the self-consciously modern age of the later nineteenth century. If indeed, as some doubters eventually claimed, Mollie Fancher's later feats were a hoax, the tale of her medical treatments might dispose one to excuse the deception. This is also where her story begins to pass twenty-first-century understanding, because it describes conditions that no longer exist as such—that have morphed into other illnesses that we recognize in their place. "Our late-twentieth-century culture," the medical historian Edward Shorter wrote in 1992, "which values individual dynamism, regards physical paralysis and sudden 'coma' (both common before 1900) as inappropriate responses."

Yet in 1866, when Mollie's case began to flower from garden-variety nervous stomach and discernible injuries into a profusion of bizarre symptoms, there existed a diagnosis that helped explain her coming paralysis, her comas (or trances), her spasms and fits, and her soon-to-be-famous fasting. It was called hysteria, and although the diagnosis was inconsistently applied to Mollie's case by those around her, it was a dominant medical conception of the late nineteenth century. As Shorter points out in his history of psychosomatic illness *From Paralysis to Fatigue,* humans must have a way of expressing the dominant emotions and anxieties of their age—and hysteria belonged to Mollie's era. To hear the narrative of her symptoms and experiences without understanding the contemporary fascination with hysteria is to try to translate her story from another language, an ancient tongue, without a glossary. Nineteenth-century hysteria opened the door to twentieth-century neurosis, and in 1866, Mollie Fancher stood on the threshold.

CHAPTER TWO

La Grande Hystérie

Perhaps no cases are more common in general practice, none more annoying, and none more dreaded than those of hysteria, in its infinite number of forms and its infinite variety of masquerade.

—S. Weir Mitchell, M.D.,
Lectures on Diseases of the Nervous System, Especially in Women, 1881

No historian will be able to account for "hysteria" who is unable to explain why these women took to their beds and stayed there.

—Edward Shorter,
"Paralysis: The Rise and Fall of a 'Hysterical' Symptom," 1986

THE HOUSE TO WHICH Mollie was carried after she fell from the Fulton Street horsecar in June 1865, and which she would never leave again, was on the corner of Gates Avenue and Downing Street. It stood on what is now considered the dividing line between Fort Greene and Bedford-Stuyvesant, two neighborhoods that have come a long way from the verdant colonial villages for which they were named more than three centuries ago.

These days, parts of both areas feel down-at-the-heel, battered by years of urban flight and the slow transition of Brooklyn from a collection of family farms to a nineteenth-century suburban town to the concrete-lined borough of New York City it is today. Bed-Stuy, as it is often called, became notorious around the country for race riots during the 1960s. One of the main avenues approaching what was Mollie Fancher's corner is now lined with Caribbean, African, and Indo-

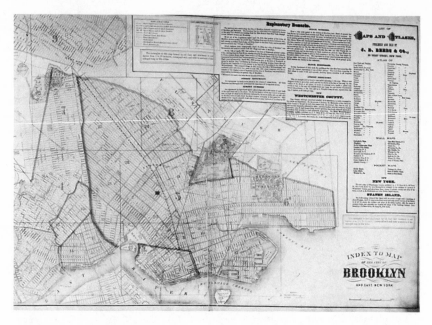

Brooklyn in 1859; the East River is at the lower left. The dark square marks the approximate location of Mollie Fancher's home, at the edge of what had been the colonial villages of Bedford Corners and Fort Greene (see page 40 for a closer view). The dotted line is Fulton Street. (THE NEW YORK PUBLIC LIBRARY)

Pakistani food shops, reflecting the immigrant cultures of the current population; the wide commercial boulevard of Fulton Street, where she alighted from the fateful horsecar, is unglamorous, even seedy. Some of the nearby avenues afford stunning views of Manhattan across the East River—the art deco Empire State and Chrysler buildings, the late-twentieth-century steel-and-glass towers reaching toward the sun— but from this part of Brooklyn they all seem very far away. These are not streets listed in current New York City guidebooks as offering Great Walking Tours with Places to See.

In the quieter streets near Gates and Downing, the surroundings become more pleasant: leafy trees line the sidewalks, and many of the nineteenth-century brownstones and row houses that survive look to be in some stage of urban renewal. A few have "No Sitting" signs on the risers of the front stairs, an injunction often ignored by men who gather to talk, smoke, and sometimes drink. Some houses have peeling paint around the windowsills, and the occasional broken or boarded-up window; others feature oval stained-glass windows in ornate wooden front doors and wispy lace curtains that evoke an earlier century. Two blocks from Mollie's corner stands an elaborately romanesque six-story building with a plaque that designates it as the Vendome, constructed in 1887 as the first multifamily apartment building in Brooklyn (and saved from the wrecking ball a century later).

At the intersection of Gates and Downing is a three-story building that at a glance looks much like that in the one known existing photograph of Mollie's house: the same slightly peaked roof, two chimneys, two rows of three windows along the front and the side, a side entrance toward the back, and most intriguing, a storefront on the ground floor, evocative of the ground-floor shop at 160 Gates where Mollie's needlework and other crafts were sold. This still-standing ghost of Mollie's house has a run-down video-and-snack store occupying the front windows. But this address is 156 Gates. Across Downing, where 160 Gates would logically have been, sprawls an undistinguished orange-brick low-rise: Public School 56. Mollie's home, where she spent decades sequestered in a rear second-floor bedroom, is no more.

This exact spot in the heart of Brooklyn (Breuckelen, as it was originally called by the Dutch) was settled in 1662 as the village of Bedford Corners; in 1668 the colonial government issued a license to one Thomas Lambertse to establish the village's first inn, or "Ordinary for Man and Beast." A century later, during the Revolutionary War, Bedford Corners was the scene of much of the fighting in the Battle of Long Island, and it was occupied by the British army for eight years. Fort Greene, the village abutting Bedford Corners about where Mollie's house would later stand, was named after Nathaniel Greene, a Revolutionary War hero who supervised the building of Fort Putnam

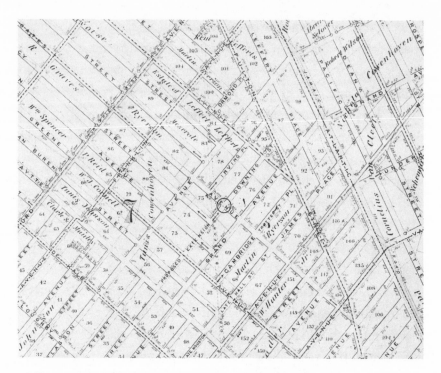

Mollie Fancher's house stood at the corner of Gates and Downing (see circle), two blocks from Fulton Street, where she alighted from the horsecar. This detail from a larger map of mid-nineteenth-century Brooklyn shows, over the grid of streets, traces of the estate lines of early settlers. (THE NEW YORK PUBLIC LIBRARY)

nearby; the fort survived the battle in August 1776, but had to be abandoned when George Washington and his men retreated across the East River.

Both Bedford Corners and Fort Greene were later absorbed into Brooklyn, which was incorporated as a city in 1834. By 1860 it boasted a massive shipbuilding industry based at the Brooklyn Navy Yard; its own railroads, ferries, and horsecar lines; numerous manufacturing businesses (including the largest hat-making company in the country); and a substantial chip on its shoulder about being a city in its own right rather than merely a smaller, less impressive cousin to Manhattan. That attitude kept Brooklyn from joining New York City as a borough until

1898. And yet bits and pieces of the past remained; as late as the 1850s and 1860s many Brooklyn street maps still printed the family names of former estate owners—Cornelius Heeney, Parmenius Johnson, Leffert Lefferts—across what had become a distinctly urban street grid.

The Fancher home at 160 Gates Avenue stood squarely in the midst of that grid when the family—James and Elizabeth, and their children Mollie, Elizabeth, and James Jr.—moved there in the early 1850s. The neighborhood then, like most of Brooklyn at the time, was peopled by what a contemporary guidebook called "the sterling middle class." Some of its residents worked locally, as storekeepers, shipyard workers, clerks, and so on, but many were part of the commuting culture, traveling to Manhattan's southern hub via the Fulton Street Ferry.

Fulton Street itself, the oldest street in the city, was described in an 1859 guidebook to New York and Brooklyn as "presenting a commanding entrance," broad and bordered on both sides with ranges of lofty brick stores. The busy thoroughfare was the city's premier shopping district, offering everything from early examples of the department store (dry goods emporiums that carried material and sewing patterns, ready-made clothing, household linens, and home furnishings) to bakers, butchers, general grocers, jewelers, booksellers, coal suppliers, horseshoers, gas chandelier warehouses, housekeeping bazaars, insurance offices, even doctors' and dentists' offices. In the 1860s, Drs. Griffin and Brothers at 257 Fulton Street offered tooth extractions "positively without pain" by use of nitrous oxide, at a price of twenty-five cents per tooth (a full upper or lower set of dentures in gold could set one back as much as twenty-five dollars). The nearby Scotch Bakery priced its best white loaf at twelve cents, the *Daily Eagle* could be had for three cents, and the play *Double Marriage* could be seen from the upper balcony of the Lyceum theater for twenty-five cents or from a front orchestra seat for one dollar.

Brooklynites were proud of the sophistication that brought them concerts, plays, art exhibits, and the latest fashions; the Brooklyn

Academy of Music, which opened in 1861, seated 2,300 and boasted a stage nearly equal in size to that of London's Drury Lane or Covent Garden. But urbanization brought its share of problems, many of them related to the infrastructure of the fast-growing city. The streets that Mollie walked on her way to Brooklyn Heights Seminary were described as "dirty" and "nasty" by newspaper columnists and politicians, and in the summer months the combined stench of human garbage and horse manure could be overpowering. Filth and sewage lined the pavements (often thrown from house windows or doors into the gutter). This refuse was blamed for frequent outbreaks of cholera, and it was not unusual for the city to experience three or four deaths from cholera each week in July and August.

The process of modernizing city services introduced fresh nuisances: Brooklyn streets were continually being torn up to lay water, gas, and sewage pipes, as well as to install ever more streetcar tracks. The design of the modern city was in the process of being invented, and there were perplexing questions to settle: Should streetlights remain on all night long, despite the expense? How should streets be paved? In the 1850s plank roads were the rage: wooden platforms that would allow vehicles to avoid mud and potholes. They proved to be disastrous—the wood quickly decayed and became useless—and many stockholders who had invested in them went broke. In 1864 the mayor of Brooklyn called instead for traprock or Belgian pavement, stones that fit together like cobblestones; and by the 1880s the latest thing was macadam, small stones compacted and bound together into a solid mass to make a roadbed, invented by British engineer John McAdam earlier in the century.

Within houses like the Fancher's, the 1850s and 1860s would have seen corresponding advances. Water systems were introduced in the late 1850s to bring water into homes and drain sewage into the East River, from where the tides would carry it out to the ocean. Kerosene lighting was giving way to gas, and Mollie's house had gas fixtures at least by the mid-1860s. The more advanced homes were turning to gas appliances to replace the wood- and coal-burning variety, and advertising in 1865 touted the great relief that gas stoves could provide in summer—allowing baking, broiling, frying, and iron-heating while giving out little ambient heat.

Mollie's father was a local businessman, well-off enough to own his own home and send his eldest daughter to an exclusive girls' seminary, but not of the class that occupied the mansions of nearby neighborhoods like "the Hill" and Brooklyn Heights. In those enclaves, gilded-age merchants such as A. M. White and Henry E. Pierrepont could survey New York Harbor from drawing rooms stuffed with bric-a-brac. The nature of the business that supported Mollie's family appears to have changed several times throughout her childhood. James Fancher, her father, was born on April 11, 1820, in Pound Ridge, New York, the eleventh (and posthumous) child of William Fancher, a farmer. James's great-grandfather was a John Fancher (or Fansher or Fanshier, as he variously wrote it in his lifetime), believed by his descendants to be a London-born Huguenot, who was one of the first settlers of Pound Ridge, in 1730. James was described in a family genealogy as a jeweler and silversmith, but Brooklyn street directories from 1849 to 1856 listed him as a jeweler and a grocer.

The story of that lonely time in Mollie's life after her mother died, in February 1855, can be known only in the outlines of dates and addresses. In 1854, Susan Crosby was working as a seamstress in Brooklyn, and was probably already living with her sister's family on Gates Avenue. There is no entry for any members of the family in the 1856–1857 Brooklyn directory the year after Elizabeth Fancher's death; James married his second wife in April 1856 in Nassau, New York. In the 1857–1858 directory, James is gone from Brooklyn (never to return), and Susan E. Crosby is listed as head of household at 160 Gates Avenue. The 1860 census describes her as thirty-five years old and a housekeeper, caring for nieces Mary Jane (Mollie), fourteen;

Elizabeth, eight; and nephew James Edwin, six. Presumably James Edwin Sr. provided the means for his first family to continue their way of life at the Gates Avenue house, which remained in the family into the twentieth century. There are hints, after Mollie's accident, of other sources of income: a small settlement from the horsecar company, commissions for the needlework and waxwork Mollie began to make, and later, the proceeds from her gift shop in the ground floor of the house. The horsecar fall, calamity though it was, eventually provided Mollie with something approaching a career.

By early February 1866, eight months after the accident, Mollie was declared to be dying. She was suffering from what was described as an "inflammation of the lungs," and on the third of that month her condition became severe enough for her physician to summon friends and her clergyman, the Reverend David Moore, to her bedside. She survived the night, but a few days later she was seized with violent spasms, and again doctors, friends, and clergy were summoned. As her grieving friends sang "Nearer, My God, to Thee" and the doctor monitored her pulse, Mollie clung to life through the night.

At six the next morning, her spasms suddenly ceased and she fell into what she and her friends later called a trance—a stillness so deep and profound that her physician proclaimed her dead. Her aunt insisted he was wrong, and forced brandy and water between Mollie's unresponsive lips. Three hours later the trance lifted and Mollie opened her eyes, but her moments of lucidity were brief. Soon she was contorted with spasms again. Those were followed by yet another deathlike trance, this one lasting three days, during which her end was again expected at any moment. This pattern—a spasm of three hours or so, followed by a trance of five to fourteen hours, sometimes longer—soon became the torturous routine of Mollie's days, to the dismay of those who loved her.

Years later, Mollie herself described the spasms in terms that

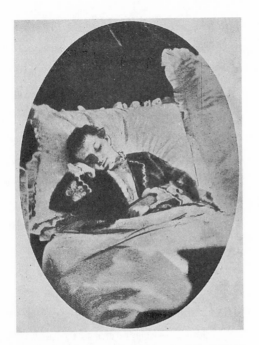

Mollie Fancher at eighteen, in the fall of 1865, as she became a "bed-case." Five months after the horsecar accident, doctors were puzzled by her condition. They predicted that death would overtake her before the winter was out. (FROM MOLLIE FANCHER, THE BROOKLYN ENIGMA)

demonstrate her flair for the dramatic. "For two months after my trances commenced," she told Abram Dailey in the 1890s, "fourteen persons were in constant attendance upon me, a relay of seven being required to hold me upon the bed during the spasms. My body and limbs were drawn together until I was almost a ball; then I leaped forward like an arrow, and would have been killed but for the protection of friends and the wadded obstructions placed in the way."

Her description of the trances was just as colorful: "As I went into a trance my body and limbs became rigid and immovable, my hands usually folded across my breast, and my eyes were open and upturned. I am told that my physicians frequently raised me to a standing position by placing their hands back of my head, without the least flexibility of my body or limbs, my body being seemingly as rigid as a piece of statuary."

To a twenty-first-century reader, this is very strange stuff. But although Mollie's case was considered odd, such symptoms were far from unheard-of in 1866. In many instances they fit quite closely the descriptions of a malady that was reaching close to epidemic proportions in the middle to late nineteenth century: hysteria, or what one French neurologist of the period called "the great neurosis."

Hysteria has existed as a word and a concept, though an often changing concept, for thousands of years. The word derives from the Greek *hystera,* "uterus," which itself derives from the Sanskrit word for stomach or belly—indicating the first ideas about hysteria as a disturbance arising from a misplaced womb. An Egyptian papyrus dating from about 1900 B.C. details odd behaviors in adult women and blames them on a wandering uterus that was applying pressure to the diaphragm. The Greeks and later the Romans subscribed to the same basic definition of hysteria; and when growing anatomical knowledge made clear that the uterus was unlikely to move about the body at will, hysteria was still associated with problems or changes in the female reproductive system (amenorrhea, miscarriage, menopause).

By the seventeenth century, physicians were challenging the strictly uterine definition of the causes of hysteria. The French doctor Charles Lepois believed that the mind and passions, rather than the womb, were the source of hysteria. He was joined by the Italian physician Giorgio Baglivi, who pointed out that the hysteric was very susceptible to her doctor's words and attitude—which suggested a mental rather than physical basis. Baglivi was one of the first to recognize the contagious nature of hysteria. At the same time, autopsies of hysterics were finding no sign of uterine problems.

Two hundred years later, in hysteria's heyday, the origins of the disease remained unclear—and Victorian doctors found themselves increasingly frustrated by its tenacious and ever more outrageous symptoms. Dr. G. L. Austin, writing in an 1883 health manual with the ominous title *Perils of American Women,* clung to the uterine theory, conceding that while hysteria could occasionally exist independently of sexual causes, it was much more likely due to a "derangement of the female sexual organs, especially of the ovaries." Another Victorian physician, Edward Dixon, writing in the 1850s, agreed that uterine dysfunction was one of hysteria's chief causes, but foreshadowing the broader understanding of hysteria that was soon to come, Dixon also noted that "the brain and nervous system are the agents of [hysteria's] most powerful manifestations."

In the middle and later 1800s, those manifestations were increasingly florid and bizarre. They also formed a blueprint of Mollie Fancher's case, matching her story symptom by symptom. One typical description of hysteria comes from a French doctor, Pierre Briquet, who kept scrupulous data on 450 patients diagnosed with the condition at the Pitié hospital in Paris from 1849 to 1859. Briquet observed a consistent progression: the onset was marked by paleness, leading to loss of appetite and loss of weight. This was often followed by sensations of pain, especially headaches and epigastric pain, and aches in the left side, spine, and abdomen, which caused a sense of strangulation. Fits or spasms were the next step. The first few of these symptoms recall the drooping schoolgirl Mollie; the next few describe Mollie's condition after her horsecar accident.

The list of symptoms didn't stop there. Hysteria was becoming so wide-ranging in its manifestations that entire books were devoted to diagnosing it. Pierre Janet, a French professor of psychology who became prominent in the early twentieth century, attempted to fully chronicle late-Victorian hysteria in his landmark work *The Major Symptoms of Hysteria.* His catalogue of symptoms was staggering, and included somnambulism (not sleepwalking as we think of it today, but a sort of amnesiac condition in which the patient functioned in a trance state, or "second state," and later remembered nothing); trances or fits of sleep that could last for days, and in which the patient sometimes appeared to be dead; contractures or other disturbances in the motor functions of the limbs; paralysis of various parts of the body; unexplained loss of the use of a sense such as sight or hearing; loss of speech; and disruptions in eating that could entail eventual refusal of food altogether. Janet's profile was sufficiently descriptive of Mollie Fancher that he mentioned her by name as someone who "seems to have had all possible hysterical accidents and attacks."

In the face of such strange and often intractable "attacks," many doctors who treated cases of hysteria in the 1800s developed an ill-concealed exasperation. Dr. Edward Dixon wrote of the prototypical hysteric: "Let the reader imagine the patient writhing like a serpent upon the floor, rending her garments to tatters, plucking out handsful of her hair, and striking her person with violence—with contorted and swollen countenance, and fixed eyes, resisting every effort of the bystanders to control her—and she will realize the scene often presented to the practitioner."

Dr. Austin began his description of the hysteric in an objective tone—the disease appeared to exaggerate involuntary movement, and diminish the power of the will—but soon gave vent to his frustration. The patient usually showed no desire to resist the hysterical feelings when they came upon her, he said, but yielded to her emotions: laughing or crying at the least provocation, exaggerating the slightest discomfort, allowing her irritation full rein. She resented hearing any advice, comfort, or suggestions of a cure from others, welcoming instead only passive sympathy, pity, or condolence. "By her suspicious, exacting, and unreasonable behavior," Austin wrote, the hysteric "makes life generally uncomfortable to those about her." Not content with that, he concluded, she was often duplicitous as well, telling her doctors that she couldn't do a certain thing, then doing that very thing the moment their backs were turned.

There were those who suspected Mollie of the latter species of fraud when her story became famous more than a decade after her accident. And in most other ways, Mollie's long list of symptoms provides a template of hysteria as it was then defined (except, perhaps, for Austin's whining-invalid persona, which no one—in print, anyway—ever attributed to Mollie). Consider the many puzzling symptoms that waxed and waned as Mollie lay prostrate in her bed in the winter of 1865–1866, beginning with her first near-death trance in February. Susan Crosby's daily diary recorded a litany of strange ailments, which Mollie herself related to Abram Dailey decades later.

Among the first was the impairment of her sense of hearing. "The only way that I could understand or hear," she told Dailey, "was by having those who spoke to me approach so near to my face, that the sound of the voice could penetrate my nostrils, and in that way communicate with my brain, or organs of hearing." Eyesight was the next to go. On February 22, 1866, she "had a terrific spasm, and my eyesight failed me entirely, and I have never recovered the same. I can see, but not by the use of my eyes. When I first became conscious of my failing sight, I was greatly alarmed, but hoped to recover it again. When I had this terrible spasm that I have just spoken of, I found it suddenly growing dark, and I supposed it was the approach of night, and asked my aunt to light the gas in my room so that I could see. She replied, 'It is lighted, darling; can't you see it?' I said, 'No, it is all dark.' Then she lighted another burner to satisfy me, and then another, but still all was dark. Then the consciousness dawned upon me that I was blind, and a sense of horror came over me, and I exclaimed: 'Oh, my God, I am blind; with all my other afflictions I am blind.'"

From February to May, Mollie lost one faculty after another. The loss of her hearing and sight, she told Dailey, "was followed by the loss of the sense of feeling. I lost the sense of touch, then the sense of smell, then the sense of taste, and then the power of speech. . . . Following the loss of these other powers, my fingers became cramped into the palms of my hands, in which condition they remained for a long time."

Her aunt's diary recorded new symptoms day after day during this period, as well as brief periods of spontaneous recovery: "On March 7th she had very severe spasms, after which she was paralyzed until the 9th, when her muscles relaxed, and she saw, heard and spoke; her hands also opened, and she remained so for several hours, possessing all her natural powers. Then they again left her."

Mollie's physical state swung from one extreme to another. Her aunt's diary recorded that on Wednesday, March 14, she had spasms in the head, was very feeble, and was not expected to live through the day. In the evening she rallied a little, though she was still feeble. By the following evening she was strong enough to speak and sing, and seemed quite happy. The next day her speech left her again, her jaws closed, and she lost her sense of touch; she could not express herself, although she appeared to be conscious. Two days later Mollie was once again "quite smart, with much unnatural strength." She spent the day writing and working, but by the evening she was delirious.

Susan Crosby's diary went on to document a mind-numbing progression of seesawing symptoms through the days and nights of the spring of 1866. Trances, fainting spells, spasms come and go. Mollie "suffers intensely with her head and heart." Sometimes the spasms are precipitated by a shock, like a crack of thunder; in "hard spasms," her body is "contracted into the form of a hoop, sometimes bent backward and then forward." At times during spasms, "her body contracted into various forms, presenting a horrible sight. Her lower limbs were twisted (in a three-twist), and her feet crossed."

Accounts of feeding are scarce, and usually amount to "a teaspoonful of wine" that Mollie "could not keep on her stomach." Her throat closed, and no food or drink could be taken; then her throat opened again for a day. Mollie later described this to Abram Dailey in her characteristically detailed way: "The spasms had closed my throat to such an extent, that it was almost impossible for any kind of nourishment to be received. The organs of the throat became so rigid, and so hard, that when struck, the sound resembled that of wood or stone." When food was introduced it was often immediately rejected, vomited back up. At one time in the spring, according to her aunt's diary, Mollie "took a small piece of cracker, and one teaspoonful of punch, which was the first food in seven weeks, that she was able to keep on her stomach."

Susan Crosby described Mollie's state in the fall of 1866: She lay with eyes, jaws, and hands closed, her right arm drawn up at the back of her head, her lower limbs in a three-twist. She had the use of part of her left arm and hand, although the fingers of the hand were closed. The only nourishment she had retained on her stomach between April 4 and October 27 had been "four teaspoonfuls of milk punch, two of wine, one small piece of banana and a small piece of cracker." With so few alimentary demands on her body, the rest of her digestive and excretory system had effectively shut down: "Since the 6th day of August," Susan's diary recounted, "the natural functions of the body for relief have not been exercised (a period of three months)."

All of Mollie's experiences, strange as they may seem from a twenty-first-century viewpoint, are echoed in case histories and medical texts of the time. Edward Dixon described in 1857 a hysterical patient whose jaw was locked for five days, "the patient being sustained by sucking milk through closed teeth." Silas Weir Mitchell, of the famous rest cure, devoted a full chapter of his 1881 *Lectures on Diseases of the Nervous System, Especially in Women* to the gastrointestinal disorders of hysteria. Mitchell detailed all kinds of glitches in the digestive systems of hysterical women, many of which were elements in Mollie's case: an apparent inability to chew; problems with the esophagus—spasms or paralysis—that made swallowing difficult; loss of appetite; vomiting. The last, Mitchell added, though it might appear a minor problem, was actually of all hysterical symptoms except multiple muscle contractions the most enduring and hardest to treat. He recalled five cases of hysteria lasting from fifteen to twenty-five years, all of them bedridden; of those, four had contractions, and three were in the habit of vomiting every meal, and had done so for years.

Mitchell found only one other digestive symptom to be as stubborn as vomiting, and that was loss of appetite, or anorexia. He used "anorexia" here in its original definition, as a simple lack of appetite without explanation, rather than as we understand it today—as a shorthand for anorexia nervosa, in which a person willfully diets and loses too much body weight with the goal of being very thin. "To call this loss of appetite 'anorexia' but feebly characterizes this symptom," Mitchell wrote. Rather, what he observed appeared to be an annihilation of appetite, a lack so complete that in some cases it seemed impossible the patient would ever eat again. In the worst cases the patient developed an antagonism to food, sometimes even going into spasms when food was pressed upon her. These unfortunate cases, Mitchell remarked, were not to be confused with the occasional patient who tried "to deceive by the pretence of fasting."

One case of extreme fasting that Mitchell treated mirrored Mollie's physical experiences in many particulars. The patient, whom he called Miss L.C., had had an unhappy love affair at age eighteen. Soon after her heartbreak, she suffered a fall in which she struck her back. Within a few weeks intense spinal irritation set in, and when braces and corsets failed, bed rest was prescribed—"a fatal remedy," Mitchell commented; "she has never since left the bed to which a physician's orders sent her." Miss L.C. graduated to a never-ending series of hysterical symptoms, including paralysis and loss of sensation in various parts of her body, contractions of the legs and feet, extreme constipation, vomiting, and finally, complete loss of appetite. When Mitchell took over her case, he monitored every teaspoon of food or fluid introduced into her body, and he was convinced that in a month and five days she never consumed, in total, more than twenty-four ounces of milk, and some water. "Everyone expected to see her die at any moment," he wrote. And yet Miss L.C.'s abstinence—thirty-five or thirty-six days in all—which almost killed her, fell far short of the six months reported by Susan Crosby for Mollie in 1866.

The physical shape of Mollie's paralyses and contortions fit the pattern of late-nineteenth-century hysteria as well—in particular the phases of "grand hysteria" described by Jean-Martin Charcot, a French physician who became world-famous in the 1870s and 1880s for his studies of hysterics. Among the general public, Charcot, a born showman, was as renowned for his lectures as for his ideas. Every week he stood before a crowd of six hundred in the lecture hall at the Salpêtrière hospital in Paris—an audience that often included the fashionable of the city: writers, doctors, actors, society people—and demonstrated his control of hysterical symptoms in patients through hypnotism. Those with the most extreme manifestations—weeping and lamentations, "passionate attitudes" of prayer or crucifixion, contortions like Mollie Fancher's—were called grand hysterics.

The hooplike spasm Mollie experienced sounds uncannily like what Charcot considered the ultimate grand movement, the *arc de cercle* (also called *arc-en-ciel*), in which the patient arched her back, balancing on her heels and the top of her head. (Charcot described it thus: "The body is bent in a bowlike curve and is supported only by the neck and the feet; the hair is dishevelled; the extremities are agitated by clonic *'grands mouvements'* of flexion and extension and the mouth is opened wide.") One of his star patients, known to her audiences only as Louise, was a specialist in the *arc de cercle*—and had a background and hysterical manifestations quite similar to Mollie's. A small-town girl who made her way to Paris in her teens, Louise had had a disrupted childhood, replete with abandonment and sexual abuse. She entered Salpêtrière in 1875, where while under Charcot's care she experienced partial paralysis and complete loss of sensation over the right side of her body, as well as a decrease in hearing, smell, taste, and

Drawings of two positions that occur during "grand hysteria," from a late-nineteenth-century French textbook. Mollie Fancher's contortions, as described by those who tended her, resembled these extreme expressions of hysteria: spasms that almost threw her off the bed, and contractures that forced her body into the form of a hoop. (GENERAL RESEARCH DIVISION, THE NEW YORK PUBLIC LIBRARY, ASTOR, LENOX, AND TILDEN FOUNDATIONS)

vision on that side. She had frequent violent, dramatic hysterical fits, alternating with hallucinations and trancelike phases during which she would "see" her mother and other people she knew standing before her (this symptom would manifest itself in Mollie).

Although critics, at the time and since, have decried the sometime circus atmosphere of Charcot's lectures, and claimed that he, inadvertently or not, trained his patients how to be hysterical, he remains a key figure in understanding nineteenth-century hysteria. He devoted his career to scientifically codifying hysteria and, most particularly, trying to isolate its source. Although he aimed his search relentlessly at organic triggers—he kept looking for a dynamic lesion of some sort that prompted hysteria—he pointed the way to the concept of psychological causation.

Charcot posited that the ultimate cause of hysteria might be an unbalanced nervous system, and suggested that a psychic trauma could precipitate hysterical symptoms. Even as he looked to the role of the mind, however, he couldn't quite let go of the idea that the mechanism was essentially physical. Thus he described a case in which a laborer (a relatively rare male patient) stood transfixed with fear before a rolling barrel that had broken loose from a pulley, and later suffered hysterical symptoms such as paralysis and loss of sensation. Charcot maintained that the laborer's fright was translated into an electrical shock that spread through the nerves and disrupted the nervous organization.

By the time hysteria really got rolling in the middle and late 1800s as an accepted, or at least a common, response to stress, the trauma involved in a case could be as unremarkable as a fall in one's drawing room. A medical historian recounts the tale of a young English lady, age twenty, who in the 1860s fell in her home and injured her knee. Four years later she could still barely walk upstairs. She became nervous and delicate, and could no longer tolerate the sound of music, something she used to love. Another young lady, seventeen years old, didn't even need to fall down. She simply awoke with a headache one day and stayed in bed. Soon she experienced pain in her spine, then pain in her lower extremities so acute that she couldn't bear the feeling of the bedclothes over her legs; then her legs drew up under her in a contracture. She couldn't bear to be moved because of the pain. She spent four years in this state, after which the pain abated enough for her to get up. But by then she had developed a genuine lack of flexibility and strength due to disuse, and could not straighten her legs.

Various forms of paralysis were an increasingly common expression of hysteria as the epidemic gathered steam. Edward Shorter, in *From Paralysis to Fatigue,* describes four types of paralysis, each of them experienced at one time or another by Mollie: spastic contracture, flaccid paralysis (catalepsy, or deathlike trance), joint pain, and astasia-abasia (inability to stand upright and walk). Shorter makes a further, two-pronged distinction in the nature of hysterical paralysis: one type occurring after psychic shock, and another adopted as a fashionable mannerism.

The former reaction, Shorter says, would now be diagnosed as grief reaction or posttraumatic stress disorder, and would involve assorted physical and psychological symptoms—but physical paralysis would not be among them. Paralysis as a response to loss, mourning, and trauma was not something that made sense to people living in either the eighteenth or the twentieth century; it was what Shorter calls a "culturally specific nineteenth-century mode of processing extreme emotion."

Fashionable paralysis too was specifically nineteenth-century; it was, according to Shorter, a learned mode of behavior. Anyone could do it—and for young women who were subject to the many constraints on behavior and movement that society imposed, paralysis often seemed the only response to frustration. Some historians, including Shorter, have proposed that one reason hysteria reached such huge proportions in the Victorian era was that its nature and symptoms, with only a little tweaking, corresponded to the current ideal of feminine perfection. Women were expected to be vulnerable and fragile—

so fainting, weakness, loss of appetite, or any other extreme response to emotional or physical shock made perfect sense.

This theorizing would have been almost meaningless to Victorian doctors, who saw hysteria as a physical phenomenon, to be understood through the workings of nerves, electrical impulses, or reproductive organs. Although Pierre Janet felt that the "psychological period" of understanding hysteria began around 1875, it wasn't until around the turn of the century that the mind was seen as the prime player in hysteria. Once that idea became established, twentieth-century historians such as Shorter and others could look back at the heights of Victorian hysteria through a cultural rather than a medical lens. What, exactly, did women gain from choosing hysteria—which was on the whole quite exhausting and limiting—as a response to stress or unhappiness?

The historian Carroll Smith-Rosenberg, writing in the 1970s, traced hysteria's popularity to a conflict in female roles. The ideal woman in nineteenth-century America was expected to exhibit a demanding amalgam of traits; to be "gentle and refined, sensitive and loving . . . the guardian of religion and spokeswoman for morality . . . emotional, pious, passive and nurturant." Not only was it difficult to be passive and strong at the same time, but while the script for women remained the same, the world around them was changing at lightning speed. Life was increasingly urban, the middle class was exhibiting new patterns of aspiration and family dynamics, women had to spend less time on the basic functions of feeding and clothing their families. Many women, Smith-Rosenberg noted, may have felt a significant amount of anxiety when forced to adapt to these changes. Hysteria may have allowed some to refuse to deal with unfamiliar demands on them, but in a nonconfrontational way; their illness was, seemingly, out of their control.

What actually happened within the family when a woman succumbed to hysteria was a subversion of the female role: rather than her being a loving caretaker, she was desperately in need of caretaking herself. Rather than her being self-sacrificing, her pathetic state demanded sacrifices from those around her. The household universe revolved around her needs. "Taking to one's bed," according to Smith-Rosenberg, "might also have functioned as a mode of passive aggression, especially in a milieu in which weakness was rewarded and in which women had since childhood been taught not to express overt aggression. Consciously or unconsciously, [the woman] had thus opted out of her traditional role."

Edward Shorter also finds the roots of hysteria in family structures. In *From Paralysis to Fatigue,* he points out that a more sentimentalized view of family life in the late nineteenth century made the family something of an emotional pressure cooker. In middle-class families with more leisure to develop relationships, problems that would never be tolerated among those living closer to the margin of existence—such problems as being bedridden, or refusing to eat—could be not only tolerated but also catered to. "The threat of disability or self-destruction thrust new weapons into intrafamily struggles for emotional control," writes Shorter. Then too, being an invalid or semi-invalid did not carry wholly negative connotations in the Victorian era. George Beard's notions of the elite, neurasthenic brainworker combined with romantic ideas of the delicate, sickly artist to subtly encourage a descent into a bedridden existence. "[Illness] caused pain and suffering, yet to the romantically influenced it marked the sufferer as one possessed of unique sensibility like a poet or a saint," writes the biographer Howard Feinstein. "Not just a physical evil, illness was to be cultivated as a romantic sign of grace."

We will never know the extent to which Mollie's physical trauma was to blame for her various ills—the paralysis, contractures, spasms, trances, and sensory problems. She might have suffered spinal or cerebral injuries that today would be revealed by X ray and CAT scan, and that would have produced neurological anomalies. But the way in which her case fit, symptom by symptom, the template of the late-nineteenth-century hysterical woman suggests that she was indeed a victim of that strange malady. One can only speculate on what might have precipitated her descent into that particular physical and emotional hell. Was it, as Smith-Rosenberg suggests, an opting out of the pressures of growing to womanhood in a conflicted and rapidly changing Victorian society? Was it anxiety over her approaching marriage to John Taylor, whom she reportedly had met at Sunday school, and the separation from her small, patched-together family that marriage would necessitate? (Mollie nobly released Taylor from his obligation to her when it became obvious that her infirmity was permanent.) Was it related to the earlier traumas in her life, the deaths and abandonment; a method of assuring the constant attention and care of numerous attendants?

That it did achieve the latter is clear from the descriptions of Mollie's spasms and the teams of people who helped keep her from injuring herself. One wonders how much of a drain she was on the household—whether she fit Silas Weir Mitchell's devastating description of "bed-cases": "the broken-down and exhausted women, the pests of many households, who constitute the despair of physicians, and who furnish those annoying examples of despotic selfishness, which wreck the constitutions of nurses and devoted relatives, and in unconscious or half-conscious self-indulgence destroy the comfort of every one about them." There is little evidence for it in Mollie's case; everybody connected with her later spoke of her fortitude, her patience, her long-suffering. Aunt Susan, of course, was the one upon whom the heaviest burden fell, and on this subject her diary is silent.

Whatever demands Mollie placed on those around her—and whatever was the true basis for her symptoms—it is impossible not to feel sympathy for what she endured in the way of cures during the winter and spring of 1866. She was treated to everything that medicine, and folklore, could devise to rid her of her spasms, which greatly alarmed her doctors, and to introduce some sustenance to her body. It is questionable whether the disease or the remedy was more agonizing. A list of the methods her doctors attempted is a catalogue of nineteenth-century medical shots in the dark, the best-educated guesses that combined emerging technology with the deepest medieval ignorance.

The first, and least damaging, plan of attack was to rub her body with alcohol. When that failed, her head was "shaved and blistered," a draconian procedure from which, Mollie said later, "my suffering was very great." Blistering, often accomplished by making chemical burns on the skin, was, like many Victorian cures, based on the theory of counter-irritation: the hypothesis that therapeutically induced pain could disrupt and relieve the cause of preexisting pain. William James became an enthusiast for blistering, and wrote to his brother Henry of how the process appeared to work on his back pain: "I have been trying blisters on my back and they do undeniable good. Get a number about the size of a 25-cents piece, or of a copper cent. Apply one every night on alternate sides of the spine over the diseased muscles. In the morning prick the bubbles; and cover them with a slip of rag with cerate, fastened down by cross straps of sticking plaster. Try a dozen in this way at first. Then wait two weeks and try a half-dozen more and so on." In Mollie's case, despite her suffering, the blistering accomplished nothing.

Next her doctors applied another popular Victorian technique, electric shocks from a battery—a technique much praised and publicized by George Beard for the treatment of ailments including neuralgia, rheumatism, dyspepsia, chorea, paralysis, and diseases of the skin. There were three types of electrotherapy, all using low voltages: faradization, or treatment with alternating current; galvanization, or treatment with direct current; and franklinization, using static electricity. Its practitioners theorized that the current created an internal massage of nerves and muscles, and revitalized a nervous system whose energy was low and listless. The therapy became popular, catching the imagination as a thoroughly modern antidote to the modern problem of exhaustion. It was said to be painless, but Alice James wrote of it rather scathingly to a friend in 1883: She was being treated "by Dr. N——, of whom I have heard great things and who certainly either in spite or because of his quackish quality has done me a great deal of good in many ways. . . . His electricity however has the starching properties of the longest Puritan descent."

Electricity did nothing to stop Mollie's spasms, so next she was put in line with the earth's electromagnetic currents: her bed was shifted so that her head pointed directly north, and her body and limbs south. She was divested of all jewelry and metallic objects, and a large horseshoe magnet was placed at her feet. Magnets had been used therapeutically as far back as the time of the ancient Greeks, and magnetism had been made popular more recently by the Viennese physician Franz Anton Mesmer in the late eighteenth century. Magnets were thought to influence the body's internal electrical energy, and to spur the body to heal itself. Mesmer's first patient had been a seemingly hysterical woman suffering from various symptoms, including blindness and paralysis of her left hand. He had her swallow a mixture containing traces of iron, then attached magnets to her legs and torso. She reportedly felt waves of energy, had a seizure, and was cured. Mollie's magnetic treatment effected no change in her condition, but at least, as she recalled later, "it occasioned me no suffering."

The doctors moved on to hydrotherapy, another popular Victorian remedy. First, sitz baths: three every twenty-four hours, for six weeks. The water was hot, often uncomfortably so, and sometimes medicated with herbs. Worse were the "steam-baths of dry alcohol" that followed: Mollie was placed in the tub, and the tub covered with blankets up to her chin. To create heat, alcohol-burning lamps were placed in the tub with her, and her skin was often burned.

When heat failed to stop the spasms and trances, as it inevitably did, the opposite was tried, sometimes in combination with heat. Mollie was put in a bath of very hot water, and her head was doused with pails of ice-cold water. Next she was rolled in wet sheets wrung out from cold water and made to lie in them until she physically protested. "I could and would endure it no longer," she told Abram Dailey years later. "Then I projected my elbows with all my strength, and burst the sheets, and was at once declared to be in another fit of insanity."

Finally, an ice-jacket was tried: a garment fit for a torture chamber, with pockets into which were put bladders filled with ice. These rested on Mollie's stomach, her spine, and the top of her head. She snapped. "I have a temper," she told Dailey, "and it was then aroused. I was satisfied that my treatment was but a series of experiments, intensifying my suffering, and preventing any chance of my recovery. I seized the bladder of ice on top of my head and hurled it across the room. This was followed by the four others sent in the same direction. Meanwhile the doctor believed I had gone insane, and I was pronounced a raving maniac. Well, I was raving. My vocabulary was insufficient to express my feelings, and I positively refused to submit to any further treatment."

Mollie took the step of firing the physician who had overseen these experiments, though she later said she bore him no ill will—that he was faced with a medical anomaly he did not understand, and felt he must do something. The spasms and trances continued. But her other doctors became ever more concerned about her rejection of almost all food or medicine that was presented to her. "How could she live without food," wrote Abram Dailey, "and how recover, or even improve, without medicines? were questions [her personal physician] naturally asked himself, and if either was forced into her stomach, in quantities to accomplish beneficial results, it was at once rejected."

If she did not begin to eat, her doctors feared, she would die of starvation. At the time, some people believed that nourishment could be absorbed externally, even through the skin, so Mollie was again put into sitz baths, this time filled with beef tea. She was also given enemas of beef tea, brandy, and milk punch (a sickroom delicacy of milk flavored with sugar, brandy, and nutmeg). Her attendants pronounced themselves astounded that she could survive on so little that resembled food. That begged the question of what, in the apparent absence of food, was keeping Mollie alive—a question that would be a defining element in the storm that broke over her more than a decade later.

Perhaps the strangest element of Mollie's case began on the first Sunday in June 1866, a year after the horsecar accident, when she went into yet another trance—but this one strikingly different from its predecessors. Mollie had, she said much later, no recollection of anything that happened for the next nine years. She characterized this period as a "nine-year trance"; yet she functioned apparently normally during that time.

Abram Dailey later chronicled that Mollie, during those nine years, wrote more than 6,500 letters, worked up 100,000 ounces of worsted, did a vast amount of fine embroidery, and constructed a great number of decorative waxwork flowers and leaves. This was especially difficult to accomplish, he reported, because for most of the period, her right arm was rigidly clamped up behind her head and the fingers of both hands were clenched together. When she needed to use both hands she would do the work above her head, carrying her left hand up to meet her right. She wrote by inserting a pencil or pen between the closed fingers of her left hand, in her fist (it is unclear whether she was originally right- or left-handed). The handwriting in her letters was said to be very regular and beautiful, and her style of composition eloquent. Mollie was also quite sociable during those nine years, welcoming strangers from far beyond New York who had heard of her case and wanted to meet her.

At the end of the nine years, Mollie went into a monthlong coma-like trance. When she came out of it, her right arm relaxed from its rigid state, her hands opened, her limbs untwisted—and she was, mentally, back in June 1866. She picked up a conversation with her doctor where she had left off, and when her twenty-one-year-old brother approached her, she didn't recognize him. He had been twelve when she went into the trance. She also didn't recognize anyone who had been introduced to her during those nine years, or the work she had done with her own hands. She was shown the diary she had written, and had to admit that the handwriting was hers. She burst into tears when she realized that she had no memory of almost a decade of her life.

"Strange thoughts came into my mind," she told Dailey later, "and strange sensations came over me. When I looked upon the wax flowers, the work of my hands, I could not realize that they had been done by me. They were repugnant to me. The sensation that I experienced was that they were the work of one who was dead. I found I could not do some kinds of the work which I had done, without learning again how. I could not realize that so long a period had passed in my life, and that I was part of the same being who had done the work, made the acquaintances, and had the experiences covering those nine years. I was, and still am, an enigma to myself. If anybody can tell who I am, and what I am, when they have heard of the remaining experiences and features of my life, I would be glad to have them do so."

What can all of this mean? The phenomenon of the lost years, though extreme, was not unknown in the context of nineteenth-century hysteria. It was called somnambulism, and it corresponds roughly to what we would now call amnesia. The *London Medical Gazette* in 1838 described the case of a young woman who went to her doctor with symptoms including unexplained pains that came and went, occasional total blindness, and a jaw clamped convulsively shut (symptoms shared by Mollie). The most peculiar feature was what her doctor termed a "hysterical somnambulism," during which his patient would sit down at the piano and play her favorite pieces, perform minor domestic chores, walk up and down stairs, get herself undressed for bed—forever unconscious of things around her, and having no memory of her actions when she emerged from the spell. One part of her mind, he concluded, was dissociated from the other.

In current psychological thinking, amnesia—that is, living certain experiences and then retaining no memory of them—is a step on the path to a larger diagnosis (one that was just emerging in the nineteenth century): dissociative identity disorder, more popularly known as multiple-personality disorder, or MPD. In MPD, the mind supports parallel states of existence (or "personalities"), each state generally (though not always) having no recollection or knowledge of the other. Anthony Walsh, a professor of psychology at Salve Regina University in Newport, Rhode Island, has looked at Mollie's case from a modern perspective, and wrote about it in the 1970s. She fits classically the symptoms of nineteenth-century hysteria, he concluded, "but a diagnosis of traumatic hysterical neurosis, conversion type, in this instance would not do justice to the richness of Mollie's neurosis." He remarked in particular on her "disintegrated self," which blossomed into a case of alternating personalities.

To Walsh, the Mollie Fancher of the nine-year trance could be seen as a secondary self, which he named the "isolated X-personality." But there was more dissociation to come. As Mollie said to Dailey in the 1890s: "I am told that there are five other Mollie Fanchers, who together, make the whole of the one Mollie Fancher, known to the world; who they are and what they are I cannot tell or explain, I can only conjecture." Dailey described five distinct Mollies, each with a different name, each of whom he met (as did Aunt Susan and a family friend, George Sargent). According to Susan Crosby, the first additional personality appeared some three years after the nine-year trance, or around 1878.

The dominant Mollie, the one who functioned most of the time and was known to everyone as Mollie Fancher, was designated Sunbeam (the names were devised by Sargent, as he met each of the personalities). The four other personalities came out only at night, after eleven, when Mollie would have her usual spasm and trance. The first to appear was always Idol, who shared Sunbeam's memories of childhood and adolescence but had no memory of the horsecar accident. Idol was very jealous of Sunbeam's accomplishments, and would sometimes unravel her embroidery or hide her work. Idol and Sunbeam wrote with different handwriting, and at times penned letters to each other.

The next personality Sargent named Rosebud: "It was the sweetest little child's face," he described, "the voice and accent that of a little child." Rosebud said she was seven years old, and had Mollie's memories of early childhood: her first teacher's name, the streets on which she had lived, children's songs. She wrote with a child's handwriting, upper- and lowercase letters mixed. When Dailey questioned Rosebud about her mother, she answered that she was sick and had gone away, and that she did not know when she would be coming back. As to where she lived, she answered "Fulton Street," where the Fanchers had lived before moving to Gates Avenue.

Pearl, the fourth personality, was evidently in her late teens. Sargent described her as very spiritual, sweet in expression, cultured and agreeable: "She remembers Professor West [principal of Brooklyn Heights Seminary], and her school days and friends up to about the sixteenth year in the life of Miss Fancher. She pronounces her words with an accent peculiar to young ladies of about 1865." Ruby, the last Mollie, was vivacious, humorous, bright, witty. "She does everything with a dash," said Sargent. "What mystifies me about 'Ruby,' and distinguishes her from the others, is that she does not, in her conversations with me, go much into the life of Mollie Fancher. She has the air of knowing a good deal more than she tells." But on another occasion, Ruby spoke to Dailey of Mollie's horseback-riding accident and other events from her teens. "She remembers Professor West, and also Mr. Taylor," wrote Dailey, "who was her beau, to whom she was engaged to be married, but [whom she] had ceased to regard with affection." (Thus Ruby provides another possible motivation for Mollie's retreat into hysteria: a wish to escape her planned marriage without having to admit that desire.) Walsh says of the animated, almost flirtatious Ruby:

"She appears to have been an entirely new personality, perhaps the one Mollie would have liked to have been."

The personalities usually emerged in that order, from Idol to Ruby. Each would eventually say she was tired, Mollie would sink into a short trance, and then the next emanation would make herself known. None seemed to know anything of the others, except what she learned from Aunt Susan or friends such as Sargent or Dailey. All four apparently became permanent though intermittent aspects of Mollie's life in 1878.

Tales of multiple-personality disorder are so strange as to have a sense of unreality about them—a lingering suspicion that this is an elaborate put-on, that no one person can be inhabited, as it were, by completely separate personalities. And in fact not all psychologists are believers. Edward Shorter contends that the diagnosis of MPD comes from a "brew of suggestibility." Evidence is mounting, he feels, that multiple personalities can be produced by the physician, or by the culture, in a patient with inchoate symptoms that he or she can't understand. "For patients who see themselves in a second state," Shorter writes, "it is a relatively simple matter to give that state a name, and then perhaps to produce other states as well, each of which has a name and a distinctive 'personality' of its own."

Anthony Walsh dated the first published case of MPD to an 1817 article, "A Double Consciousness, or a Duality of Person in the Same Individual," which appeared in the *New York Medical Repository*. Shorter describes a slightly later case, that of a young Frenchwoman named Estelle L'Hardy in the 1830s, which has similarities to Mollie Fancher's circumstances. Estelle was devastated by the death of her father in a cholera epidemic when she was seven years old; two years later she suffered a fall on her back and developed a series of what Shorter feels were psychosomatic symptoms. She sometimes was paralyzed and felt chilly; when in her "other state" she demanded ice-water baths to cure her paralysis. That state evolved into a separate personality, named Angeline, who directed the doctors in her treatment.

Shorter places MPD in the context of the Victorian fascination with the altered mental states of hysteria—and the apparent ability of certain doctors, Charcot for one, to induce somnambulism or a second state of mental awareness through hypnosis. "For students of psychosomatic illness," Shorter writes, "the point about multiple personality disorder is that a climate of suggestion can elicit not merely physical symptoms such as paralysis, but fashionable mental symptoms as well." He makes the very telling observation that the occurrence of MPD declined greatly between 1900 and 1950, only to be revived by the publication of *The Three Faces of Eve* in 1957. By the end of the twentieth century, it had become again "a common form of dissociation, supposedly resulting from 'child abuse.'"

A somewhat less skeptical Walsh characterizes MPD as remaining "a mysterious sport of nature—for most psychologists, psychiatrists, and physicians live long and active professional careers without ever encountering a single case." Twentieth-century psychological theory, he adds, usually points to an early childhood environment that was bizarre, restrictive, or broadly hysterical as a strong factor in MPD. One thing remains clear, Walsh writes: "Multiple personality has long been associated with hysteria."

The historian Carroll Smith-Rosenberg has theorized that psychoanalysis is "the child of the hysterical woman," and it was a case that in some respects echoes Mollie Fancher's, the case of the famous "Anna O.," that launched Freud into his theories on hysteria and hypnotism. Anna O. was being treated by Freud's mentor, Josef Breuer, in the early 1880s, for various hysterical symptoms (again, shared by Mollie): areas of numbness, contractures of the right arm, partial paralysis of the other three limbs, nervous cough, and problems with hearing and vision. Breuer's technique was to hypnotize her so that she would relive the trauma that caused the hysteria; once that was done, Anna's symptoms disappeared. His experience, which he shared with

Freud, led the two to publish their opinion, in the 1895 *Studies on Hysteria,* that hysterical patients were reexperiencing an original psychic trauma—that their physical symptoms were not random but were expressions of the original causal event.

Freud and Breuer's theory signaled the beginning of the end of the age of hysteria. Their thinking pointed the way, quite convincingly, toward a psychological—that is, mind-based rather than physiologically based—definition of hysteria. Their logical demystification coincided with Charcot's death in 1893, and the overblown balloon of Victorian hysteria collapsed to earth. Flamboyant hysteria almost immediately disappeared from the Salpêtrière. Charcot's inpatients, the stars of his lectures, stayed on and gradually "forgot" their symptoms, or left the hospital and lived normal lives on the outside. In 1901 a disciple of Charcot's came up with a cynical definition of hysteria: "any symptom that can be induced by suggestion and abolished by persuasion."

Although it's not precisely true that hysteria completely evaporated in the twentieth century—remnants of it have been reclassified as various neurotic phenomena—the more florid aspects of its Victorian incarnation appear to be gone forever. The sudden, inexplicable paralyses; long-lasting muscle contractures; loss of the use of one's senses; and especially the fits and spasms that twisted the body into weird positions—these are extremely rare today. What made these manifestations suddenly decline? Some medical historians hypothesize that once doctors stopped believing in the symptoms, the patients stopped presenting them. Others suggest the symptoms vanished because the unique psychosocial context—the complicated and frustrating role of the Victorian woman—vanished.

Still others propose an explanation by the "psychological literacy" theory: that as Freudian and Jungian ideas, and other basic tenets of psychology, have become more widely understood by the general public, the more obvious, primitive acting out of stresses has become more subtle, more inward. We have become more sophisticated in our ways of expressing mild mental illness—that is, neurosis. In this way, hysteria may have fostered much of our thinking about psychosomatic disease, and more broadly our thinking about the ways in which the mind deals with psychic distress. Many aspects of nineteenth-century hysteria are known now by other terms: depression, schizophrenia, dissociative disorder, histrionic-personality type, and factitious-illness disorder.

If Mollie Fancher's experiences seem to partake of several characteristically Victorian preoccupations—railway neurosis, invalidism, hysteria—they also forecast new ways of thinking about the mind that pointed to the twentieth century. More than a decade after the accident that made her an invalid, those new ways of thinking could be found, improbably, on the front pages of New York's newspapers.

CHAPTER THREE

"Dead and Yet Alive!"

The girl is simply a miracle. She says she is a miracle, and I know she is one. The entire scientific world should know all about her, and I hope the time will come when it will.

—Professor Charles E. West, in the New York *Sun,* November 24, 1878

M OLLIE'S STORY was too rich and strange not to find its way ultimately into print. When it finally hit—despite her pleas for privacy—it hit big. In the absence of *20/20* and reality TV, the curious and the bored had in the late nineteenth century a plethora of broadsheets (some so broad that one could and often did take a nap beneath their wide pages). Brooklyn alone had several major newspapers, including the *Daily Eagle, Daily Times,* and *Daily Union-Argus.* New York City claimed the *Times, World, Sun, Herald, Tribune, Evening Post, Star,* and lesser rags.

Even the more staid papers made room for a few colorful tales. Readers of the *Eagle* could chuckle over "Neighborly Amenities," in which Mrs. Matilda Fahey was fined five dollars by a judge for permitting herself the luxury of pulling the hair and scratching the face of Mrs. Ann Riley. The ladies lived in the same house, number 16 Pacific Street, Brooklyn, "and are consequently mortal enemies." Amid more solid news of cholera epidemics, impeachment dramas, attempted lynchings, and steamship disasters were nestled stories of the uncon-

71

ventional, the shocking, and the sad: "A Priest's Marriage: He Falls a Victim to the Attractions of a Pretty Widow" and "Suicide of a Young Woman—She Takes Arsenic and Dies" (the coroner decided to investigate the case in order to find out "why the young woman should thus desire to leave her friends here for an unknown future").

If a story was spectacular enough, it could cross state lines. The tale of "Tragedy in St. Louis—Infidelity and Shooting Affair" was too wicked to remain local; it reached the New York papers the very next day. It told of Abraham Dyson, a respectable man of forty-five, his attractive young wife, and Charles Rappe, the gay and dashing young music teacher who rented a room in the same house as the Dysons. Friends warned Dyson that his wife was becoming too friendly with Rappe, and finally Dyson, who gave it out that he was going away on business, instead armed himself with a revolver and hid near his wife's bedroom. Convinced of her guilt, he rushed the room, but stumbled against a coal bucket. The lovers heard him and barred the door, so he went outside, climbed in the window, and shot Rappe in the chest. When a police officer arrived, he found the wounded Rappe and Mrs. Dyson pinning Dyson to the floor; Rappe was trying to wrest the gun away. Dyson was arrested, and Rappe was not expected to live. Amid such tales, the Mollie Fancher story had fewer immediate hot buttons— no sex or murder—but more staying power. It took two forays into print before the story gained a foothold. Once it did, it began to embody the angst of the age.

The first story to appear about Mollie was the *Eagle* article of June 7, 1866, a year after the horsecar accident, which used Mollie's case to deplore the overactive "nervous energy" of the times. The reporter, not bylined but said by Abram Dailey to be a Colonel William Hemstreet, did not reveal Mollie's name but gave the details of her story, with some errors. He also saturated his article with commentary about the societal evils that brought her to such a pass. Dailey did not mention how Mollie's situation reached Hemstreet's ears; the reporter mistakenly wrote that Mollie was living with her father, mother, and several siblings. He described her as "a fine-looking, capable, young lady, and of great apparent promise. She is what would be termed *spirituelle,* with light hair and complexion, a fragile figure, pale countenance, large sparkling eye, with a forehead and features indicative of thought rather than execution."

Hemstreet also mistakenly wrote that Mollie continued her schoolwork until the time of, and even after, her horseback-riding accident (while "looking more like parchment than flesh and blood"). He then described with fair accuracy her multitude of symptoms resulting from the final horsecar misadventure, but followed these with the first indications of something that was to help split her observers right down the middle, according to their beliefs: her "clairvoyant condition." While in a trance, he wrote, "she is powerfully clairvoyant in her faculties. She can tell the time by several watches variously set to deceive her, read unopened letters, decipher the contents of a slate, and repeat what 'Mrs. Grundy says,' by serving up the gossip of the neighborhood. She appears to possess the faculty of second sight to a remarkable degree." Hemstreet connected Mollie's apparent clairvoyance or "other sight" to the waning of her physical senses—as if they were being replaced by something less tangible.

Mollie herself described the inception of her special powers to Abram Dailey in the 1890s. Her second sight—her sense of seeing without the use of her eyes, in her words—began to develop around May 1866, three months or so after her blindness set in. First she seemed to have a consciousness of the position of things around her, and the movements of people, without actually seeing them. Then she began to perceive the face of her small gold watch, which hung over the mantelpiece on the opposite side of the room, at a distance that would defy even ordinary eyesight, not to mention the blindness Mollie claimed. Soon after that, she amazed her aunt by "reading" a letter. Susan Crosby had, since Mollie lost her sight, fallen into the habit of opening her letters and reading them aloud. One day in the spring of 1866, Mollie insisted that her aunt hand her the letter that had arrived in that day's post. Susan replied, "Why, darling, you know you can't read it," but Mollie persisted. According to her own account, she took it in her hands and read it to her astonished aunt. Once Mollie's friends heard of her feats, they began playfully to test her special vision. She astounded those around her by telling them what they held in their hands, and even what was hidden in their pockets.

Mollie reportedly kept her eyes tightly closed most of the time, even when exercising her second sight. One friend, Alice LePlongeon, often visited with her husband, a physician who was fascinated by Mollie's case, and later told Abram Dailey that they were both convinced that Mollie could "see" quite clearly even though her eyes were blind. Once the LePlongeons brought photos to show her, and Mollie, lying with closed eyelids in the darkened room, made comments about the pictures. "She even pointed out a portrait of myself in a very small group," Alice LePlongeon said, "where my face was hardly bigger than the head of a common pin. We had not told her that my figure was there." Alice also described Mollie's intricate needlework, and other friends told of her deftly unknotting tangled strands of wool worsted, threading fine needles, and watching and exclaiming about a tadpole swimming in a glass case that was placed on the far side of the dark room—all with her eyes closed.

Mollie's mysterious eye problems led to one of the most salient, and peculiar, aspects of her daily life. What visitors mentioned about Mollie's room—almost the first thing they commented on, in fact—was the darkness of the place. Mollie maintained that the light pained her eyes (although some wondered why a blind person would be bothered by light), and the curtains were customarily drawn and the gaslights kept low. The duskiness made her special sight all the more remarkable to visitors, who themselves could not see things around them that Mollie described minutely. One visitor's tale, written in a letter from a friend

Mollie Fancher in 1874, nine years after her injury, and four years before her story hit the front page. Her face and hands give no evidence of her reported fasting, which at this time was said by friends and family to have persisted for eight years. (FROM *MOLLIE FANCHER, THE BROOKLYN ENIGMA*)

of Mollie's, Louis Sherk, to Abram Dailey, struck an especially spooky note. Sherk told of his first visit to Mollie. He had been invited because his brother had performed magnetic treatments on her at the request of her doctor. Sherk's visit took place, he recalled, "upon a dark and stormy day." He was wrapped in a cloak, wearing a slouch hat. He entered the downstairs hall of the house at Gates and Downing and heard his name called to go upstairs.

"The room in which Miss Mollie was lying was very dark," wrote Sherk. "There was no fire in the room and it was cold and chilly. . . . On account of the darkness I could not distinguish Miss Fancher's features at the time. She took hold of my hand and passed into a trance state, and when she came out of it she was covered with cold perspiration."

Dailey described Mollie's eyes as being almost continuously closed, or with just a little white showing at the bottom, for at least the first nine years of his acquaintance with her. Gradually they began to open occasionally, but they were still apparently unseeing. Even when threatened by sudden movements near her eyes, Mollie remained impassive, with no instinctive recoil or fear. Doctors called in to examine her eyes, according to Dailey, concluded that they were sightless. "The arteries and veins are scarcely perceptible," he wrote, "and indicate that an insufficient supply of nourishment is afforded to the organs of sight to give them strength for ordinary use."

Instead, Dailey wrote, Mollie saw from other parts of her body. "That she could and can see from the top of her head and from her forehead, cannot permit of a reasonable doubt," he claimed. He also described her method of reading books with her fingers, simply absorbing the contents of the printed matter. Once Mollie was commissioned to embroider a rose design for a lady visitor; she sketched a spray of roses, selected needles and silks, threaded the needles without hesitation, and sewed the design—all with her eyes "fast shut." The visitor exclaimed, "Oh, Mollie, your eyes are in the ends of your fingers."

Soon after Mollie's actual sight apparently failed, in the spring of 1866, her sense of touch became more sensitive, and later observers suggested that her senses had been transposed—not an unprecedented idea at that time. This had been reported in various other cases, some of classic hysteria. Estelle L'Hardy, the young Frenchwoman who was among the first recorded cases of multiple-personality disorder, also had various psychic phenomena (in addition to her intermittent paralysis and other hysterical symptoms). She claimed that her senses were transposed around her body—to her stomach, fingertips, elbow, and shoulder—and that she could read a printed text with her fingers.

By the mid–nineteenth century, with the rise of mesmerism, the idea developed among practitioners and many doctors that trance could exalt or transpose the senses. When many bodily functions were suppressed, as in a cataleptic "crisis" or self-hypnosis, the theory ran, electrical energy could become so focused in one sense, such as vision, that the cataleptic patient could see through solid objects (the back of a clock, for instance, as Mollie presumably saw through) or read minds. Vision might also be transported, say from the eyes to the stomach or fingers, and become meshed with a sense of touch sensitized and concentrated enough that fingertips could "read" text.

Such theorizing gives at least a context, though hardly a sense of reality, to stories like the one published in *The World* in the late fall of 1878, during Mollie's second and much more sensational period of fame. On December 1, in the midst of the Mollie brouhaha, the newspaper ran a long letter to the editor from a Chicago doctor who signed himself "J.D., M.D.," detailing a case that he compared in many details to Mollie's. It involved Emma Parker, daughter of a distinguished lawyer, who at the age of eighteen was injured in the heel when she stepped on a tack. One misfortune followed another: her leg swelled to huge dimensions for a period of six months; once the swelling abated, her limbs became paralyzed; soon afterward the muscles of her mouth became paralyzed and she could neither eat nor speak. "By degrees the original paralysis extended throughout the patient's system," the doctor wrote, "so that in two or three years the avenues for impressions from the outer world were wholly, or seemed to be wholly, closed for her." She lay in bed speechless and unable to move.

Then the strangest aspect of her case emerged: those close to her came to understand that when she wanted food, Miss Parker would make a low moan from the extremities of her toes and a bass grunt from her right heel, the one that had been wounded. These transposed sounds were only the beginning. After a while, music was heard from Miss Parker's toes. "We were naturally then at a loss to find out how it was that new tunes by Harrison Millard—who was her favorite before she sank into the condition which I have described—could resound from her feet," Dr. J.D. commented. "Still there was the fact, and it was left to us as men of science to account for it." This he did by explaining that Miss Parker's sense of hearing must have been transferred to her lower extremities. Some might say that it was impossible for toenails, even in the direst situation, to give out sounds. But facts were facts, and the evidence of one's own eyes and ears could not be refuted.

The story gets better. While Miss Parker lay in bed, oblivious to the world around her, listening, when she was not in a trance or pseudoslumber, to the music played from her toes, she developed another singular talent, one reminiscent of Mollie's case. She was able to perceive what was happening outside the house. She could "see" her father going down to court, and even place him in a specific street at a specific time. When she expressed with her toenails (in a popular tune or a hymn) that she desired beef, it was certain that the butcher was about to arrive; she could even tell when he was before the door. (Dr. J.D. does not reveal how Miss Parker could communicate her sightings to others if she was not able to speak.) In the same breath as the tale of the butcher and Miss Parker's longings for meat, however, the doctor conveys another conundrum of the young woman's condition: her friends claimed that she had not eaten in the year since her encounter with the tack. Her esophagus, like the rest of her body, was in a state of complete prostration. This reported fast did not keep Emma Parker from appearing to the doctor to be "as hale and hearty as she was before her accident," despite her bedridden sensory deprivation.

Miss Parker's musicality improved, and even spread to other body parts. Dr. J.D. knew that New York doctors would scoff at his story, but he was constrained to tell the truth: Miss Parker whistled the tune of "Lily Dale" audibly through her eyelids; she literally breathed the notes through her eyes, and he heard them "in dulcet strain." Where there is music, harmony cannot be far behind, and eventually Miss Parker evolved into a barbershop quartet. "She became able after a few years to sing soprano with her right heel, while her left did duty as alto," Dr. J.D. reported. "When her feet were removed from under the coverlet, the two would sing the 'Quis est homo' with the most telling effect, and in other songs it was necessary only to lift her elbows from under the cover to make one of them do the basso and the other the tenor. Meantime she herself lay as still as the dead." To read such a tale today is to wonder whether this was an elaborate joke perpetrated on *The World,* and yet the letter was played straight. More than a century ago, it was possible to conceive of the universe as a thing containing many great unknowns.

The other manifestation of Mollie's "second sight" or clairvoyance that fascinated those who knew or read about her—and that echoed the claims of earlier cataleptics—was her reported ability to have out-of-body experiences, to see beyond her room into the world at large and observe people who were far away. According to Abram Dailey, Mollie would often surprise friends with her knowledge of things they had done out in the world that she could not have witnessed. Once, for example, a friend of the family, a Mr. Townsend, arrived to join his wife at Mollie's house after a ferry trip across the East River. He began joking with Mollie, and she told him, "See here, old fellow, be very careful; that was a very pretty young lady that you were escorting across the ferry, and you seemed to be very much interested in her." Mr. Townsend blushed, and admitted that he had come across on the ferry with a young lady of his acquaintance. Mollie said she had been with him, unseen, and she was able to describe the young woman who had accompanied him. Dailey wrote that such scenes were repeated often, that Mollie told of being with friends when they were a thousand miles away, detailing their actions and surroundings. The details were so accurate, he added, "that to doubt her powers would be absurd."

To believers in such nonphysical travel, the most riveting aspect of Mollie's experiences was her professed ability to visit, in spirit, the Great Beyond. She often described to friends her encounters with loved ones who "are said to be dead" (her phraseology itself making clear that life after death was an open question to her). "When I come out of my trances," she told Dailey, "I sometimes am grieved because I have been taken away from brighter and better conditions in another world. At times, at least in spirit, away from the scenes of this world, I am with friends in most heavenly places. My consciousness of these things is, to me, as real as the experiences of my life upon this earth. I often see my mother and other friends around me, and in my dreary days of sickness, pain and suffering, and when my spirit is depressed, I can hear her tender voice speaking to me words of cheer, bidding me 'bear up, and be brave, and . . . endure.'"

Mollie's purported experiences among the spirits of the dead resonated deeply with believers in Spiritualism, which was then reaching its apex. Spiritualism billed itself, in what might now be seen as an oxymoron, as the "scientific religion." Through one of the oddest combinations of ideas put together by any group of philosophers, nineteenth-century Spiritualists did their best to co-opt scientific language and methods to explain an atavistic belief in spirit communication that reached back thousands of years. In an age that, according to one historian, "wanted to believe that its universe operated like an orderly machine," this pseudoscientific approach to spirituality was a winning ticket.

At its height in the 1860s through the end of the century, Spiritualism claimed such adherents as Abraham and Mary Todd Lincoln (who tried to contact their dead son, Tad, through séances); the psychologist William James (a driving force behind the founding of the American Society for Psychical Research to "investigate" Spiritualism); John Roebling, the designer of the Brooklyn Bridge; and Mollie's biographer Abram Dailey. The central belief of Spiritualism was that the soul, or spirit, could be separated from the body and live on after death, and that spirits could be contacted through human mediums. The primary ritual of the religion was the séance, the most colorful of which featured table-lifting and other feats of spiritual kinesthesia, and in which a medium would claim to be speaking to dead family members or, sometimes, famous figures from history.

Mollie's claims, both to live without nourishment as a kind of bodiless soul, and to cross the border and communicate with the dead, made her the perfect standard-bearer for Spiritualism—a role that she persistently rejected. "It has been charged and stated," she told Dailey, that his biography of her was being written "in the interest of what is commonly known as Spiritualism. Nothing could be further from the fact, in so far as I am concerned; and I believe the same to be true as regards others interested in this publication. The work is being done in the interest of the medical and scientific world and at the earnest request of friends. I have been repeatedly asked to attempt to act the part of a medium for spirit communications, and I have invariably refused to attempt anything of the kind, because I do not consider myself capable of answering any such requirement."

Colonel Hemstreet's 1866 *Eagle* article, which launched Mollie not only into the view of the general public but also into the hungry maw of the Spiritualists, put the two elements that would become the most celebrated—her clairvoyance and her abstinence from food—at the bottom of a long subhead. But the next time her name reached the headlines, twelve years later, the fasting and second sight captured top billing. The stage was set, at last, for a long run.

Mollie Fancher's greatest fame began, not in Brooklyn or New York City, but in Buffalo, in upstate New York, in the fall of 1878. The leading ladies of that city organized an art loan exhibition, which opened on October 1, that featured artwork and crafts from across the country and around the world. The exhibition was big news in Buffalo, launched with great fanfare in the press and offering musical performances almost every evening. *The Buffalo Daily Courier* hailed its first night as a brilliant success, guaranteed to reap a bountiful harvest of money for charitable causes and to demonstrate that Buffalo was one of the richest art depositories in America. The *Courier* published an article about the show nearly every day of its run, which ended on October 26 (after being extended twice). The first, and longest, article detailed each collection and made mention of, in the local artists' room, "some very fine embroidery which is said to be the work of a blind girl living in New York who has eaten nothing for several months."

It was some of Mollie's handiwork, and apparently it attracted no small notice. On October 22, the *Courier* ran a long article, headed "Mollie Fancher: A Romance from the Loan Exhibition—Fourteen Years Without Food / A Marvelous Invalid—A New York Story Authenticated by Buffalo Witnesses." As the paper reported: "Many visitors to the local room of the Art Loan Exhibition have remarked in one of the cases a specimen of very fine satin embroidery surmounted by the photograph of a very beautiful woman, evidently an invalid and blind, reclining upon a bed. The work is exquisitely done, but the chief interest in this exhibit lies in the history of the worker, whose picture it is that lies upon it. This history is so strange, so romantic, so at defiance with all scientific precedent that we should hesitate to publish it did it not come to us backed by the best of authority."

The article went on to paraphrase a long piece published two days before in the *New York Herald*—coverage that had been stimulated probably, in circular fashion, by gossip filtering down from the loan exhibition. Mollie's story may have been a fresh sensation in Buffalo, but it qualified as old news in New York, a fact that some newspapers derided even as they eagerly pitched in to cover it one more time. "A dull interval in the world of journalism is very apt to be marked by a revival of the story of Miss Fancher of Brooklyn," complained New York's *Evening Post*. "The revived story does not vary in any important particular from the story which has been told many times during the last thirteen years. Miss Fancher lives apparently without bodily nourishment, although for a great part of the time her condition scarcely can be called that of life." At the same time, *The Brooklyn Daily Eagle* tried to establish precedence by reminding its readers that it had been the first to unearth and publish Mollie's story—she was, after all, a local girl—"with much minuteness of detail" and with regular updates.

This time, however, the Fancher tale took hold in a new way. Fasting itself, rather than clairvoyance or Spiritualism, now took the lead. "Life Without Food," proclaimed the *Herald* headline, followed by stacks of subheads: "An Invalid Lady Who for Fourteen Years Has Lived Without Nourishment / The Laws of Life Defied / What the Physicians Say of the Remarkable Case / A Sad and Romantic History." (*The Herald* appears to have initiated a pattern of exaggeration in its subhead, by inflating the period of Mollie's reputed fast from twelve to fourteen years. According to Mollie's friends and family, she ceased eating in the spring of 1866—which in the fall of 1878 would put the fast's duration at twelve and a half years. The mistake was repeated by other newspapers and commentators, until fourteen was cited interchangeably with twelve as her number of years without food.)

"In a modest, secluded house at the corner of Myrtle avenue [*sic*] and Downing street, Brooklyn," the story began, "lives an invalid lady afflicted with paralysis, with a history so remarkable and extraordinary that, notwithstanding it is vouched for by physicians of standing, it is almost incredible." The most fantastic element of the case was Mollie's claim to have lived absolutely without food or nourishment for more than a dozen years—a claim her family had supposedly kept secret to protect against the visits of the curious and incredulous. Although the reporter was not admitted into the house to see Mollie or her aunt directly, he did speak to several people who knew her well, among them an unnamed woman intimate with the family who gave a description of Mollie.

She lay, the friend said, in a dark room, in a gloom to which one's eyes gradually became accustomed. The room was brightened by the presence of flowers, birds, and books, although such decorations would be of little use to the blind woman. Mollie, despite her years of pain and starvation, retained a girlish beauty. Her face was framed by rather short blond hair that curled close to her head, parted slightly on the side and combed back from her face in almost a jaunty manner. Her cheeks were full, her mouth and nose delicately molded, and her teeth white, small, and even. The friend estimated that Mollie would, under ordinary circumstances, weigh about 130 pounds, but gave no hint of her actual weight. The full cheeks do not suggest emaciation. Yet, the friend insisted, to her knowledge Mollie had lain since 1865 in the same room and in very nearly the same position, and had not eaten any nutritious food since 1866.

The *Herald* article described at length the evidence of second sight, and introduced an element that was to become a rallying point as time went on: the idea that Mollie was a true miracle—not only something beyond ordinary human experience, but perhaps supported by divine power. The first hints of that came from R. Fleet Speir, Mollie's personal physician, a prominent Brooklyn practitioner whose grandfather had erected a homestead, the Fleet Mansion, on the corner of Fulton and Gold streets. Dr. Speir had graduated with highest honors from the medical department of the University of New York, made a tour of European hospitals, and returned to the United States with the new technology of plaster-of-Paris splints, which he later taught to Union Army surgeons during the Civil War. Speir assured the *Herald* reporter that no solid foods had passed the woman's lips since the paralysis that followed her horsecar accident. Early in her case, he had feared that she would die of starvation, and had sometimes forced her to take a teaspoonful of water or milk by using an instrument to pry open her mouth. But that was painful to her, and he finally desisted, astounded by her continued survival. "The case knocks the bottom out of all existing medical theses," Speir observed, "and is, in a word, miraculous."

NEW YORK HERALD, SUNDAY, OCTOBER 20, 1878.

LIFE WITHOUT FOOD.

An Invalid Lady Who for Fourteen Years Has Lived Without Nourishment

THE LAWS OF LIFE DEFIED.

What the Physicians Say of the Remarkable Case.

A SAD AND ROMANTIC HISTORY.

One of the first of many sensational newspaper stories that made Mollie Fancher a household name. This New York Herald *article inflated Mollie's twelve years of fasting to fourteen, and offered a voyeuristic glimpse into the "well guarded secret" of her darkened bedroom.*

Speir hadn't give up his medical theses without a fight. He employed his own professional tools of deception to discover whether Mollie was eating secretly, several times giving her unannounced emetics to detect any evidence of food in her system. He even occasionally crept into the house at eleven or twelve at night to see whether he might surprise her snacking or sneaking out of bed. But always his findings were the same: her stomach was devoid of food, and she was at all times in the same condition, lying in the position she had occupied for her entire invalidism. Other doctors were at first inclined to laugh, Speir said, and "call me a fool when I told them of the long abstinence and keen mental powers" of his patient. But everyone who actually saw her, he added, was convinced.

Another of Mollie's physicians, Dr. Robert Ormiston, told a similar tale of mystification. "It seems incredible," he said, "but from everything I can learn Mollie Fancher never eats." Nearly everything about her diagnosis eluded him; he couldn't classify her case with any of the ordinary complaints he had encountered in the course of his medical practice. He hypothesized that spinal trouble, the presumed result of her horsecar fall, explained the paralysis and physical infirmities. But why should her nervous system be so abnormally developed, some of it seemingly dead, and other senses so keen and intuitive? Most striking of all, Ormiston said, "her tenacity of life for fourteen years [he had, it appears, adopted the *Herald*'s exaggeration], utterly without sustenance enough to feed a baby for a week, appeals strongly to my unwilling belief in supernatural visitations."

The *Herald* reporter had opened his story by calling Mollie's case "almost incredible." But the rest of the article was free of editorial comment, allowing sources to speak for themselves. What were readers to make of these odd details, of the reports that this woman who was said to have eaten nothing for twelve or so years had full cheeks and a beautiful face? Despite their intermittent tests of whether she did or did not eat, did her medically trained physicians really believe that anyone could live without food for that amount of time? The public challenging of those ideas would turn Mollie's story from curiosity into cause célèbre, after the publication of a personal account by a reputable person who had known Mollie for years: Professor Charles West, head of the school where she had been a student until her illness.

For this, *The Buffalo Daily Courier* had an exclusive, and an enviable one. Professor West was well known in Buffalo as the former principal of Buffalo Female Seminary, and had been deluged with questions about Mollie once the art loan exhibition began. He responded with a long letter, and evidently gave his permission for it to be published in the paper. This was the final dose of gunpowder needed. Headlined "Mollie Fancher," it ran on November 10, 1878. Her fasting figured in the subhead: "Dr. West's Account of a Most Remarkable Case / Twelve Years Without Food / Extraordinary Physical and Mental Conditions / Clairvoyance and Other Preternatural Faculties / 'Nothing to Die.'"

West's lucid account covered all the basic threads of Mollie's story except the multiple personalities, an aspect that must have been carefully guarded by friends and family, because it never reached the newspapers, even at the height of her fame. To tell her story adequately, West began, would require a treatise, but he managed to paint a vivid picture of the teenage Mollie he had known when she attended Brooklyn Heights Seminary. She had been a sweet girl, of a delicate and nervous temperament, highly esteemed for her pleasing manners and gentle disposition, as well as an excellent scholar. Before she left school because of her failing health, she had excelled in what West termed *"belles lettres."* He had fallen out of touch with the family, but when he learned of her invalidism from a Brooklyn newspaper article—probably Colonel Hemstreet's 1866 piece—he called at Gates Avenue and subsequently became an intimate visitor.

Perhaps one reason, beyond West's firsthand knowledge of the family and his prominence as head of an exclusive seminary, that his account carried the weight it did was that he approached Mollie with an attitude of some scientific skepticism. He kept a journal of his visits, jotting down observations of her symptoms. "I have used all the sagacity I possess to detect any fraud or collusion," he wrote the *Courier,* "but I have never seen anything to excite my suspicion or mar my confidence in her integrity. She is a lovely Christian girl and shrinks from any public exhibition of herself." West included short excerpts from Aunt Susan's diary describing Mollie's physical changes, and then added his own, presumably eyewitness, descriptions. In these he did not appear to stumble, educated man though he was, over the seeming inconsistencies in her story—for instance, the miles of worsted and embroidery and wax flowers she was said to have made during the nine years she was paralyzed, when her muscles would relax only under the influence of chloroform.

Mollie's food intake merited its own section of West's story, subtitled "Lived Without Food." There he reiterated the claims that her stomach would not retain anything; that even water, fruit juice, and other liquid, when introduced into her mouth, did not reach her stomach. His physical descriptions were explicit. "In the early part of her illness [her stomach] collapsed, so that by placing the hand in the cavity her spinal column could be felt. There was no room for food. Her throat was as rigid as a stick. Swallowing was out of the question."

Her mental state, he went on, was equally extraordinary. For someone so apparently incapacitated, Mollie was surprisingly active and involved. Until the end of 1875, according to West, she had written 6,500 notes and letters, clutching a pen or pencil in her clenched left hand. She kept a daily journal, except when in trances that lasted longer than twenty-four hours, and once wrote a poem of ten verses in as many minutes—"her thoughts," in West's words, "flowing with the rapidity of lightning." Mollie also took on the responsibility for keeping the accounts of family expenses since her illness began.

From West came the first full description of Mollie's work in embroidery and wax, in which she reproduced intricate designs of leaves and flowers not only without using a pattern, but while reportedly blind. She would cut velvet leaves to decorate pincushions, holding the scissors with her knuckles and shaping the leaves so uniformly that they looked as though they had been cut out with a punch. In the early years of her illness, West said, Mollie created more than two thousand such leaves. "She never studied botany or took a lesson in wax-work," he added, "and yet she never mistakes the forms of leaf or flower. Leaves with their ribs or views, their phylotaxis; flowers, with calyx, corolla . . . are given with a most truthful regard to nature."

West's acceptance of her clairvoyance was similarly complete. She could see whatever she wanted to; distance posed no barrier. She routinely found lost objects, dictated the contents of sealed letters, saw friends in remote places. West admitted, in his last paragraph, that these phenomena strained belief—that their rationale must be sought outside normal human experience: "The incredulous will not accept it—and it is not surprising. Miss Fancher is not to be judged by ordinary laws. The state is abnormal—a species of modified catalepsy, which has deranged the ordinary action of mind and body. It is a rich mine for investigation to the physiologist and the psychologist; and with them I leave the case."

The case did not rest for long. The Mollie Fancher story, finally, had legs. As many papers later pointed out, not much about her condition had changed since her first exposure in the press more than a decade before—except that the claims of fasting now extended over a much more dramatic period of time. The story had always possessed inherent potential for controversy simply from its content. What it hadn't had were the combatants who would take up arms on either side. These were about to be supplied, in spades. The most influential of them had not been ready for prime time in 1866, but in 1878 they were poised for their entrance.

The reaction to West's account in the Buffalo *Courier* began the following week, with an editorial in the *New York Herald* entitled "Hysteria." Its approach was skeptical; there had always been stories of girls subsisting for protracted periods without food, it held, but they always proved to be impostures. When these girls were put in hospitals where they could be monitored, they got hungry. The mistake about Mollie Fancher was in understanding the claims to mean she ate nothing at all for twelve years; instead, she was said to live "virtually" without food—meaning she ate enough to live. The piece ended cheekily: "It seems that this patient, if she consumes nothing else, is terribly destructive of worsted and note paper."

A week later, on November 24, the story had its breakthrough: seven columns across the top of the front page of the Sunday New York *Sun,* crowned with a sensational headline. "Dead and Yet Alive!" it proclaimed. "The Extraordinary Case of Miss Fancher of Brooklyn / Facts Verified by Abundant Testimony / A Mental Sight That Is Not the Claptrap of Clairvoyance." If the *Eagle* had been first on the scene in Brooklyn, and the *Herald* first in New York City, the story ended up belonging to *The Sun*—at least for the following week, as day after day its reporter hunted down experts willing to comment on Mollie, and day after day the other papers played catchup, often reduced to reporting *The Sun*'s findings. The paper added several crucial elements: an utter completeness, including numerous interviews with people familiar with the case, and colorful anecdotes of Mollie's feats; an instinct for combat that led the reporter to seek out opposing views; and writing that stood high above the other papers in storytelling, verve, and detail. Unfortunately, as newspaper articles of this era were seldom bylined, the name of the reporter who tracked Mollie's story for *The Sun* is lost.

"Dead and Yet Alive!" recounted Mollie's story in great detail and in fairly credulous fashion. The lead, in a few broad strokes, vividly set the scene in Mollie's bedchamber. "In Downing Street, Brooklyn, has lain for thirteen years Miss Mary J. Fancher, much of the time in a trance-like condition, with feeble heart pulsations, sluggish and almost imperceptible respiration, and the chill of death upon her flesh. At times she has been transformed into a cheerful, vivacious, intelligent, entertaining young woman, and then she has relapsed into speechlessness, blindness, deafness, and entire paralysis of the senses. She has developed most astonishing powers, resembling second sight or clairvoyance, reading with ease the contents of sealed letters, describing articles in hidden packages, perusing books while absolutely blind. Sometimes her powers are voluntary, at other times they are unconsciously exercised. So little nourishment has she taken that it may be said she lives without food. She is surrounded by persons of social standing and refinement, and has always been exceedingly sensitive to any public mention or knowledge of her condition. She has ever repelled any effort to couple her manifestations with those of clairvoyants; has begged to be allowed to live and die in the retirement of her home, unmolested by strangers, and accessible only to her friends."

The writer named for the first time some of the people who had taken an interest in Mollie's case, and it was an impressive list: the Reverend Dr. Joseph T. Duryea, pastor of the Classon Avenue Presbyterian Church, who would have much to say about Mollie's soul; the Reverend Dr. Henry J. Van Dyck, pastor of the Clinton Street Presbyterian Church; James B. Smith, "the well-known architect"; the Reverend Mr. Moore, former pastor of the Washington Avenue Baptist Church; the Reverend Dr. Prime, editor of New York's *Observer;* her many physicians: Drs. Speir, Ormiston, Mitchell, Kissam, and Crane; Henry Parkhurst, the astronomer; and of course, Professor West. The very presence of such names in a sensational story like this may have played a major role in elevating Mollie's case beyond the lurid into the realm of philosophical discussion.

The article went on to recount the by now familiar elements of Mollie's physical and mental condition. About her food intake the writer commented: "She has eaten altogether since that day—nearly thirteen years ago—not so much food in the aggregate as an ordinarily healthful girl of her age would eat in forty-eight hours." The story also added much context to Mollie's social situation—the writer seemed eager to establish her as a respectable, upper-middle-class Brooklynite rather than a publicity-hungry member of society's fringe. He described her "modest yet comfortable home" surrounded by the fashionable avenues of that part of Brooklyn known as the Hill, and her intelligent and ladylike bearing. Those who had studied her case, he wrote, had concluded that such an unmistakably truthful lady, with such an abhorrence of publicity, surrounded by friends of unquestionable position and with no apparent desire to enrich herself or her friends by the use of her gifts, could not possibly be intentionally deceiving people.

The most powerful element of the piece was the writer's description of Mollie and the dramatic value of his anecdotes. He obtained the physical details of Mollie's state from doctors and friends willing to speak to him, and turned them into something almost cinematic. (Although one has to wonder, as with the cinema, how much is strictly accurate and how much embellished.) He described her trances, which yielded many of her most astonishing clairvoyant revelations. She would suddenly start, as though charged from an electric battery, and instantly become rigid in every joint and muscle. Her face would take on sometimes a most pained expression, and at other times a look of positive pleasure. More often, though, it resembled the face of one who was dead; those unfamiliar with her trances often thought she had died. A deathlike pallor would creep over the already pale face, and not the slightest movement could be perceived in her muscles. She would almost cease to breathe, her body would become chill, and the pulsations of her heart would slow and weaken so as to be hardly detectable. The initiatory movement would often raise her into a half-reclining position, in which she would remain as still as if she were made of marble.

"Every one who has seen her in this condition speaks of the beauty and pathos of the scene," wrote the reporter, "the ashen complexion; the brown, fine waving hair streaming toward her shoulders, yet not reaching them; the faultless features, neither wrinkled nor drawn nor wasted, and yet not rounded and ruddy as in her school-girl days." One hand and graceful arm would be transfixed in position at the instant of attack, perhaps pointing upward, perhaps extended to receive a visitor's salutation, perhaps folded over her breast. The other arm would remain bent behind her head as though she were resting on it; her eyes were always closed. Mollie would remain thus for half an hour, for half a minute, even occasionally for twenty-four hours. When the trance ended she would be exhausted, her breathing labored, and she would settle back on her pillow with a marked expression of either acute sorrow or great pleasure on her face.

Curious new tales were revealed in the *Sun* story. For instance, although Mollie loved dogs and cats, birds, and even squirrels, her pets never survived for long. (Some of the "men of intelligence" who met her wondered whether in some inexplicable way she drew the life out of them.) Friends who visited might walk into Mollie's room, see her doing nothing, and ask why she was idle. Oh, I am reading such-and-such a book, Mollie would reply. "Well, where is it?" "Under the bedclothes, here," she would say, producing it and describing its contents.

One incident involving her embroidery provides an insight into not only her special sight, but also the way in which Mollie's circle of friends continually aided her and devotedly ran errands for her—and how she didn't hesitate to ask their help. In order to produce a "peculiarly delicate effect" in a piece of embroidery, Mollie needed a shade of worsted that was available only in Manhattan. She asked a gentleman friend to stop by the shop and pick it up for her, and being especially anxious about the selection, gave careful instructions about which color to purchase. In due time her friend returned with the parcel of new worsted. "You've bought the wrong shade, I am sorry to say," she told him the moment he stepped inside the door, and while the new worsted was still in his pocket.

"It's just according to sample, Miss Mollie. The salesman was very particular to compare them."

"Yes, he may have thought so, but it's a shade too light, and it will not do," she replied.

The worsted was produced from her friend's pocket, and the pattern in which it was to be used was put by its side. Those in the room could not detect a difference, but Mollie continued to insist that it was too light. "Take it back, please, when you are passing the shop, and the expert there will convince you that I am right," she said. Back went the gentleman with the worsted.

"You gave me the wrong shade," he told the clerk.

The clerk examined it and denied the mistake.

"Call your expert," said Mollie's friend, and the expert came.

"It is a lighter shade than the sample," was the expert's decision, and he quickly produced the proper one.

"This is just right," was Mollie's greeting, as the second parcel, with the correct shade, was handed to her unopened.

After this tale the article gave examples of Mollie's "following" people down streets and onto horsecars, seeing people at the door before they rang the bell, even seeing her lost dog return to her through rainy streets. Once a friend of Mollie's secretly visited a medium; the friend was convinced that Mollie's special powers were like those of clairvoyants, and she wanted to meet one so that she could compare the two. Mollie had a horror of clairvoyants, and was so sensitive to being classed with them or suspected of employing their methods that she wanted nothing to do with them; even a mention of them pained her. The friend first stopped in at Gates Avenue to see Mollie, then went to a clairvoyant's house nearby. After having tested the clairvoyant's powers to her satisfaction, she drifted into a general conversation in which Mollie's case was mentioned. After she left, she was so fascinated with her experience that she decided to return to Gates Avenue. She found Mollie sobbing.

"What is the matter, dear?" the friend asked soothingly.

"You have been to see a clairvoyant about me, and it makes me feel so badly," Mollie replied. She proceeded to narrate exactly the route her friend had taken, and at what address she had rung the bell and been admitted. The details, according to the friend, were absolutely correct.

When the *Sun* reporter approached the Reverend Joseph Duryea, a prominent figure in Brooklyn and in the Presbyterian Church, the minister advanced a theory about Mollie that would resonate with devout people of both mainstream and Spiritualist persuasions. Duryea, who was descended from an old New York family, had a musical as well as a philosophical bent, and later became a professor of biblical theology and then philosophy at Wellesley College; he also edited and published a *Presbyterian Hymnal* and *The Psalter for Use in Worship*. When asked by the *Sun* reporter how to account for Mollie's powers, he proposed a species of body-soul separation that could help explain both her clairvoyance and her existence without food.

"The child cannot deceive," Duryea said. "She does not wish to practice imposition. But her physical changes have in some manner released her mind from the imprisonment of the body, and she does with it what other mortals cannot do with theirs. Here she is deprived first of hearing, then of sight, then of speech, her throat paralyzed—sealed up so that nothing could be passed through it—in such a state that you might as well expect her to swallow a ramrod as a piece of bread; her abdominal organs in the same condition. The mind or spirit was absolutely confined. May it not with a mighty effort have burst away, and, once partly freed from the confines of the physical body have been governed by other and higher laws than those that control it while under the bondage of the body?"

When the reporter asked Duryea whether Mollie's case was well known in Brooklyn, the minister not only assured him that it was, but added that he himself used it often as a spiritual example to others. Her experience was living proof of the separation of the spirit and the flesh, and the superior power of the former over the latter. "I have followed her closely," Duryea added, "and always with no more deep wonderment at her peculiar manifestations than admiration of the sweet, contented cheerfulness of her disposition, the purity and simplicity of her life, and her steadfast hope."

The *Sun* article was a bombshell, a hometown coup that sent other newspapers scrambling. Each had its own strategy. The *Evening Post* tried to put itself above the fray with a supercilious item about the perennial nature of the Fancher story. The *Brooklyn Daily Union-Argus* ran a laconic and Brooklyn-centric item: "The case of Miss Fancher, the Brooklyn trance-lady, which is paraded at such length in the New York papers, was written up a dozen years ago in the journals of this city. Most of the singular features of her case had then been made manifest, and the narrative now looks like a restoration of an old picture." Other papers sent reporters out to interview the sources quoted in the *Sun,* and published much the same story. Most of the papers— the *World,* the *Herald,* the *Tribune,* Brooklyn's *Daily Eagle, The New York Times* (which credited its story directly to "yesterday's *Sun*")— expressed some skepticism yet felt compelled to repeat many of the anecdotes of the wonders Mollie was reported to perform. Various theories were brought forth: that she ate very little simply because her physical needs were so minimal; that the loss of certain senses heightened the remaining ones so greatly that she could hear and see things ordinary people couldn't.

The *Sun* editors must have immediately recognized what they had in their hands, because they kept their reporter on the move every day that week. The day after "Dead and Yet Alive!," while other papers rehashed its revelations, the *Sun* ran a reaction story that fundamentally changed the nature of the debate. In it, a reporter called on several New York physicians who were known to treat cases of nervous disease, and obtained from them opinions that directly, and sometimes harshly, questioned the reality of the tale. One of these physicians, William A. Hammond, was to become Mollie's chief adversary.

In the hands of the *Sun* reporter, Mollie's tale was transformed from possible mystical sensation to possible scam, and thus litmus test for medical sophistication and gullibility. The new *Sun* story, "Miss Fancher of Brooklyn—The People of Two Cities Talking of Her Wonderful Powers," began with journalistic self-aggrandizement, to the effect that the previous day's article had "excited universal interest; hardly anything else was talked about in the two cities." The reporter outlined the central reason that Mollie's case could not be dismissed out of hand as claptrap—the reason, essentially, that reporters were still on the story. That a woman should exist for so long practically without food, without natural sleep, and possessing such powers of clairvoyance, seemed almost incredible. Yet it seemed equally far-fetched that men of such stature, intelligence, and discernment as those figures in her life who defended her could be so mistaken or deceived. In the interests of truth and fairness, then, it was only reasonable to venture beyond Mollie's own physicians and seek the perspective of other experts. Thus began the maelstrom.

Some of the doctors the reporter contacted did not want to comment on the case without investigating it firsthand; others were saving their opinions for later expression in medical journals—an indication of how seriously the Fancher story was being taken. But Dr. Meredith Clymer, approached by the reporter while leaving his home, spared him a few words: "I have read *The Sun*'s account of the Brooklyn girl, and I think it is undoubtedly a case of hystero-catalepsy, and a very interesting one too." He went on to describe similar cases in which patients were quite cunning and deceptive, including one not far from Brooklyn whom he was currently treating. The girl in question would lie so rigid that three men could not bend a joint in her limbs, yet the moment she was alone, she would jump out of bed. When anyone entered the room she immediately lay rigid again.

Clymer was politic about the physicians involved in Mollie's case, most of whom were known to him, and all of whom stood well in their profession. Yet, he added, they were not experts in the peculiar disease of hysteria. "Even the honestest men," he warned, "are liable to be imposed upon in such cases." The next doctor the *Sun* reporter interviewed, E. C. Seguin, likewise characterized Mollie's case as one of hysteria. "These patients are sometimes very tricky. I had one in the hospital who said she could not eat anything; food was nauseating to her. But one day I gave her an emetic, and up came a nice lot of nuts."

It is a sign of the *Sun* reporter's lively instincts that he saved the best for last: his interview with Dr. William Hammond. He wisely wrote the interview as a dialogue, call and response between writer and doctor, bringing their conversation to life like a passage in a play. When asked what he thought of the previous day's *Sun* story about Mollie, Hammond boomed, "What do I think of it? Why, that it is a perfect humbug—a clear case of deception, sir." The reporter pressed: What about the testimony of so many prominent and learned men in her behalf? "I don't mean to say that the gentlemen named are not honest in their opinions. But I know that they are all deceived—lied to by this hysterical girl. There is deception in it all," said the doctor. "It's all a humbug. Why, my dear fellow, she isn't the first girl that has deceived learned and good men. There are plenty of cases of simulative hysteria, and Miss Fancher's case is one. I haven't seen her, never heard of her before, but I have heard of so many other similar cases that I do not hesitate to speak strongly about it."

Hammond went on to describe the famous case of another girl who claimed to live without eating, Sarah Jacob, "The Welsh Fasting Girl." When she was ten years old, Sarah began to exhibit many of Mollie's symptoms: pains in her stomach, spasms and fits that Hammond defined "of a clearly hysterical character," and a diminishing appetite. Soon her parents were proclaiming that she ate nothing at all, and as the months went by, even her clergyman came to believe this was true—that she had lived without food for sixteen months. A committee who watched the girl for fourteen days reported that the fasting was genuine, that there was no deception. "However," said Hammond, "the reports of this case show that the watch was a very careless one, the parents having access to the child at all times." A noted physician came from London to examine Sarah and found her to be "a pretty, plump child, with rosy cheeks and lips, and sparkling eyes," Hammond recounted. "He found by his examination that her condition was such as to show the impossibility of her being the subject of an exhausting disease, or even of her having been in bed continuously for nearly two years, as her parents asserted." The London doctor's diagnosis: simulative hysteria in a girl having a very strongly developed propensity to deceive.

The doctor's remarks, published in the London *Times,* ignited so much interest in Sarah's case that a team of nurses was sent from Guy's Hospital in London to conduct a professional watch. The result was disastrous. The watch began on December 9, 1869, with her parents' sanction. Soon symptoms of starvation appeared: after five days she looked pale and anxious, her eyes were sunken, her nose pinched. The family's vicar urged the Jacobs to stop the watch and allow Sarah to obtain food in whatever way she had secretly used before. They stood by their daughter's fasting, saying she had been this weak before and would not eat in any case. As the days crawled by, the parents were repeatedly urged to call off the watch; they refused, as did the girl herself. "Sarah became weaker and weaker," Hammond told the *Sun* reporter, "and on the seventeenth of December died—actually starved to death. Yes, sir, starved to death." The parents were tried for manslaughter; Mr. Jacob was sentenced to twelve months' hard labor and Mrs. Jacob to six months' hard labor.

"This case," said Hammond, "shows plainly how all the facts which science has gathered go for naught, even with educated persons, when brought face to face with the false assertions of a hysterical girl and two ignorant and deceitful peasants. If we know any one thing, it is this: that there can be no force without the metamorphosis of matter of some kind. Yet here was a girl maintaining her weight, actually growing, her animal heat kept at its due standard, her mind active, her heart beating, her lungs respiring, her skin exhaling, and all this, as many persons supposed, without the ingestion of this material by which alone such things could be. Why, it is ridiculous, preposterous. Upon my word, if that girl over in Brooklyn should die in any of those experiments made with her, I'd have every one concerned in the matter indicted for manslaughter."

With this pronouncement, Hammond rose from what the reporter described as his "immense and ancient chair" to retrieve a volume from a shelf. "Two years ago I wrote about this thing in a book on spiritualism and nervous derangement," he told the reporter, "in which I spoke as I have spoken to you. In addition I said this." Hammond read directly from his book: "Such is the tendency of the average human mind to be deceived that it would be perfectly possible to reenact in the city of New York the whole tragedy of Sarah Jacob, should ever a hysterical girl take it into her head to do so, and there would not be wanting, even from among those who might read this history, individuals who would credit any monstrous declarations she might make." Hammond looked up from the book. "That sounds like prophecy, don't it?" he asked, smiling.

Hammond then offered a direct challenge to Mollie's claims of clairvoyance (he would soon add a similar one to her fasting). He would bet $3,000 that she could not describe a check that he would enclose in an envelope. The check would be for some amount over $1,000, he said—and if she could divine the exact amount and the name of the bank it was drawn on, he would give her the check. "I tell you," he added, "those people in Brooklyn are of two classes—those who lie and those who are deceived. Mind you, I do not say that Miss Fancher is to blame, that she does all this intentionally. Hysteria prompts deception. It is a characteristic of the disease. She has probably not will enough to overcome the desire to deceive. But she should be aided in every way to overcome the desire, not assisted in her deceptions."

With this, the *Sun* reporter had his sensation of the day—and perhaps he was not too surprised, at that. Not only was Hammond known for his unfettered tongue, but he had also gone on record in recent years against many of the very causes and theories that were being advanced in Mollie's case. Now, at the prime of his career, Mollie had suddenly fallen, like a prize plum, into his hands.

CHAPTER FOUR

Dr. Hammond's War

It seems that no proposition that can be made is so absurd or impossible
but that many people, ordinarily regarded as intelligent, will be found to
accept it and to aid in its propagation. And hence, when it is asserted that
a young lady has lived for fourteen years without food of any kind, hundreds and thousands of persons throughout the length and breadth of a
civilized land at once yield their belief to the monstrous declaration.

—William A. Hammond, *Fasting Girls: Their Physiology and Pathology,* 1879

THE MAN WHO HELD FORTH for a reporter from his "immense and
ancient chair," and who pronounced his opinions with an almost
baiting vociferousness, was in 1878 a towering figure in New York
medicine—was in fact, wrote one medical historian, "one of the best
known medical men in the United States." But just a dozen years before, as Mollie's case was first reaching the newspapers, he had been a
disgraced practitioner, starting from less than zero at the age of thirty-
six. He came to New York and opened a medical office in 1864, and as
he much later told an interviewer, "When I arrived here I had nothing
and was obliged to borrow money from whosoever would loan it to me
in order to support myself. There were times when I really did not
know how I was to get my next meal."

Hammond owed his temporary downfall, in part, to the same un-
bound arrogance and lack of politesse that characterized his remarks
about Mollie—and that was to unleash the defensive wrath of his
philosophical opponents in the Fancher case. This was a man who en-

tertained not the slightest doubt of the rightness of his positions, and who certainly never allowed someone else's sensibilities to get in the way of his expressing them. Mollie had in Hammond a formidable adversary.

William Alexander Hammond was born in Annapolis, Maryland, in 1828, the second son of parents who united two old lineages. His father, a physician, was descended from John Hammond, who emigrated from the Isle of Wight to Annapolis in 1685, and whose family received large grants of land in Anne Arundel County, Maryland, from the British crown and from Lord Baltimore. Hammond's maternal ancestors had gone to England from Normandy with William the Conquerer in 1066; Mrs. Hammond's uncle William Pinkney was a celebrated American lawyer, ambassador, and senator. Hammond studied the classics with private tutors and grew interested in medicine, and at sixteen went to New York to study and apprentice with a well-connected family practitioner in the city.

When he arrived in New York, the teenage Hammond was lanky and awkward, with a pronounced stammer—not at all the hyperarticulate orator he was to become in later years. He received his M.D. degree from the Medical College of the University of the City of New York (later New York University) in 1848. At the time, medical education was not the nearly decade-long trial that it is today: two years of an ungraded curriculum sufficed to make a student a doctor, and clinical work, although encouraged, was not required for a degree.

After his marriage in 1849, Hammond joined the U.S. Army as an assistant surgeon, a post he held for ten years in frontier stations in what are now New Mexico and Kansas—and this was to lead to both his greatest prominence and his most painful disgrace. Hammond was an innovative medical thinker, especially interested in hygiene and hospital administration, and by 1862 his efforts to improve conditions in wartime hospitals had attracted the notice of the recently created U.S. Sanitary Commission. Members of the Commission urged that he be appointed the new surgeon general of the Army with the rank of brigadier general, and President Lincoln, despite a few dissenting voices, including that of Secretary of War Edwin Stanton, gave Hammond the job. Those in the medical profession who knew of his work and research applauded the appointment, but *The Philadelphia Inquirer* editorialized: "Dr. Hammond will have, although a dignified, yet a somewhat unenviable position. Those jealousies from which no profession or station is free, will undoubtedly beset and surround him as they have others."

That turned out to be a vast understatement of Hammond's two-year stint as surgeon general. He attacked the job with great energy, and was later credited with introducing revolutionary improvements in hospital sanitation, more professional standards of health care, and more skillful and humane treatment of the sick and wounded. His work is cited as the reason that the mortality rate in the hospitals of the Union Army during the Civil War was lower than that of any other army hospitals of the era. While leaving his mark on military medicine, Hammond spent his evening hours producing three books over two years, *A Treatise on Hygiene with Special Reference to the Military Service, Physiological Memoirs,* and a manual for military surgeons.

As highly skilled and effective as he was in his work, however, Hammond had a serious flaw: a dearth of political and personal sensitivity, which was to dog him his entire life. One biographer, Jack Key, wrote that Hammond was at his worst "arrogant and pompous, with a high regard for his own dignity. He had a sharp tongue, which was easily and often employed." His self-regard and outright bragging stunned and even offended those with whom he came into contact. And in Secretary of War Stanton—described by Key as at his worst "arrogant, insolent, overbearing, harsh, and easily given to hatreds"—he appears to have met his match in pugnaciousness. "It was inevitable that Hammond's unusual personality would excite the disapproval of such an autocratic person as [the secretary of war]," wrote Key. "Their official and personal relations early became strained, and there was constant friction in the conduct of business between the two."

No one has pinned down what earned Hammond the secretary's apparent dislike, but it is likely to have been a combination of two elements: the doctor's energetic reforms and withering criticism of the Army's medical state of affairs before he took over, and his general style of personal arrogance and confrontation. In later defending himself against what he said was the "persistent enmity" of Stanton, Hammond described an encounter that serves to explain why the two men clashed at once, and why Stanton's hackles were thereafter evidently forever raised.

"I gave [Stanton] to understand," Hammond related, "from a very early period of my official career, that I, for one, would not quietly submit to the insolence which he constantly exhibited toward his subordinates. Two days after my appointment, he sent for me. I went to his office, and the following conversation took place. His tone and manner were offensive in the extreme, being that of one who is determined to crush out if possible all opposition: 'What are Dr. Bellows and the Sanitary Commission about?' asked he. 'I don't know, sir,' I answered. 'I want to tell you,' he said, 'that if you have the enterprise, the knowledge, and intelligence, and the brains to run the Medical Department, I will assist you.' 'Mr. Secretary,' I replied, 'I am not accustomed to be spoken to in that manner by any person, and I beg you will address me in more respectful terms.' 'What do you mean?' he exclaimed. 'Simply,' I said, 'that during my service in the army, I have been thrown with gentlemen, who, no matter what our relative rank was, treated me with respect. Now that I have become Surgeon-General, I do not intend to exact anything less than I did when I was an Assistant Surgeon, and I will not permit you to speak to me in such language as you have just used.' 'Then, sir,' said he, 'you can leave my office immediately.' I accordingly left it, and I have never entered it or his house since, except upon strictly official business."

Within a year of Hammond's appointment, Stanton was quietly moving to have him dismissed. He selected a commission to examine the affairs of the medical department, headed by ex-governor Andrew Reeder of Kansas, an old enemy of Hammond's (the two had tangled over land grants when Hammond was serving in Kansas). The commission also included someone whom Hammond had recently denied a position—and who had taken his complaint to Stanton. Rumors circulated about irregularities in Hammond's department, and a group of prominent East Coast doctors organized an attempt to save his job. They sent an anonymous letter in support of Hammond to the *Medical Times,* and the publication ran an editorial that portrayed the investigation as having "an appearance of a secret and deliberate conspiracy against the Surgeon General directly, and against the medical department indirectly. . . . A united effort should be made to restore him to his legitimate position, or secure him a fair and impartial hearing."

Stanton hesitated, but Hammond's bluster and uncompromising sense of right and wrong once more hindered his own best interests. George Templeton Strong, a member of the Sanitary Commission, described in his diary how Stanton told Hammond, through intermediaries, that "he would abandon the persecution if Hammond would consent to let bygones be bygones. To which Hammond responded that he would be glad to do so if the Secretary would apologize, but that if the Secretary wouldn't, he must have a court-martial. . . . He proposed to try his own case, without counsel, against which preposterous course I gave him advice gratis, most emphatically."

Hammond, bent on a very public vindication, rejected all advice and prepared his own case against charges that do indeed sound trivial: that he personally ordered a quantity of blankets rather than have a medical purveyor make the purchase; that the blankets were overpriced and of poor quality; and that he lied to someone about why he was passed over for a post. Even so, Strong wrote, while Hammond was optimistic, he himself "did not expect an acquittal, though I am confident his case is honest and good. Some impulsive blunder of his will probably spoil it, and Stanton is an ugly adversary."

Although the case dragged on for months, the court needed less than two hours to reach a guilty verdict. President Lincoln issued an order that confirmed the result: Hammond was dismissed from the service in official disgrace. Many other doctors supported him and felt he had been judged unfairly, but the respect of his colleagues did not appease Hammond; he would not rest until he had put his entire case before the public. One reason he was penniless by the time he returned to New York was that he spent several months after his court-martial writing, self-publishing, and distributing a seventy-three-page booklet that told his side of the story. The document reverberated with Hammond's overwhelming sense of importance and of the injustice perpetrated against him.

A Statement of the Causes Which Led to the Dismissal of Surgeon-General William A. Hammond from the Army; with a Review of the Evidence Adduced Before the Court took the reader through every phase of Hammond's experiences with Stanton, defended his work as surgeon general, and included letters exchanged between various principals, and even question-and-answer sequences from the court proceedings. Hammond claimed that his appointment, at age thirty-four, was resented by older members of the corps. "It will be easily seen, then, that I had a difficult undertaking before me, even with everything in my favor. With the persistent enmity of the Secretary of War, to whom I had a right to look for official support and countenance, the task was almost insurmountable." For having placed saving lives above saving money, he later wrote, "I was accused by the wicked and the ignorant of useless extravagance."

Hammond was a master of the unhesitating heap of insults against those who had angered him, during this earlier period and in the more mature years of his career. About Reeder, the head of Stanton's investigatory commission, he wrote: "Inimical to me in the highest degree, unscrupulous, dishonest, cowardly, and ignorant, no man in the country could have served [Stanton's] purpose better." About Stanton, Hammond had apparently stored up every incident of disrespect. "It would be impossible for me to detail the hundredth part of the insults of all kinds I was compelled, to some extent, to bear. . . . Every advance which I made toward him was repelled with harshness. . . . As an example of his littleness of mind and forgetfulness, the following letter is adduced. . . . To show the depth to which the Secretary of War could descend to gratify his malice, the following correspondence is given. . . ."

On the last page, Hammond reached the heights of righteous indignation: "I have never, however, despaired of the eventual triumph of my cause. I know it rests upon the sure foundations of truth and justice; and I shall continue to pursue my path through life with the knowledge that it is crime, not punishment, which brings disgrace. . . . The time will come when such wickedness as I have endeavored to expose in this statement will meet with its due reward. Till that hour arrives, I shall not bear myself any the less proudly, by reason of the temporary triumph of my enemies; but, conscious of right, will patiently wait for the full vindication which is sure to come."

That vindication was a long time in coming. In the meantime Hammond applied his prodigious energy to establishing a private practice. He decided to focus on the rising specialty of neurology, having become fascinated during the Civil War with symptoms of nervous exhaustion in soldiers—what would later be called battle fatigue. Neurology was at that time in a transitional phase. It had existed for centuries as the study of the brain and the nervous system, and cases of head injury, convulsions, paralysis, epilepsy, and the like were understood to fall under its rubric. Hammond, along with other Victorian physicians interested in nervous ailments, began to expand the discipline to include such symptoms as insomnia, phobias, vertigo, and general malaise, as they burgeoned in the increasingly anxious late nineteenth century—symptoms that today would often be considered psychological rather than physical. But even as neurology moved into treating symptoms that sometimes appeared emotional or mental, its theory remained solidly rooted in the physical. It was assumed that the cause, as well as the treatment and cure, would always be found in the body: the rest cure for nervous exhaustion, spinal treatment for various hysterical symptoms, and so on.

When Hammond decided to define himself exclusively as a neurologist, he took on another challenge: to establish neurology as a legitimate specialty in its own right. In this, characteristically, he was going against tradition. Until the mid–nineteenth century very few practicing doctors identified themselves as specialists, for the term was often associated with quackery; almost all well-educated physicians maintained a general family practice. Now, more than a century afterward, specialization has become the norm in medical practice.

Even as Hammond paved the way for the wide-ranging specialty of neurology, however, its identity began to shift, in effect to split in two. Hammond and other Victorian neurologists dignified nervous ailments by taking them seriously and proposing that they were medical conditions that could be treated scientifically—that the hysteric could be systematically cured, that mental healing could be a scientific discipline—only to see the territory stolen away by a new specialty: psychology, the study of the human mind and behavior, and its offspring, psychiatry, the science of therapeutically treating mental, emotional, and behavioral disorders. Hammond has been described as a transitional figure in the history of neurology, poised between treating the mind and treating the body. Mollie Fancher's case itself even embodied that split: Were her symptoms the result of physical injury, spinal or otherwise, or were they an expression of emotional hysteria, the invention of a troubled mind?

By the end of the century (and Hammond's life; he died in 1900), neurology was approaching its present-day definition as a specialty confined to the mechanics of the nervous system. The symptoms of neurasthenia—a central part of Hammond's practice—were being classified solely in psychological terms. But during his lifetime, Hammond's neurological ideas served him extremely well. A few months after his arrival in New York, he already had a steady roster of patients at his office on West Thirty-fourth Street in Manhattan, presenting a broad spectrum of symptoms from phobias to paralysis. He owed his flourishing practice in part to referrals from peers in the profession, who despite his military debacle respected both his clinical skills and his scientific research. In 1866 he took a teaching position, as lecturer on diseases of the mind and nervous system at Columbia's College of Physicians and Surgeons, which added to his patient list. The next year a post as professor of the same subject was created for him at Bellevue Hospital Medical College.

In the 1870s, Hammond took command of his new specialty, producing a string of firsts. In 1871 he published the first neurology textbook, *A Treatise on the Diseases of the Nervous System,* and took the lead in creating the New York State Hospital for Diseases of the Nervous System, the first American hospital devoted solely to neurological disease. The following year he helped organize the New York Neurological Society, the first such association in the country. He became a leader in promoting postgraduate medical study at a time when doctors often went out into the world to practice their profession woefully unprepared; he created a postgraduate faculty at his alma mater, and later helped establish a separate institution, the Post-Graduate Medical School.

Throughout this period Hammond squeezed in an impressive amount of writing and editing, skills of which he was quite proud. He contributed to the founding of several medical periodicals, including the *Quarterly Journal of Psychological Medicine and Jurisprudence, New York Medical Journal, Journal of Nervous and Mental Diseases,* and

Neurological Contributions. In addition, he turned out fiction in his spare time, one novel in 1867 and six during the 1880s and 1890s.

By the late 1870s, Hammond was established and moneyed enough to indulge a continuing obsession: to overturn his court-martial and formally clear his name. He petitioned Congress, bills were introduced in both the House and Senate, and the Senate and House Committees on Military Affairs agreed to review his case. The result was an exoneration by an act of Congress on March 15, 1878, and an annulment of the court-martial sentence by President Rutherford Hayes. Hammond now had the absolution he had so confidently predicted fifteen years earlier; his name was placed on the retired list as surgeon general and brigadier general, effective August 27, 1879. Hammond waived his right to the customary retirement pay. His fortune had long been secured by his practice, and his annual income in 1878 was reportedly a then princely $60,000.

A decade later, in 1888, a colleague described Hammond in the *Virginia Medical Monthly* as "perhaps among the busiest of active practitioners in America. . . . [His] investigations and records have established him as the father of, and *the* authority in, American neurology." But his forceful presence and personality, which sometimes crossed the line into belligerence, even outright hostility, made Hammond a man who, as Jack Key wrote, "was either loved or hated but never ignored," who attracted both an active following and active enemies. A maverick with a lifelong lack of what Key termed diplomatic restraint, Hammond had a habit of blithely defying tradition and following his own instincts. Toward his friends and colleagues he was fiercely loyal, even if the expression of his support was sometimes outrageous in itself. When Silas Weir Mitchell, creator of the rest cure and a close colleague and friend of Hammond's, was turned down for chairs of physiology at Jefferson Medical College and the University of Pennsylvania, for example, Hammond wrote a letter of protest that appeared

William Alexander Hammond, Mollie Fancher's first and perhaps most vociferous adversary. In November 1878, he called her case "a perfect humbug— a clear case of deception." (NATIONAL ARCHIVES AND RECORDS ADMINISTRATION)

in several medical journals, in which he concluded: "I am disgusted with everything and can only say that it is an honor to be rejected by such a set of apes!" Although he could be charming and gracious when pleased, once he was angered Hammond didn't seem to know how to simmer down.

He was a larger-than-life character, a man who, in the words of one old friend, "filled the room when he entered it." Key described him physically as "a man of commanding presence, possessed of extreme self-confidence and remarkable personal magnetism. He was uncommonly large, 6 feet 2 inches tall and 250 pounds. He had a powerful voice, a pleasing delivery, and a flow of language that made him a popular speaker."

In 1882, four years after the Fancher uproar, a reporter for *Harper's New Monthly Magazine* vividly depicted Hammond's public lecturing style—and his stature in the medical world—in an article about medical education in New York: "A portly gentleman enters the stage, who from the firmness of his tread and the erectness of his body might be a general reviewing his troops. He is massively built, and has a full round face, a clipped head, and a heavy mustache. He is dressed in a fashionable frock-coat and light trousers. His hair is nearly gray, and as he strides across the stage, waiting for the applause to cease, he looks more like a general than ever. His manner somehow implies that time is very precious with him, and he talks in a rapid but rather husky voice. . . . He is a voluminous writer of books on his specialty, a famous entertainer, a frequent diner-out, and an omnivorous reader of newspapers and popular magazines. Very few men combine the successful pursuit of science and literature with the pleasures of society as Dr. Hammond does."

Hammond was indeed something of a bon vivant, known for his dinner parties and for his conversational skills in the private and public arenas. A physician friend of his, D. B. St. John Roosa, recalled at a memorial for the late Hammond that he had been "a great host—to dine as his guest was a pleasure, such as you will rarely have even with the most genial and intellectual of hosts." And despite his absorption in work, Hammond also knew when to set it aside. "It is a sad thing for a hard worked doctor to go to a dinner after a long day's work and hear about a new kind of tumor, or a new discovery or about some mistakes in diagnosis committed by a fellow practitioner," Roosa said. "These are not interesting. Hammond did not do that; he was broad enough to carry you away from such things and lead your mind into pleasant channels, and thus he became a solace and a rest to his guests."

Roosa remembered a dinner party of Hammond's attended by several visitors from Philadelphia, including Silas Weir Mitchell. As soon as the dinner began and the soup was served, the Philadelphians present asked for champagne. Hammond said, "In New York we don't give champagne until late in the dinner." One of his visitors replied that in Philadelphia the dinner began with champagne, and that in fact no other wine was served. "Who's giving this dinner?" Hammond retorted, and his guests jovially replied that they knew he had good champagne, why wouldn't he serve it to them? At this, Hammond threw New York custom out the window, brought out the champagne, and served it for the rest of the meal.

At another dinner, Roosa recalled, Hammond played a wicked practical joke on a medical writer by convincing him that his book had been placed under a ban by the Catholic Church. The author had mentioned in his book the dark ages—a term sometimes used by Protestant writers of the day to designate "the time when the Catholic Church had absolute domination," according to Roosa. When Hammond told him that his book had been "put in the Index Expurgatorius," the man "turned visibly pale." Hammond let him suffer for about fifteen minutes before delivering him from his misery.

Visits to Hammond's house and office were made even more colorful by his taste in decorating, which tended toward the exotic. He was famous for a statue of the Buddha in his front hall, which gave Roosa a sense of dread in the late hours of the evening. Dr. J. G. Hopkins, up from Atlanta to meet with Hammond on a patient's case, described his consulting room with a jaundiced eye for the *Atlanta Medical and Surgical Journal* in 1884. "Having sent in my card, and [Hammond's] readiness to receive me being announced, I entered his consultation room. The first object which fixed my gaze was the monarch himself, perched upon a large armed chair, the back of which, stretching far above his hoary head, bore the image of an Egyptian female and many unmistakable evidences of antique art. The walls and ceiling of the apartment were elaborately frescoed in a style which reigned supreme in the days of Pompeii. Over 3,000 volumes bedecked the space between doors and windows, and in every nook and corner could be seen the work of the skilled sculptor, such as woman-headed horses and many other objects of the mythologic age. . . . A gorgeous polycolored chandelier o'erhung the table and desk in the center of the room at which Lord Hammond communes with his prey."

His bedside manner bore, on occasion, a strong resemblance to the autocratic Lord Hammond of the metaphor. Dr. Hopkins related Hammond's treatment of the patient he had brought from Atlanta for help with an unnamed ailment: "The patient got no better. . . . The Doctor insisted that he was cured. Finding that he could not make the young man acknowledge that he was better, but rather [that he] insisted that he was worse, he simply said, 'Tis all damned nonsense, and I shall write your father to send you to the asylum. Do you suppose God is going to help you and you sit down on your tail and not help yourself?'"

Hammond's explosiveness attracted controversy like a magnet. Just before he became a prominent figure in the Mollie Fancher affair, his name had been in the popular press for another imbroglio: he brought a libel suit against another doctor, John Gray, editor of the *American Journal of Insanity,* for publishing a speech that Hammond said defamed him. The speech was given by Dr. Eugene Grissom, superintendent of the Insane Asylum for North Carolina in Raleigh, who spoke not only against Hammond's attacks on the asylum system and treatment of the insane, but against him personally. Grissom's speech was titled "True and False Experts," and he firmly and openly placed Hammond in the latter class. Grissom accused Hammond of selling his testimony in court cases, and of having given wildly contradictory opinions to suit the exigencies of each case. "The false expert is no man at all, but a moral monster," Grissom declared; Hammond and others like him were "poisoners of the fountains of justice."

Hammond shot back an open letter to Grissom that was characterized by *The Buffalo Daily Courier* as "considerably more sarcastic than that of his assailant, and, we should say, equally libelous." Hammond's letter showed off his acclaimed rhetorical talents, making what the *Courier* called an "ingenious argument to prove that Dr. Grissom is insane, at the close of which the suggestion that he should be confined in his own lunatic asylum is rejected as altogether too cruel a procedure to be thought of!" Next came an "appendix" from Grissom, remind-ing Hammond that he had neglected to refute the specific charges brought against his professional and personal character. This prompted a second open letter, as Hammond appeared constitutionally unable to let an attack remain unopposed. Said the *Courier,* "Dr. Hammond loses his temper and flings the whole dictionary of vituperation at his antagonist." Eventually, all sides involved—Hammond, Grissom, and the journal's editors—published position papers and the libel case was dropped.

What underlay Hammond's famously imperious manner was an ab-solute conviction that he was right. Self-doubt was an alien emotion to him, and his self-assurance was at times almost amusing. "I liked his en-thusiasm," said Dr. Roosa at Hammond's memorial, "and his unwitting exaggerations of what he could do, which were as honest as the beliefs of any person on the face of the earth. He talked as if he thought there were no problems in medicine which he would not ultimately solve."

The medical problem posed by the case of Mollie Fancher in 1878 was an especially tantalizing one for Hammond. He was then at his peak—well known, respected, ready for combat. And Mollie happened to embody, simultaneously, two of his pet peeves, about which he had written in the past: the claims of Spiritualists and those of fasting girls. Now was his chance to use the power of his voice in the name of sci-ence and against superstition—and now, finally, people might listen.

William Hammond's public challenge to Mollie Fancher in the November 25 *Sun*—to prove her clairvoyance by "reading" what was written on a check enclosed in a sealed envelope—brought the public-ity about her case to a new level. It was no longer simply a marvel to be believed or not, but now a contest and a confrontation between the doctor and the mystic. All the local newspapers covered Hammond's remarks, and conflicting opinions abounded. The *Tribune* sent a reporter to Professor West's house on the evening of the twenty-fifth to ask whether he thought Mollie would submit to the test. "I do not know that she would," he replied. "She has always been unwilling to gratify curiosity seekers, especially where a money consideration was concerned, but she might consent in this case, in order to convince an expert, such as Dr. Hammond."

The Brooklyn Daily Eagle editorialized that "Dr. Hammond makes a proposition which, if she is sincere, Miss Fancher can assign no possible reason for refusing, and which will go far toward definitely settling [the question of] her clairvoyant powers. . . . Here is a fair challenge. Dr. Hammond thinks that if she succeeds he will have very cheaply learned of the existence of an occult force in nature of whose existence he is at present very skeptical. Since Miss Fancher can have no objection to the test, if she is honest, she ought to submit to it. If she declines it, or accepting it fails, the public will have good grounds for discrediting marvelous stories told."

Mollie's friends and supporters may have sensed the tide turning in the wake of such matter-of-fact skepticism. In any event, Hammond's challenge galvanized many of them to tell their own tales, firsthand, of her feats. The newspapers saw a feast laid out before them, seemingly weeks' worth of juicy material and irresistible tidbits from both sides, perhaps even name-calling and vilification. With the volatile Dr. Hammond involved, such excitements were always a possibility. And Hammond himself must have realized he was on to a good thing, because within three weeks he had repeated his challenge to Mollie— first made conversationally to the *Sun* reporter—this time as a formal wager, complete with conditions spelled out point by point. This he did on December 14 in the *New York Herald,* in response to a letter to the editor from Henry Parkhurst, a prominent member of Mollie's camp.

Until Parkhurst wrote his letter to the editor of the *Herald,* published on November 30, he had been one of Mollie's more reticent friends. The astronomer, who lived two doors from her on Gates Avenue, frequently visited her and her aunt. A *Sun* reporter approached him at his home on November 26, and Parkhurst was polite but firm; he laughed and said, "I'm glad to see you, but you won't get anything out of me. You see, I hold the position of an intimate personal friend to Miss Fancher's family, and I say nothing without her permission." But he couldn't resist a few comments when asked his opinion of what the New York physicians were saying. Parkhurst laughed again and said, "You didn't bring that check of Hammond's, did you? I wish you had. The reading of it would be an easy thing for her to do, compared with what she has done." He went on to describe the letters he had been receiving asking whether the first *Sun* story about Mollie had been true, including a heart-rending letter from a man whose son was missing: he asked Parkhurst's help in getting Mollie to use her second sight to find him.

When Parkhurst lapsed into silence, the reporter persisted, remarking that Mr. Parkhurst was a hard man to interview. Again, Parkhurst couldn't resist saying more. He described an encounter he'd had with another reporter a few days before. "He asked me if Miss Fancher did really make waxwork, embroidery, and the like, although blind. I answered this as I had all his questions, that I had nothing to say. And all the time, he was sitting where you are, leaning against that tidy, and his arms resting on those other two, all the work of Mollie. But these are simple pieces of work. There are many more elaborate pieces of workmanship that she has done in this room now." The reporter jumped up to examine the tidies (another word for antimacassars), and saw wax flowers and examples of needlework in the room. But Parkhurst would say nothing further about who made these.

When the reporter asked how Mollie had reacted to the *Sun* article, however, Parkhurst did give a hint that she was relaxing her strictures about publicity. "Not unpleasantly," he responded. "Heretofore, when anything has been written about her, she has been much distressed, but now she does not seem to be annoyed." The growing skepticism in the newspapers may have roused Mollie's ire, because only three days later Parkhurst revealed, with her explicit permission, the details of tests he had conducted of her powers years before. This he did by writing a long letter to the *Herald*. It is unclear why he chose it above other papers— if anything, its editorials had been among the more disbelieving—but one pictures the editors of the *Sun* gnashing their teeth that, having gotten to Hammond first, they suddenly lost their scoop to a competitor.

Parkhurst's letter recounted at length an elaborate experiment he said he had conducted of Mollie's clairvoyance in June 1867. Curious as to whether her gifts entailed mind-reading of the people around her or actual second sight, he had an assistant fold and seal a piece of printed paper into an envelope so that Parkhurst himself was unaware of what it contained. He then had two other witnesses examine the envelope and the wax seal on it before he gave it to Mollie. She gave it back, apparently unopened, and told him various numbers and words that, she said, appeared on the paper inside; when the envelope was opened, it was found that she had been correct.

What was conclusive evidence to Parkhurst was to Hammond a botched and unscientific experiment. He responded with a letter to the editor of the *Herald,* in which he stated that Parkhurst's test did not satisfy him as to Mollie's powers, as she could have opened the envelope without disturbing the seal and read the contents. His own re-iteration of his challenge to Mollie, he wrote, was prompted not only by reading Parkhurst's remarks but also by the great deal of talk about the case and by the fifty-seven letters he had received "asking me to investigate it. . . . I have stated very explicitly that I regard the whole matter as a humbug of the most decided kind, but I have never asserted the impossibility of the young lady's alleged performances. On the contrary, I hold nothing to be absolutely impossible outside the domain of mathematics. But possibilities and realities are very different things, and I certainly will not accept as true any such phenomena as those asserted to have been associated with Miss Fancher unless they are proven."

He outlined his proposal, for the record: that he place a certified check for a sum of money exceeding $1,000 inside an envelope, which Mollie would be allowed to hold if she liked. She would have half an hour to describe the check—number, date, on what bank drawn, amount, and signature. If she succeeded, the check would be hers, or he would donate it to any charity she liked. His additional conditions were these: that the experiment be conducted in the presence of Hammond and two other members of the New York Neurological Society; and that the envelope should at no time pass out of his sight.

"If Miss Fancher succeeds in this test I will admit that heretofore in my denunciations of such performances as hers I have been in error," Hammond wrote grandly, "and that there is a force in nature which ought to be further investigated. I will pay the money not only without chagrin, but with great satisfaction, and will consider that I have received full value." Such grace in defeat seems easy for Hammond to foretell when he obviously did not anticipate any such outcome. "If she fails," he went on, with his more characteristic thunder, "as I am quite sure she will, I shall not hesitate to continue to denounce her as an imposition in this as well as in her assumed abstinence from food."

Sensing perhaps the rising public interest, Hammond added a bonus: another test, this one of Mollie's fasting. "I know something about 'fasting girls' and their frauds," he asserted, and in order to expose Mollie's deception suggested a one-month watch, day and night, by relays of members of the New York Neurological Society. The very real possibility of her starving to death, as in the case of Sarah Jacob, was to be avoided by giving authority to her physician Dr. Speir to feed her forcibly if she appeared to be in danger. "I will give her $1,000," Hammond wrote, "if at the end of that month she has not in the meantime taken food voluntarily or as a forced measure to save her from dying of starvation."

Hammond's challenges unleashed a fresh torrent of response. Newspaper editorialists tended toward skepticism of Mollie's powers. *The Brooklyn Daily Eagle* called Hammond's proposed test of her fasting claims "very simple and gentle," and predicted: "We fear that the cause of occult science will not gain much from Dr. Hammond's offers, nor will his bank account suffer much depletion." But while the editors tended toward irony, their letters-to-the-editor columns overflowed with high emotion, much of it in defense of Mollie, on grounds ranging from mysticism to common decency.

The first volleys were personal, coming from friends of Mollie's who were horrified at Hammond's "coarse and ungentlemanly manner" in writing of her. Two letters, both signed anonymously and published in the December 19 *Eagle,* defended Mollie's refusal to rise to his bait. "The very thought of such a man coming in contact with her in any manner is utterly repulsive to all her friends," wrote "one of Miss Fancher's friends." "While it is a matter of utter indifference to those who count themselves among her friends what Dr. Hammond's opinion may be, it is exceedingly painful to them to have her made a subject of his remarks, unless he can adopt a different tone in his published letters."

This person was clearly close to Mollie's case, because the writer went on to give Mollie an out, by placing her most remarkable feats in the past. The author of the letter explained that the experiment Henry Parkhurst described had been conducted nine years before, and that Mollie's condition had undergone a change since then to a state "more natural and less marked by such phenomena." The friend concluded dismissively: "If Dr. Hammond wishes to hear no more of the case, her friends are no less desirous of hearing nothing more from him, and he may rest assured that he had better confine his denunciations of a lady he knows nothing about to a very limited sphere."

The second letter in the December 19 *Eagle,* signed "D," which also claimed to be from a friend of Mollie's, focused more on Hammond's challenge to her fasting than on that to her clairvoyance. "I style it abuse and insult," the correspondent wrote, "for any human being to propose to invade the privacy of the afflicted lady's sick room for one month, to watch her every movement day and night, and give her one thousand dollars if, at the end of that time, she is not proven to be an imposter. . . . To be an imposter one must have some motive, and Miss Fancher certainly can have none." This friend echoed early newspaper accounts in pointing out that behind Mollie's odd claims stood the testimony of physicians, scientists, and ministers of high reputation, as well as that of a great number of refined and cultivated friends. If such corroboration did not command as much respectful attention from the public as did Dr. Hammond's proposition, "then the public must be very stupid."

With these personal defenses came two substantive countercharges to Hammond, the first a dissertation on transposition of the senses and spiritual mysteries, the other a turning-of-the-tables by Parkhurst himself, both published in the *New York Herald* on December 18. The former was a letter from "M.H." in Brooklyn, who wrote from the point of view of a doctor (speaking of similar cases met in his own practice) without admitting to being one. "It cannot but be well known to the learned gentleman," M.H. stated, "that transposition of the senses does undoubtedly attend certain abnormal conditions of the brain and nervous centres. And that there is a law of compensation which enables certain unfortunates who are deprived of the use of the ordinary senses to obtain impressions and knowledge through unusual channels is a fact too well known to be called in question." M.H. himself had encountered a case of catalepsy (trance) in which "the auricular nerves were transferred to filaments, permeating the surface of the gastric region" (in lay terms, the sense of hearing "seemed to be transferred from the ears to a certain spot on the abdomen"). "Careful experiments," M.H. added, "established the fact."

M.H.'s conclusion about Mollie, though, was in the end more mystical than medical. He sounded a theme that would gather strength as the contention about Mollie's significance went on: that "in Miss Fancher the immortal is really held to the mortal part by most fragile threads," that she was somehow beyond normal human experience—that she was living, breathing evidence of the possibilities of an old-fashioned transcendental mysticism. Few ideas were more antithetical to Hammond and the crop of scientists he was leading toward the twentieth century. These doctors represented the creed of so-called materialist medical thinking, a philosophy that focused on empirical observation of the material, physical world; nothing unseen could be considered real. In fact, nothing irked William Hammond more than illogic and superstition. To indulge in such atavistic nonsense as belief in miracles and mysteries was to live like an ignorant savage in an age of science and knowledge. When a reporter asked him how Mollie could manage to deceive the learned clergymen who supported her cause, Hammond immediately retorted, "Oh, that's nothing. Clergymen are the most gullible men in the world!"

In a book debunking Spiritualism published in 1871, Hammond had laid out his philosophy—the worldview he was trying so hard to get across to the ignorant masses in 1878 by using the case of Mollie Fancher: "[Man] has learned to doubt," he wrote in *The Physics and Physiology of Spiritualism,* "and, therefore, to reason better; he makes experiments, collects facts, does not begin to theorize until his data are sufficient, and then is careful that his theories do not extend beyond the foundation of certainty, or at least of probability, upon which he builds." That foundation was seriously undercut by belief in miraculous creatures like Mollie Fancher, creatures who could live without sustenance and see through walls and into sealed envelopes.

M.H. attempted to chip away at that foundation with an argument that by the close of his letter became frankly religious. The question of whether Mollie was miraculous or merely sick, mentally and otherwise, was becoming more concrete. Amid the barely post-Darwinian confusion that was Victorian spirituality, M.H. returned to the comforts of old-time faith in the person of Mollie Fancher.

"What does Dr. Hammond want us to believe?" he asked. "Must we set aside all practical experience, as well as the traditions of Christianity and every other form of religion known to ancient or modern times? Has not fasting, physical suffering, purity and innocence of life, and the entire subjugation or extinction of all animal appetite, ever in the past enabled mortals to burst the ordinary bounds of the senses in the pursuit of spiritual or other truths? . . . Have we ever had any seer, or prophet, or saint, or holy men or women who have been exalted above their fellow creatures by piety, or suffering, or natural endowment, so that they could hear and see and know of things unseen, unheard and unknown to others less morally purified? Or must we eschew all such possibilities and come down to the plane of materialism—to hard, everyday fact and sensuous knowledge only?" In other words, to the bleak, closed new world of spiritually empty scientific "truth" that Hammond advocated.

Juxtaposed to such cosmic ideas, Henry Parkhurst's letter, which directly followed M.H.'s, comes off as picayune. It began on a grand footing, comparing the situation of Mollie's supporters to that of Galileo discovering the moons of Jupiter—"I can imagine a sceptic calling him a humbug of the most decided kind, and declaring that unless he would show four moons to the planet Venus to a committee of three members of some society he must consent to be denounced as an imposter." But Parkhurst quickly arrived at his main purpose: to challenge Hammond to prove his main objection to Parkhurst's experiment, namely that there was no way of knowing for sure that Mollie had not opened the envelope, read the contents, and closed it, despite the wax seal over the envelope's flap. It is here that both scientists, the neurologist and the astronomer, come to resemble a pair of eight-year-olds throwing sand at each other in a playground brawl.

Parkhurst proposed to prepare and seal three envelopes and give them to a committee, which would then hand one to Hammond—who would open, reclose, and return the envelope. The committee would troop back to Parkhurst with all three envelopes, not revealing which one had been opened. "If I fail within three days to designate which of the envelopes was opened I will admit that my former test was insufficient," wrote Parkhurst; Hammond would have shown that Parkhurst was not sufficiently an expert to know whether a sealed envelope had or had not been opened. Parkhurst's offer would remain in effect until midnight on December 31—Hammond's exact deadline for Mollie to accept his own challenges—"and if not taken up by that time, let us hear no more of Dr. Hammond's opening envelopes and reading their contents without disturbing the seal."

Dr. Hammond's letter to the *Herald,* however, was hardly the last that was heard from him, either on the matter of sealed envelopes or on that of living without discernible nourishment. And not only because Hammond was so demonstrably a man who could not walk away from a battle until it had been absolutely won—preferably, and almost always, in his favor. Hammond needed to continue his attack on Mollie Fancher and on the various personages who supported her because what she represented struck at the heart of his life's work. He was dedicated to taking science into an objective and strictly medical future. The deepest veins of the Fancher story, by contrast, seemed to lead directly into an ancient bedrock—into the shadowed ignorance and superstition of a benighted past.

Even as the letters columns continued to resound with salvos from both sides of the Mollie Fancher debate in December 1878, Hammond had returned to material he had written several years before on the subject of fasting girls and was revising it to comment directly on Mollie. His volume *Fasting Girls: Their Physiology and Pathology,* published in early 1879 by G. P. Putnam's Sons, laid out for posterity his stand on the notion that anyone could live without food. The first lines contain the essence of Hammond's worldview (and self-view): Since "hundreds and thousands of persons throughout the length and breadth of a civilized land" had fallen under the spell of the "monstrous declaration" that a young lady could live more than a dozen years without food, it was up to Hammond himself to set the record straight.

The cure for popular ignorance was, in this instance, quite simple, according to Hammond: fasting claims, whether historical or contemporary, were the result of hysteria. There was nothing magical or mystical or spiritual about it, for these claims were merely the ravings of girls or women suffering from an identifiable disease. This was a medical matter, not a religious one. The only mysterious element was the credulity of the public—especially in such a modern and enlightened age. "If a weak emaciated girl asserts that she is able to exist for years without eating, there are at once certificates and letters from clergymen, professors, and even physicians, in support of the truth of her story. The element of impossibility goes for nothing against the bare word of such a woman, and her statements are accepted with a degree of confidence which is lamentable to witness in this era of the world's progress."

Hammond surveyed the history of other cases of fasting claims, touching on tales of medieval religious abstinence as well as more recent examples like that of Sarah Jacob (whose story he told in great detail), and then arrived at his motivating force: "The Brooklyn Case." Part of his motivation, it becomes clear, was to announce to a larger public his views on the case and defend his own actions in it. "Some of the letters which have appeared in response to a proposition I offered," Hammond wrote, "have accused me of dragging the young lady before the public. It will be seen, however, that her friends and physicians are responsible for all the publicity given to the case."

Of those physicians, Hammond appeared to take delight in relating a few of the more contentious comments from Mollie's Brooklyn doctors. He quoted from the November 26 *Sun,* which had reported: "Dr. R. Fleet Speir, one of Miss Fancher's physicians, smiled last evening when . . . asked . . . what he thought of Dr. Hammond's opinions on the case. 'I probably have just as high an opinion of Dr. Hammond's opinions as Dr. Hammond has of mine,' he said."

After indulging in such personal sidelights, Hammond arrived at his principal point, which was to present a logical—and physical, or materialist—account of what was going on with Mollie Fancher. It appeared, he wrote, that her accident had caused some spinal, and perhaps nerve and brain, injury that confined her to bed. Because she was confined thus, and "her bodily temperature [was] low, and [she was] passing a good deal of her time in trances or periods of insensibility, the requirements of the system as regarded food would necessarily be limited. But this is the most that can be said. She *did* breathe, her heart *did* beat, she required *some* bodily heat, and the various other functions of her organism could not have been maintained without the expenditure of matter of some kind. During abstinence from food the body itself is consumed for these purposes, and there being no renovation, no supplies from without, it loses weight with every instant of time until death finally ensues."

Hammond next presented what he knew best, the god of his particular universe: scientific knowledge, gained from observation. He offered a history of human understanding of starvation, or "inanition," in which the bodily machine does not receive enough fuel. The machine model of thinking about the human body was a new and refreshing one to Victorian scientists, and even now it sounds surprisingly modern—akin to the late-twentieth-century discovery that many forms of mental illness are mediated by chemicals such as serotonin. Hammond described this human machine as "constructed for the purpose of working," and defined "every act of perception or sensation, every thought, every emotion, every volition" as an act of work. To perform that work, there must be force, and that required a source of energy.

He extended the metaphor, a favorite with Victorians at the height of the Industrial Revolution: "The engine may be perfect, the water may be in the boiler, but unless there be force in the form of heat there will be no steam; and there will be no heat unless there be fuel in a state of combustion." While a weak, emaciated, inactive girl who passes all her time reclining in bed will require far less food than a strong, able-bodied, active man working as a plowman, she will still absolutely require something: "a mouthful of bread, or a little tea and toast. . . . The function of calorification may be almost nothing. Still there must be some food taken."

This was proven fact, and Hammond backed it up with experimental evidence. A French researcher, Chossat, had performed tests on various animals and found that, on average, death resulted when the body lost four-tenths of its original weight; a body weighing one hundred pounds could thus waste away to sixty before expiring. At the extreme, five-tenths, or one-half, appeared to be the limit of weight loss that the body could support and still survive. To put those results into a time frame, in order to relate to Mollie's purported twelve or so years, Hammond cited examples of involuntary human starvation—Belgian colliers trapped in a coal pit for twenty-four days with only water to drink; French workmen in a cold, damp vault for fourteen days without even water. When the men emerged in the latter case, their pulses were slow and weak, their "animal heat" greatly reduced, and respiration barely perceptible. Scientists attributed their survival without water to the humidity of the air in the vault. A collier trapped for twenty-three days, the last thirteen without water, died three days after being rescued. Hammond concluded that "in ordinary cases absolute deprivation of food and drink cannot be endured by a healthy adult longer than ten days, and death generally ensues before the end of the eighth day."

What, then, of Mollie? The crucial thing to understand about her, Hammond asserted, was yet another organic fact: that she had a disease, that disease being hysteria. And among the symptoms of the disease of hysteria—a symptom just as far beyond the control of the patient as the symptom of pain is beyond the control of a pleurisy patient—was "a proclivity to simulation and deception. . . . To say, therefore, that she simulated abstinence and deceived us to the quantity of food she took, is no imputation on her honesty, or questioning her possession of as high a degree of honor and trust, as can be claimed by any one. Other women naturally as moral as she, have under the influence of hysteria perpetrated the grossest deceptions."

Hysterical women, Hammond added, also appeared able to go without food and drink somewhat longer than the average person. Hammond himself had had several patients do without one or the other, sometimes without both, for anywhere from one to eleven days with little if any suffering. As soon as there was any suffering, they did not hesitate to break their voluntary fasts; Hammond here betrayed his attitude toward hysterical women, saying that "real suffering is a condition which the hysterical woman avoids with the most assiduous care."

In Mollie's case, because of her hysteria and her trances, which slowed her physical needs, he declared himself willing to believe that she had indulged in frequent long fasts—and that "it is just possible that she might, by remaining quietly in bed in a state of partial or complete trance—a hysterical condition in which the waste of the tissues is greatly reduced—exist for a month without food or drink." Hence his use of the one-month period in his challenge to her, he added, was not outrageous; it gave her, in fact, the benefit of the doubt. Perhaps she could do it.

"But," Hammond continued in his more characteristic bombastic style, "when it is gravely said that 'for a period of nearly fourteen years she has lived absolutely without food or nourishment of any kind,' we are forced to declare, in the interest of science, that the statement is necessarily absolutely devoid of truth." He allowed himself a brief excursion into his philosophy of scientific proof, a subject central to his thinking—and to his reasons for pursuing so avidly the putative claims of a hysterical woman: "All the teachings of science and of experience are against the claim." Natural science, he explained—patiently, for the lay reader—was necessarily founded on experience and observation. We would not initially know, looking at a bear for the first time, that the animal could go into retirement at the beginning of winter and remain till spring in a condition of semi-existence and without food. We could learn through observation the natural law that "all bears go through the same process, that it is a law of their organism to do so, and that their reduced functional actions are maintained by the consumption of the fat with which in the beginning their bodies were loaded."

By the same logic, everything we have learned about humans and starvation, he continued, would tell us that Mollie Fancher could not have lived fourteen years without food. If, by some amazing fluke of nature, her body had managed to break every known physical law, then her case ought to be investigated, as Hammond himself (he reminded his readers) had suggested. This he wrote in the last paragraph of *Fasting Girls,* which ended with wording that suggested a trial in a court of law: "If Miss Fancher has lived fourteen years without food, or even fourteen months, or weeks, she is a unique psychological or pathological individual, whose case is worthy of all the consideration which can be given to it, not by superstitious or credulous or ignorant persons, but by those who, trained in the proper methods of scientific research, would know how to get the whole truth of her case, and nothing but the truth." Needless to say, one of those trained and rigorously scientific people would have to be Hammond himself.

But there was another practitioner Hammond considered worthy of joining him in evaluating Mollie Fancher's case, and that was George M.

Beard, a fellow neurologist and the creator of the concepts of American Nervousness and neurasthenia. The two doctors, temperamentally mismatched, had occasionally been at loggerheads in the past, but the serendipity of Mollie's fame gave them a common enemy. What Beard saw in her case, as Hammond did, was a chance to defeat the primitive forces of superstition once and for all.

CHAPTER FIVE

The Nervous American

If Mollie Fancher can do what is pretended for her, then all science goes
for naught. We must begin all over, and she should be worshipped as
God, for she has divine attributes.

—George M. Beard, in the New York *Sun,* November 26, 1878

In their unplanned partnership to oppose Mollie Fancher,
William Hammond and George Beard made for a psychological odd
couple. Both were highly respected doctors and scientists, Hammond
perhaps a bit more so because of his former title of surgeon general
(despite the court-martial) and his wide clinical practice. They shared a
bombastic approach to the Fancher case. But in terms of character, they
represented opposite extremes of the eccentric scientific personality.
Where Hammond was excitable, Beard was calm; where Hammond
took everything intensely personally, Beard cultivated a philosophic distance and irony; while Hammond systematically built up a large practice
and a considerable fortune, Beard jumped from enthusiasm to enthusiasm and spent every penny practically before it was earned. They did,
however, both enjoy a nearly unshakable conviction that they were right
in most things—and an absolute lack of hesitancy about saying so.

They had been known to part company on certain issues of scientific
philosophy (Hammond had once said of one of Beard's ideas, "If the
doctrine of Dr. Beard was to be accepted, I should feel like throwing

132

away my diploma and joining the theologians"). But in the matter of Mollie Fancher, they stood as one—and stood so far above other dissenting voices in the vehemence of their comments that, as the fireworks continued, "Drs. Beard and Hammond" came to be recognized as a single entity. What they represented was, quite simply, the future of medicine and of psychiatry.

George Miller Beard, like Hammond, was descended from a comfortably established family. He was born in Montville, Connecticut, in 1839; his father, the Reverend Spencer Beard, was a Congregational minister, and his grandfather had been a doctor. George's schooling involved the top establishments: he prepped at Phillips Academy; graduated from Yale College in 1862 and studied for a year at Yale Medical School; spent two Civil War years as an assistant surgeon in the Navy; and graduated from Columbia's College of Physicians and Surgeons in 1866. While a medical student, he met a fellow student and fraternity brother, A. D. Rockwell, who was to become his medical partner for eight years. Rockwell later was the source of many personal details of his colleague's life and character, after Beard's rise to fame and untimely death from pneumonia in 1883, at the age of forty-three.

It is Rockwell's reminiscences that convey most vividly Beard's quixotic personality, and no details are more telling than those about Beard's youthful struggles with spiritual questions. They may help explain not only Beard's antipathy to the Spiritualist pseudoreligion that crested during his adult years, but also the fiercely unsentimental and scientific worldview that propelled him into the Fancher fray. One story about the young Beard appears, in its first incarnation, in an unpublished, handwritten letter sent by Rockwell in 1905 to another doctor who knew and wrote about Beard, Charles Dana. The letter, now found tucked inside a printed copy of Rockwell's 1883 eulogy, *The Late Dr. George M. Beard: A Sketch,* in the Rare Book Room at the New York Academy of Medicine, reveals the young Beard as a brooding, conflicted, and surprisingly religious figure.

In the letter, Rockwell described a diary Beard kept from age sixteen through his graduation at Yale, which Beard's daughter showed to Rockwell after her father's death. What he read indicated a man reared very strictly and teetering on the verge of unbelief. The diary, Rockwell wrote Dana, "reminds me very much of that kept by 'Geo Eliot' in her early days—both of them had been brought up according to the strict letter of the law, both were decidedly morbid and both gradually grew into a saner atmosphere." Beard in these years was a true son of a minister; according to Rockwell, he "worried about his soul a good deal, scored himself for loving the vanities of life, and was perpetually reminding himself that 'the places that now knew him would soon know him no more forever.'"

Rockwell then related how Beard wrote of taking a Sunday walk near Manhasset Bay, Long Island, where he was then living: "He deplores the wickedness of those he sees fishing or sailing and speaks of it as a sad commentary on human nature." One can picture the "preternaturally grave" young man watching other young people relaxing lightheartedly on a warm summer Sunday, the day he was brought up to think of as solely and exclusively the Lord's. And perhaps this young man both deplored and envied them—the surreptitious envy driving him to "worry about his soul" and to remind himself that these pleasures, like all other human endeavors, would soon pass away.

Rockwell's letter contains another anecdote of Beard's developing religious thought, also from his diary: "In his junior year he notes the fact somewhat humorously but regretfully that those who go to prayer meeting seem to be the dullest men in his class." Rockwell concluded, "All this of course was quite new to me and most interesting. When I first met him in the early [1860s] he was unobtrusively agnostic."

By the time Rockwell was looking back on his own life in his autobiography, *Rambling Recollections,* which was published fifteen years after his letter to Dana (and nearly forty years after Beard's death), he had incorporated this new insight into what he already knew of Beard's character. It made perfect sense to Rockwell that the "most unusual man" he had met in medical school had been this conflicted creature just a few years earlier. In his autobiography he put together eye-opening tidbits from Beard's diary with what he knew of Beard's childhood and inherent personality. What he produced was a raison d'être for the secular, perhaps somewhat cold scientist Beard became in maturity—the man who was later to write and speak sternly and unforgivingly of Mollie Fancher's character and motives.

Because Beard's father was a clergyman, Rockwell wrote, "George was reared in all the strictness and strait-laced orthodoxy of the times." His diary made clear the effect of this strictness—"How the youthful soul can be submerged in gloom and deprived, through a well-meant but hurtful theology, of its birthright of joyous, helpful living. We see a keen intelligence backed by high moral principles, coming gradually into its heritage of rational living, but not without scars." Rockwell traced that philosophical sea-change through Beard's diary entries. Early on, there were moralistic diatribes like the comments about that summer Sunday near Manhasset Bay, and fears that he would become a moral castaway, but as his later teen years passed, his severity and introspection seemed gradually to relax.

Rockwell flagged Beard's question about his Bible study and prayer meetings—"Why is it that these meetings are not better attended by the brighter and quicker-witted men of the College?"—as a midway point on his spiritual journey or transformation. By the time Rockwell met him, Beard appeared to have reached the end point and settled on a practical agnoticism, in which, Rockwell wrote, "in regard to the affair of the soul and its future, he neither affirmed nor denied. 'The great beyond' was to him 'unknown and unknowable' in this life."

Beard had strayed so far from his early orthodoxy in the direction of knowable fact that the dogma of Christian faith no longer made any sense to him. Rockwell recalled Beard's once saying that if he were now to take up the Bible for the first time and attempt to read it, especially the Old Testament, he would be able to make neither head nor tail of it. To Rockwell, this illustrated the trend of Beard's mind, "his waning interest in studies outside the practical affairs of human thought, and his rebound or revolt from the hampering teachings of early days." All well and good, except that even Rockwell—who obviously loved Beard and greatly admired his intellect, who wrote that Beard had changed the current of his life—felt that perhaps the rebound had been too powerful, and had taken Beard into a barren philosophical place.

His friend, Rockwell wrote, inwardly resented his lengthy thralldom to the ultrastrict Christian mores of his childhood. "The pendulum which had swung so long in one direction made an equal arc in the other. While giving up every vestige of belief in the supernatural, he might have made more of the soul of man and of human emotion and sentiment. Nothing seemed to interest him much in literature or books but pure science, accuracy of statement, mathematical precision or certainty." The transformation of Beard's personal religious beliefs makes it easy to see why the Spiritualist movement would be particularly irksome to him. His work as a doctor and scientist was based firmly, maybe even obsessively, on hard evidence, fact, proof—those were the gods of his philosophy. Spiritualism offered none of that, while daring to call itself scientific.

Beard devoted his short but very productive life to the glorification of proof. Even as he lay dying, while still in his prime, his mind wrestled not with mortality or fear but with scientific observation. His last words were, "Oh, that I had the strength to write out the thoughts of a dying man." *That* would be evidence worth having, the best kind, in Beard's view: not just any old proof from any available observer, but evidence from a trained, skeptical expert who knew the science behind the phenomena. The kind of expert who could comment knowledgeably, and who could also detect fraud where it existed—fraud like Mollie Fancher's wild tales, which seemed so easily to buffalo the average, gullible citizen.

That this single-minded searching after proof and fact may have resulted at least in part from a personally wrenching rejection of religion in his own life makes Beard look like an incarnation of his time. Dogmatic religion, with its ancient and unquestioning faith in miracles and the supernatural, was seeming increasingly irrelevant in the late nineteenth century. Those at the frontiers of post-Darwinian modern thought—the brain-workers, as Beard would come to call them—were instead putting their faith in what was knowable, and in the cultivation of that knowledge. That knowledge, not some unknowable God, would save mankind. In Mollie Fancher, Beard, the archetypal nineteenth-century thinker, confronted what he saw as the essence of archaic ignorance.

The odd thing about Beard—so odd as to be hard to believe, were it not for the numerous anecdotes that back it up—was that amid all his gloom and severity he was a man who dearly loved a joke. Rockwell described it this way: "Underneath his deep solemnity of countenance there lurked such a sense of humor, at times subtle and elusive and again so explosive and rollicking, as to amuse, mystify or disturb, according to the occasion or type of mind affected." Charles Dana, who met Beard in 1881 at the height of his scientific prowess and fame, described him similarly as having "a continual undercurrent of humor."

That undercurrent was such a surprise, such a contrast to his stern demeanor, that Beard garnered a reputation for eccentricity. Many people who didn't know him well, wrote Rockwell, saw him as an enigma—there was such incongruity between the intense seriousness of his usual facial expression and the thoughts that came out of his mouth. He was a slender man of medium height, who in his maturity sported the thick muttonchop sideburns of the time, which offset his receding hairline and high, broad forehead. The photograph of Beard that illustrates Dana's and Rockwell's memoirs, taken when he was forty-two, displays the solemnity that both his friends mention: his face

George Miller Beard, "the father of neurasthenia." A self-contained man with a half-hidden streak of impish humor, Beard joined William Hammond in attempting to expose Mollie Fancher as a fraud, or at best as seriously deluded: a template of the neurotic, hysterical female. (GENERAL RESEARCH DIVISION, THE NEW YORK PUBLIC LIBRARY, ASTOR, LENOX, AND TILDEN FOUNDATIONS)

appears empty of expression; he stares off to the side at a middle distance rather than at the camera; his strong nose and small, pursed mouth are sharply outlined. This man meant business—and indeed, he was astonishingly prolific in his forty-three years.

But Beard was also a man who couldn't resist ribbing his more circumspect colleague Rockwell. Once, upon returning from an extended trip to Europe, he walked unexpectedly into Rockwell's consulting room and found him in conference with the same patient he had been treating when Beard had come to say good-bye three months before. "I can see Beard now," wrote Rockwell later, "with his hands thrown up, saying, 'For the Lord's sake, have you been treating that man ever since I have been gone?'"

Beard was most pressingly in need of his sense of humor when it came to another odd aspect of his personality: his inability to manage his money. To him money was an inconvenient detail; he was apparently unconcerned about amassing any wealth, and equally unconcerned about going into debt. When he came into a little cash—as, for instance, when he was commissioned by the publishers Charles Scribner's Sons in 1869 to rewrite a large medical tome—he immediately planned how he would spend it. In that case, he finished the job in

record time and left straightaway for Europe, promising his then partner Rockwell that he would return with much fresh information from
prominent scientists in England, Germany, and France. "Some would
have placed [the writing fee] in the bank for a rainy day," wrote Rockwell. "But this was against the principles of Dr. Beard, for with him
money was a thing not to be hoarded but to be spent." He left for Europe
with eight hundred dollars and returned (to an empty bank account)
with fifty cents in his pocket.

This insouciance in regard to finance made creditors a steady fact of
Beard's existence. Rather than give in to embarrassment or despair
about this, Beard sometimes indulged in some fun with it. Once he was
visited in his office by someone in a prominent position at a booksellers' with which Beard had a large and long-standing debt (lesser
debt-collectors for the firm having previously had no luck squeezing a
nickel out of him). Beard happened to go through a lot of books because of another impractical habit: when he found something he
wanted to quote, he clipped it out instead of copying it, and thus
ended up with a library full of mutilated volumes.

When the booksellers' agent arrived, Beard ushered him in with ef-
fusive greetings, telling him how glad he was to see him, without letting
him get a word in. When the collector was finally able to state his business, Beard—already a little deaf; the condition would later worsen—
cupped his hand behind his ear and pretended to misunderstand the
man's point, making an irrelevant reply. The man repeated his demand
with growing asperity, and Beard, still with his hand at his ear, replied
that he had no complaint to make: the firm had always served him well,
and he would continue to buy his books there and would recommend
it to his friends.

"Thus at cross purposes," wrote Rockwell of this incident, "the dialogue was kept up for some time, the collector with increasing heat
pressing his claim and Beard, with that look of vacancy on his face,
which he knew so well how to assume, failing seemingly to understand.

Finally the exasperated collector started for the door with great disgust depicted on his face. Beard followed, insisted on shaking hands with him, asked him to come again, saying that he remembered that he owed a trifling bill for books, and in due time would pay it, which he failed not to do."

On another occasion, Beard, an easy and fluid writer, was inspired by the constant importuning of debt collectors to compose an ironic essay about them. Never published in his lifetime, this extract was found among his papers after his death: "I congratulate myself that few persons at my time of life have succeeded amid severe discouragements in honestly acquiring so admirable a band of creditors. . . . It has been said by those who regard themselves as wise, that you must winter and summer with a man before you can know him, but I will recommend a shorter and surer road to acquaintanceship—the getting in debt to a man, or allowing him to get in debt to you. Such delicate relationships bring out, as I have noticed, the finer, subtler, and least suspected qualities of human nature, that would never reveal themselves to any other test whatever; indeed, no man can be said to know himself until he has been either a debtor or a creditor.

"Not the least of the charms of the relationship of debtor and creditor, if one may judge from his own experience, is its permanence; in this feature it is certainly superior to wedlock, or any other earthly relation. Marriages are followed too often by separations, divorces, or at least by infidelities; but my creditors or their representatives are never long away, and they never sue for a divorce, and are faithful unto death."

Beard's sense of the ridiculous marks perhaps the strongest distinction between his personality and that of his prickly fellow scientist William Hammond. Both faced numerous challenges, sometimes even hostility, from their professional community. Not only did they inhabit a contentious and rapidly expanding period of scientific discovery, but both men pushed the envelope, daring to explore areas that had previ-

ously been considered outside the purview of respectable doctors. Hammond's response to criticism was explosive; Beard's was calm, placid, distanced, sometimes ironic.

"Nothing could or ever did disturb his serenity," recalled Charles Dana in a sketch of Beard written on the fortieth anniversary of his death. "He lived in a kind of enchanted atmosphere of synthesizing mental activity"—the classic absentminded professor. "I never saw him angry and he became eloquent and earnest, but never excited," continued Dana. "He met all his critics and all assaults on his character with a joke or with philosophic calm. He always thought he was right in his scientific conclusions and social views. He argued for them, but never quarreled. . . . He never indulged in personal criticism or said an unkind word against any one."

To compare that quietly sure manner with Hammond's loud and angry self-defense against critics is to wonder whether there was a key difference in inner confidence between the two men. Both took an unquestioning stance on the rightness of their own ideas, but Hammond perhaps protested a bit too much (or too emotionally). Beard was the master of soft-spoken assurance, as illustrated by his unflappable appearances as an expert witness in court cases. In one trial, a lawyer ran up against Beard's imperviousness after hours of trying to break down his assertions. Finally the lawyer burst out in exasperation, "Then it is to be presumed that all authorities who differ from you in this matter are in error." Beard answered, "It is to be presumed that they are."

If Hammond's method was to attack the character and motives of those who disagreed with him, Beard's was to restate his stand without raising his voice. This positiveness of statement, as Rockwell termed it, made him some enemies. Many who encountered Beard felt, according to Rockwell, that it "could proceed only from intense and offensive egotism. That Dr. Beard was egotistic, in the sense of placing a high value on his own interpretation of certain phenomena in physics and

psychology as against the opinion of non-experts in these realms of science, cannot be denied. It was, however, the egotism that comes from the consciousness of a clearer and keener insight." Beard's philosophy of self-defense, in Rockwell's view, was: "I never argue, I simply assert." This was, Rockwell said, "the result partly of a natural disinclination for polemics, and partly of a settled conviction that the surest way to establish the truth, as he understood it, was boldly and persistently to reiterate it."

Beard's immovable sense of surety, combined with his wry sense of humor, was called into service with greatest urgency in the late 1870s, not long before he became a key figure in the Mollie Fancher controversy. Suddenly, after years with a booming medical practice and thriving scientific reputation, his professional ascent stalled. Rockwell later blamed the decline in Beard's practice and fortunes on his admirably selfless, but impractical, "ever-restless instinct for research . . . along lines which could in no possible way bring in any return."

Rockwell and Beard had enjoyed success early in their medical practice by popularizing electrical treatment for all types of ills. In the 1860s, when they were beginning their clinical careers, electrotherapy was languishing in a medical ghetto of quackery. As Rockwell recalled in his autobiography, "The whole subject was a veritable *terra incognita,* and to touch it, as one worthy friend remarked to me, was to imperil one's professional reputation." But when he encountered a patient in his practice who had apparently been treated effectively with electrical current for a brain inflammation, he became intrigued, and approached his friend Beard on the subject.

He learned that Beard, "with his usual curiosity in regard to every strange and misunderstood thing," had already investigated using electricity on himself while at Yale. He had suffered in college from persistent indigestion and nervousness—making him perhaps the first official victim of the neurasthenia he was later to make famous around the world—and as a budding materialist physician along the lines of

Hammond, he saw physical treatment as the cure for all mental ills. He had tried applying electricity to himself from "crude induction coils," and had found the results promising. The two practitioners decided to test electrical therapies on charity patients for a variety of ailments. Within two years, Rockwell and Beard were publishing the results of their studies, a series of five articles in the *New York Medical Record* that later became a book, *Medical Use of Electricity, with Special Reference to General Electrization as a Tonic in Neuralgia, Rheumatism, Dyspepsia, Chorea, Paralysis, and Other Affections Associated with General Debility.*

The two had great hopes for their research, Rockwell wrote at the end of his career; they felt they were issuing new and important work. As it happened, the interest their studies excited both in the United States and abroad far exceeded their highest expectations. Soon large numbers of regular, paying patients were being referred to them by other doctors who had read of their results and been convinced of the treatment's efficacy. Patients as distinguished as Cornelius "Commodore" Vanderbilt, at the time perhaps the richest man in the country, came to Rockwell and Beard for treatment.

In an article published in 1869, Beard described the rather daunting procedure: "The feet of the patient are placed on a sheet of copper to which the negation pole is attached, while the positive, either a large sponge or the hand of the operator, is applied over the head (the hair being previously moistened), on the back of the neck, down the entire length of the spine, down the arms, over the stomach, liver, bowels, down the lower extremities—in short, over the entire surface of the body, from the head to the feet, but with special reference to the head and spine." (Beard neglected to mention whether any of this was painful.) Of thirty cases that Beard and Rockwell treated and followed, twenty considered themselves either "cured" or "greatly benefitted." The other third of the patients felt either "slightly benefitted" or "not perceptibly benefitted."

For the relative success of such a modernistic treatment, however,

Beard had only the most primitive of explanations. The first sounds distinctly medieval: "The electric current may directly improve the quantity and quality of the vital force, in accordance with the theory of the correlation and conservation of forces." The second was marginally more sophisticated, and equally speculative: "The violent and repeated muscular contractions that are produced during the operations of general electrization greatly increase the processes of waste and repair"—a phenomenon that Beard called "passive exercise."

The two doctors applied their innovative electrical therapy in a happy partnership for eight years. But in 1876, one thing after another went south. First, the two quarreled over office space. Beard, who had been keeping an office in Brooklyn for morning appointments, abruptly announced his intention of spending morning hours at their shared Manhattan office. Rockwell objected, arguing that the office had room for only one doctor at a time. When Beard persisted, an exasperated Rockwell suggested that perhaps they had better separate their practice—and Beard immediately agreed.

At the time they were in the midst of producing the second edition of their book on the medical uses of electricity, and their physical separation exacerbated the clash of two growing egos. The proof sheets for the book were sent back and forth between offices, with each doctor making changes that the other erased—especially when it came to the question of who had originated what idea. "We very frequently disagreed as to where the credit should be placed," recounted Rockwell. "Where I had written 'Dr. Rockwell' he would erase it and write 'Dr. Beard,' to whom he thought the credit belonged, and I in my turn would re-erase and so the unseemly conflict ran on to the disgust of the printer, and to the detriment of our pockets." They were charged a considerable sum for their extensive changes.

Beard and Rockwell eventually made up their differences and reestablished their friendship, though not their partnership. But other, more worldly things went wrong. While the first edition of their book on electrotherapeutics had done extremely well, in England and Germany as well as the United States, the second was a flop. No one was buying, the medical profession seemed to be drawing back again from the idea of electrotherapy, and both of their clinical practices fell off.

Beard became so discouraged that he decided to change entirely the direction of his work; he told Rockwell he had never really cared for the details of the practice of medicine. What he wanted to do was to bring science to the level of the average mind—to become a popular lecturer on scientific subjects—something he had already tried to accomplish by publishing articles in mainstream magazines such as *The Atlantic Monthly*. Three things, he felt, were needed to draw audiences: good stories; "splurge," or a good show; and most important, "absence of thought." To try to make people think would be "a deadly obstacle to popular success."

The one element Beard didn't take into consideration was that he was by nature not a splurger but a thinker. His lecturing career had an inauspicious beginning and a short life. Rockwell warned him that he did not have a good voice and was not a graceful speaker, but nonetheless Beard hired a hall on Third Avenue in Manhattan with a capacity of one hundred fifty, and announced his first presentation. Rockwell even tried to help by having his own minister announce the lecture from the pulpit on Sunday. The lecture was attended by exactly three people: Rockwell, the janitor of the hall, and a boy who slipped in and sat in the last row. Beard calmly presented an hourlong talk, losing the boy about halfway through. It took a few more months of speechifying, occasionally to a larger crowd, to persuade Beard to return to what was his natural strength: investigating and theorizing, activities that would lay the groundwork for twentieth-century psychiatry.

When George Beard took on Mollie Fancher in late 1878, he was heading into the most productive and innovative period of his medical career. His mind worked in such sweeping ways—Rockwell called him "sort of a genius"—that he tried to pin down the nature of scientific discovery itself, to get at the essence of what makes humans understand the world scientifically. What constitutes or proves "discovery" of some new principle or phenomenon? How can we judge evidence? Can we always trust our senses? Can just anyone testify meaningfully to medical or scientific fact, or only a trained observer?

Whether he admitted it to himself or not, the Fancher case must have seemed like a gift to Beard. It would allow him to present favorite themes of scientific discovery and testimony to the general public, and it was a ready-made opportunity to regain some of his former prestige and professional momentum—in a manner more suited to his talents than his ill-fated lectures had been. So it was that when the intrepid *Sun* reporter approached Beard on Monday, November 25, the day after the big front-page story on Mollie (and the day Hammond's first remarks on the case appeared in the paper), Beard had already been thinking long and hard about her. He was at that moment in the process of finishing an article about Mollie for *The Medical Record*. Both his written comments and his remarks to the *Sun* reporter would soon bring him plenty of attention, some of it antagonistic.

The reporter found Beard ready to talk. "I have been interested in the Fancher case for some time," he said, "and I have written much on the subject of nervous disorders and hysteria, so that I guess I can answer your questions. The subject is not sprung on me." He went on to say that he had in the past spoken directly with Mollie's physician Dr. Speir, with an eye to examining her case firsthand. "He answered that she wasn't giving any remarkable manifestations then, and that the family did not desire an investigation. In short, I was coolly set back."

Beard was quite cool himself about testing Mollie. "A proper investigation would cost $1,000, and would take three months or more. The girl must be taken away from all her friends and confined, just as though she had committed a crime. That is, so that her friends could not act in collusion with her. Then could be ascertained without the shadow of a doubt whether she ate or not. Whether she was deceiving or not."

Beard brought up one of his favorite scientific subjects—one equally admired by his colleague Hammond. "I claim that people are divided into two classes," he told the reporter, "experts and non-experts. A non-expert has no right to pretend to authority. I don't know anything outside of my line. I am no mathematician. It would be foolish for me to write for the public a paper on the binomial theorem"—as foolish, presumably, as for non-experts on nervous disease to dare to assert that Mollie Fancher lived without food, and was clairvoyant.

Perhaps, Beard conceded, Mollie's senses were heightened as a result of her being in a trance—a topic he had investigated at length—because the nervous activity of her brain might be concentrated in one region of that organ. But clairvoyance, mind-reading, prophecy? "I know that she doesn't have [those abilities]," Beard declared. As an expert in his field, he clarified, he was authorized to recognize ridiculous claims. "I don't have to investigate. It is not scientific to investigate such pretensions. Suppose a hysterical girl tells a mathematician that two and two make seventeen. Does he go to work investigating to see whether it is true or not? He knows it's false."

But, the reporter interjected, what about the testimony of Mollie's seemingly honest doctors, friends, and family members?

Beard's response would touch a nerve in anyone who had given Mollie the benefit of the doubt. "The testimony of a non-expert amounts to nothing," he said. "If we accept non-expert testimony there can be no science. The first step in any science is the rejection of all average non-expert human testimony relating to it." Even the physicians studying Mollie's case, he asserted, were not expert enough in assessing evidence and seeing through either intentional or unintentional deception on the part of the subject. "These physicians in Brooklyn are my personal friends," Beard added. "They are able men in their line, but they are not experts, and their testimony goes for naught. The number who

147

testified to Mollie Fancher's wonderful performances makes no difference. A naught has no value, two naughts has no value, five hundred millions of naughts has no value."

So sure was Beard of the falsity of the Fancher claims that if she were proven to be authentic he would be ready to throw all of his knowledge out the window. If that were the case, "then all science goes for naught," he said. "We must begin all over, and she should be worshipped as God, for she has divine attributes." Beard, agnostic that he was, knew the power of that statement. He also knew how unlikely it was that he would ever have to practice such worship.

With this daring pronouncement, Beard had the public audience he had craved. In his own bylined *Medical Record* article, which appeared four days after the *Sun* interview, he had the opportunity to frame the Fancher story wholly within his own philosophy. The document he produced—the one he was approving in page proofs when the *Sun* reporter visited him—placed the rule of reason and logic above all else, at times not very politely. It was a manifesto of a new medical age, and Beard knew it.

The root of Beard's particular genius (and perhaps of his egotism as well) may have been his ability to put even his own science into a context, a place in history—and the future. It is almost as if, in his short life, he was able to rise above the confused squabbles of the day and look up and down a timeline of scientific discovery. This he did repeatedly in his *Medical Record* article about Mollie, as though her case prompted him to think in larger terms. The thorough study of the nervous system that this case demanded belonged, he wrote, "to the science of the present and the future"—a future in which he surely saw himself figuring prominently. As for the matter of clairvoyance and "allied delusions" raised by Mollie's claims, it was "the witchcraft of the nineteenth century," and the excitement about the Fancher case "by the very extravagance and stupendousness of its claims [would] do more than any course of abstract reasoning could possibly have done to hasten its decline."

Beard saw Mollie, as well as himself, as an agent of history—a way to point other doctors and thinkers down the right path of objectivism, and away from mysticism. "The Fancher case will have been of value," he said, "if it shall do no more than impress on the professional mind the importance of a re-study and re-building of the logic of medicine." But what his article did, instead, was to galvanize his enemies by its very forcefulness.

Beard confessed himself relieved to be writing to an audience of scientists, who would be more likely than the average newspaper-reader to appreciate his main point: that medicine and science were comprehensible only to those trained very specifically for their practice—a viewpoint that would come to dominate the rigidly specialized system of doctoring in the twentieth century. The great movement of the nineteenth century was to take medical treatment out of the hands of generalists and "irregular" practitioners (including holistic and faith healers) and into the expensively trained hands of experts who were adept in one area of study. As just such an expert, Beard gave his informed diagnosis: "In ordinary neurological language this case of Miss Fancher would be designated as hysteria of a traumatic origin, with contractures and attacks of ecstasy, which, like catalepsy, is but another term for one of the many phases of trance."

There was only one other possibility, Beard added, in a statement that would inflame Mollie's supporters more than any other. If she wasn't hysterical, which would at least absolve her of responsibility for her actions, she was simply an out-and-out premeditated liar. "Unsought-for evidence has been brought to me from various quarters—from physicians and from clergymen as honorable and as able as any whose names have appeared in connection with this case—that Mollie Fancher intentionally deceives; that she lives on the fat of the land; that the fancy articles she professes to make are made for her; that her reading without eyes is done by trickery. . . . In nearly all the claims of this character that I have had opportunity to investigate, the deception was found to be intentional; the experience of other observers in Europe and this country is, I believe, the same."

Together, the *Sun* interview and the *Medical Record* article put Beard on the map as Hammond's semi-official partner in an energetic public campaign. The *Sun* reporter took the natural next step: he went back to "Miss Fancher's friends" for a rebuttal the day his interview with Beard was published, and wrote an article under that title for the next day's edition. The most expansive in Mollie's defense was once again Professor West, whom the reporter found in his parlor at Brooklyn Heights Seminary (after "passing through a bevy of pretty girls"). In West's remarks can be heard a slight prickliness on the side of Brooklyn, which is echoed in some of the Brooklyn newspaper stories. "So the medical men of New York City don't believe we know what we are talking about over here," he remarked. "That our testimony is of no value in this case because we're non-experts, and that we are all wrong when we say we have seen these things! Well, what of it? What difference does it make whether they believe it or not? It doesn't alter the facts in the case."

The facts, West insisted, were what he himself could see, as a physicist and chemist. "I have subjected her to severe tests, but I have never been able to see the faintest traces of deception. She lay there, bedridden, for nine years in one position. Was there any deception in that? I can place my hand on her abdomen and feel her back bone. Is there any deception there?" West registered a complaint against Beard and Hammond that others were beginning to raise: For scientists who swore by empirical evidence, was it not contradictory that they were judging this case sight unseen? "The trouble with these physicians, Hammond, Beard, and the rest," he said, "is that they are arguing from a theoretical standpoint. Their theory is all right, perhaps, but how do they know that it applies to this case, which they have never studied? They haven't seen the girl do these things, and yet they presume to say that she can't do them, because it is contrary to some theory of theirs. . . . The fact is, they don't know anything about this case."

The *Brooklyn Daily Union-Argus* weighed in on the same day, and in similar fashion, with a sardonic unsigned item linking Beard and Hammond: "Ex-Surgeon-General William A. Hammond, an eminent authority on psychological subjects, who never heard of the case of Miss Fancher until within a week, and who has never seen her, pronounces her a humbug. Dr. George M. Beard, whose learning is approximate only to that of the eminent Dr. Hammond, says, 'It is not scientific to investigate such pretensions.'. . . If 'a little learning is a dangerous thing,' let such pigmies in wisdom as Prof. Parkhurst, the Rev. Dr. Duryea, Prof. West, Dr. Speir, and others, of this city, be grateful that, whatever their present peril, they are not exposed to such awful risks as are Drs. Hammond and Beard."

The newspaper commented again in December, after Beard's *Medical Record* article, sounding a defensive note. "How would it suit Dr. Beard," it editorialized, "to have a scientific investigation of the characters of the Rev. Drs. Duryea and Van Dyke [*sic*], Profs. Parkhurst and West, Drs. Ormiston and Speir, and other gentlemen of this city, whose veracity and intelligence have hitherto been unchallenged? It is evident that somebody is woefully deceived about this business." Days later, the other major Brooklyn paper, the *Eagle,* quoted Beard's infamous "living on the fat of the land" passage, in a letter to the editor signed by one Edwin W. Carr of Brooklyn. "I have to say—and to say most emphatically—that when Dr. Beard makes the above statement he states what he knows to be an untruth," wrote Carr, who did not divulge his connection to the Fancher case or the source of his knowledge. "When a man descends to a lie to strengthen his argument, it must be a very weak one. If what he says is true, then he is in duty bound to give the names of these 'clergymen and physicians' who have not, as yet, been heard from for themselves."

Letters to the editors of various newspapers flew furiously after Beard's comments, most of them from writers who remained anonymous. The exchanges sometimes became so heated that correspondents felt compelled to write repeatedly, carrying on acrimonious dialogues to the entertainment of both editors and readers. One of these recurring characters was "Speculum," who wrote to the *New York Herald* from Brooklyn. He said he used a pseudonym because he was a "man of family" who "may possibly die rich," and he was afraid his belief in clairvoyance cast enough doubt on his mental stability that his will might be contested after his death. He was driven to contribute his thoughts about the case, he said, by his disgust with "several so-called experts." The only ones he named were Hammond and Beard.

These experts' treatment of the Fancher case, Speculum wrote, was "most uncharitable and unscientific, and savors more of the police detective than the physician." What's more, "the intense self-satisfaction and arrogance of some of the critics is amazing. . . . It is beyond the laws of nature; [Dr. Beard] has been specially privileged with a complete edition of them. I must own that it is hard to keep cool in discussing with such writers."

Speculum pinpointed a flaw in Beard and Hammond's theorizing about testing Mollie's powers—in particular, her clairvoyance. There would never, he predicted, be a conclusive end to the question, because there would always be an even more skeptical expert to disbelieve the other experts' proof. "Supposing Miss Fancher's friends accepted this bet [Hammond's check-in-the-envelope challenge] and she read the enclosure correctly, how much would the case be altered? Thousands think themselves smarter than Dr. Hammond or Dr. Beard, and would require the test repeated with their envelopes. The celebrated Professor Gregory, of Edinburgh University, a teacher and writer of acknowledged merit, investigated the subject of clairvoyance for years and was thoroughly convinced of its truth; but does Dr. Hammond or Dr. Beard believe it on that account? Does the fact that the late Professor Elliotson, of London (one of the best physiologists and physicians of his day), after years of experiment, was a thorough believer settle the question? Certainly not. And the conversion of Dr. Hammond or Dr. Beard could not settle the question any more than the belief of their at least equally gifted fellow physicians just named." So much for Beard's hope for the "re-study and re-building of the logic of medicine" as a worthy result of the Fancher affair.

Another recurring correspondent to the *Herald,* "M.H." of Brooklyn, also took issue with the two self-styled experts. In his third letter to the *Herald,* with a few quick brushstrokes, he addressed the huge cultural issue that underlay the struggle over the meaning of Mollie Fancher like a vast subterranean reservoir: faith in the ancient tenets of religion versus the atheistic ethic of modern science. In an age that was just beginning to comprehend the shattering implications of Darwin's vision, many thinking people still clung to the logic-defying beliefs that had once been unquestioned. If, as Beard and Hammond stated so unwaveringly, the powers of fasting and "vision" claimed for Mollie violated immutable natural laws that had always been the same, "what, then, are we to do with the Bible?" M.H. wondered. "With Moses and the prophets? With the apostles and disciples? With all the saints in the calendar? In fact, with any and all forms of religion?" It was the very question that George Beard had wrestled with as a student. He had chosen his answer long before; now his mission was to show the world that he was right.

Beard was especially eager to debunk, or at least redefine, Mollie's trances and clairvoyance, because the nature of trance had become for him a pet cause. Trance could be considered mystical—as in the biblical prophets, or the Spiritualists he so disliked—or a medical phenomenon in which, as Beard wrote in *Nature and Phenomena of Trance,* "the organism becomes a mechanism." Beard was dedicated to proving that the latter conception was the only acceptable one: a purely scientific, mechanistic state, in which the conscious will is withdrawn as a result of a "concentration of nervous activity in some one direction, with corresponding suspension of nervous activity in other directions."

Beard's ideas about trance led to interesting conceptualizations of the nature of consciousness and of what he termed "the involuntary life"—a precursor of sorts to Freud's theories of the unconscious, which the great psychoanalyst would not refine until at least a decade later. Beard's most powerful legacy to psychiatry had to do not with his explication of trance, however, but instead with his vision of American Nervousness, a disorder caused by the mechanistic nature of civilization itself.

Beard's most significant leap forward was to synthesize and define what was in the 1870s a swirling pool of symptoms. People felt sick in ways that they couldn't understand, and that didn't seem to yield to familiar treatments. They had what they called "sick headaches"; muscular aches and paralysis; nausea and indigestion; insomnia; phobias and vague fears; chronic fatigue. Beard was determined to connect these symptoms in some meaningful way, with a description that spelled out both cause and cure. He began to do this in a speech to the New York Medical Journal Association in 1869, which was published in April of that year in *The Boston Medical and Surgical Journal* (precursor to *The New England Journal of Medicine*).

Beard called his phenomenon neurasthenia, or "exhaustion of the nervous system," his term based on Greek root words meaning "nerve," "strength," and "lack." His first step, as any self-respecting inventor or entrepreneur would understand, was to establish that he got there first, to plant the flag of ownership: "The morbid condition or state expressed by this term," he wrote, "has long been recognized, and, to a certain degree, understood, but the special name *neurasthenia* is now, I believe, for the first time presented to the profession." Neurasthenia was "most frequently met with in civilized, intellectual communities"; it appeared to be the price we had to pay for enjoying progress and refinement.

Beard described the typical American neurasthenic as a delicate, nervous person, often highly intelligent and artistic, who is somewhat emotionally unstable but whose disturbance falls short of serious mental illness. Beard's neurasthenic was in effect the neurotic Woody Allen persona transported to the nineteenth century—worried, narcissistic, urban, twitchy—with a high-strung, creative sensibility often overwhelmed by the demands of a hyperactive modern society.

A dozen years after his first article about neurasthenia, Beard explored that society and its demands in a much broader work: his *American Nervousness*, published two years before his death. Here, in a book Beard himself described as more philosophical and popular in nature than his previous work, containing a quarter-century's worth of his research and thought, he edged ever closer to modern psychological thinking. Why was this nervous exhaustion on the rise? he wondered. Why did it seem to strike brain-workers more than others?

Beard found the culprit in modern society's recent introduction of five elements, each representing an enormous change in how people experienced the world and their place in it. The first, steam power, moved man and machine at a greatly increased pace. The second element was the press, which put daily information about the entire world into people's hands as never before. The third, the telegraph, transmitted ideas and news rapidly, and therefore closed distances between people and between towns. The sciences, Beard's fourth element, were in the nineteenth century discovering how the physical universe operated in ways that challenged ancient faiths. Last, "mental activity of women," representing middle-class women's evolving role in a society that had begun to free them from the household, challenged ancient ways of structuring society on the most basic level. Who wouldn't be nervous?

Americans had an extra element that predisposed them to neurasthenia, Beard added: the very freedom and opportunity that defined their national character. "Civil and religious liberty, and the great mental activity made necessary and possible in a new and productive country" carried a burden of anxiety. The potential offered by a place where ostensibly anyone could become president, where land stretched seemingly endlessly just waiting to be conquered, could also be a potent source of psychological stress. While in older, more hierarchical countries people lived in a spirit of routine contentment and repose, in America there was at all class levels "a constant friction and unrest—a painful striving to see who shall be highest; and, as those who are at the bottom may soon be at the very top, there is almost as much stress and agony and excitement among some of the lowest orders as among the very highest."

Beard seems to be on to a twentieth-century conception here—our casual, automatic assumption of a connection between emotional stress and neurosis—and yet he couldn't shed the materialist ideas of his time. He still saw the disorder as physical in nature, as an actual disease of the central nervous system, and he laid out his hypothesis in vague terms that would make little sense to a twenty-first-century chemist or biologist: "My own view is that the central nervous system becomes dephosphorized, or, perhaps, loses somewhat of its solid constituents; probably also undergoes slight, undetectable, morbid changes in its chemical structure, and, as a consequence, becomes more or less impoverished in the quantity and quality of its nervous force." He considered this a molecular disturbance, something that would show up under the microscope in studies of patients who died in a neurasthenic condition. "All forms of insanity," he wrote, "are dependent on *some* central morbid [i.e., diseased] condition."

In other ways as well, *American Nervousness* was despite its prescience very much a document of its time. Mixed in among Beard's acute observations were occasional absurdities that revealed cultural preconceptions. "The eyes," he wrote, "are good barometers of our nervous civilization. . . . The savage can usually see well; myopia is a measure of civilization." And: "The excessive nervousness of Americans seems to act as an antidote and preventive of gout and rheumatism, as well as of other inflammatory diseases."

The beauty of American women claims its own chapter subhead— "Relation of Nervousness to Beauty"—and a great deal of hyperbole. "In no other country are the daughters pushed forward so rapidly, so early sent to school, so quickly admitted into society; the yoke of social observance (if it may be called such), must be borne by them much sooner than by their transatlantic sisters. . . . Their mental faculties in the middle range being thus drawn upon, constantly from childhood, they develop rapidly a cerebral activity both of an emotional and an intellectual nature, that speaks in the eyes and forms the countenance; thus, fineness of organization, the first element of beauty, is supplemented by expressiveness of features—which is its second element; by the union of these two, human beauty reaches its highest." So it seems the "mental activity of women" in America had some positive side effects, at least.

Woven in among Beard's laments about the sometimes excruciating price of civilization was a sly sense that it might be a badge of honor to be neurasthenic. Just as an earlier generation of Romantic poets and artists had cultivated an aura of sensitivity and physical delicacy, Victorian neurasthenics—especially as defined by Beard—could be seen as refined and brainy. "Savages" and "lower orders" did not suffer from nervousness; nervous diseases "increase with the increase of culture."

Indeed, Beard described the inner life of the neurasthenic as virtually Wordsworthian—emotionally tuned to a higher pitch, able to perceive with greater acuity not only the strife of existence but also the

157

"glory in the flower," the splendor of everyday life. Perhaps the greatest compensation for having "this type of [psychic] organization" was that the "very fineness of temperament, which is the source of nervousness, is also the source of exquisite pleasure. Highly sensitive natures respond to good as well as evil factors in their environment. . . . If they are plunged into a deeper hell, they also rise to a brighter heaven; their delicately strung nerves make music to the slightest breeze; art, literature, travel, social life, and solitude, pour out on them their selected treasures; they live not one life but many lives, and all joy is for them variously multiplied."

Such romantic notions and flowery language may have been one reason that Beard's concept of American Nervousness was not at first universally accepted. One founder of the New York Neurological Society described Beard as a Barnum of American medicine, and wrote of his book that it "was not worth the ink with which it is printed, much less the paper on which this was done." The historian Charles Rosenberg has written that some of Beard's colleagues regarded him as a charlatan, evidently more concerned with establishing his reputation than with providing evidence for the existence of neurasthenia. But by the early 1890s, Rosenberg adds, the diagnosis of nervous exhaustion "had become part of the office furniture of most physicians." More than one hundred years later, Beard, though obscure, is generally regarded as the first to outline and study what is today seen as neurosis.

Beard's conception of the nervous American as highly strung but artistically and spiritually sensitive sounds like Mollie Fancher—the schoolgirl who devoted herself too intently to her studies, the dyspeptic teenager with fainting spells and no appetite, the injured young woman who had hysterical fits when thunder crashed or a fire wagon passed by; but who also wrote poetry, embroidered untiringly, and in her trances rose "to a brighter heaven." Mollie was in some ways the ultimate neurasthenic, a genuine victim of the modern age because of the horsecar accident, and suffering from an affliction that fit all the criteria of hysteria, one of Beard's symptoms of neurasthenia.

Mollie also embodied the tension between old and new, between ancient, slow-moving ways and the modern rush of civilization, that Beard blamed for American Nervousness. She could be seen either as a saintly spiritual phenomenon or as the neurotic hysteric that such forward-thinking doctors as Hammond and Beard claimed she was. But there was another realm, beyond the ken of American Nervousness, in which Mollie stood at a crossroads between ancient belief and scientific reason: the realm of eating or not eating, fasting or starving. In anorexia as well as nerves, a new understanding of psychology was emerging, one that hinged on the mind and not the body.

CHAPTER SIX

Feeding on Air

It is ungenteel to have much of an appetite, especially for young misses, destined to circulate in fashionable orbits.

—The Ways of Women, 1873

It is sometimes quite shocking to see the extreme exhaustion and emaciation of these patients.

—Sir William Withey Gull, *Anorexia Nervosa (Apepsia Hysterica),* 1873

IN HER 1882 ADVICE MANUAL *Eve's Daughters; or, Common Sense for Maid, Wife, and Mother* (one title of many in her Common Sense in the Household Series), Marion Harland told of a worrisome dinner-table conversation she had had with a fashionable young lady. The exchange was so common, she added, that she could detail dozens of similar cases—each with the same cautionary and appalling aftermath.

"Do you always eat so little?" asked I, once, of a beautiful girl, who had been my *vis-a-vis* at a dinner-party.

"Seldom more, I think; I am fresh from boarding-school, you know. Most girls get out of the habit of eating at such places."

"You dined to-day, on three spoonfuls of soup, half a cracker, an olive and a bunch of raisins," pursued I, surveying the rounded cheeks and brilliant bloom. She was very dear to me, and I could not forbear the remonstrance. "My child! do you know that such fare will injure the coat of your stomach?"

"The stomach is what Carlyle calls it—a diabolical machine," she returned lightly. "If I could lose mine entirely, in addition to ruining it, I should be happy to renounce it and all its works. It and its appurtenances are a vile clog upon human happiness and human progress. A regular meal, comprising soup, fish, meat, vegetables and dessert—invariably gives me a headache and flushes my face painfully."

A few years later, the regimen—a popular one among delicate, upper-class females of the late Victorian era—had taken its inevitable toll. Harland described the young woman's condition with appropriate melodrama: "At twenty-five," she wrote, "when she should be in the prime of womanly beauty and vigor, she is a prey to chronic neuralgia and frequent carbuncles—the sure indices of poverty of blood. Her bloom has gone and her buoyant spirits are depressed by the dread of permanent invalidism. She is, also, a confirmed dyspeptic—a mysterious dispensation to one who never ate heartily in her life."

The relationship between young women and food was, in the late nineteenth century, growing fraught in a way it never had been before. The act of eating had, until then, been fairly straightforward. Most people worried simply about having too little to eat, or too little to eat that was good, or fresh, or unadulterated. If you could afford it, you were likely to eat a lot, in as much variety as possible. Victorian menus and cookbooks bulge with a mind-boggling array of soups and aspics and removes (the main meat or poultry course, which "removed," or came after, the soup and fish courses). Edith Wharton's *The Age of Innocence,* set in the 1870s New York of her youth, describes an at-home dinner for two men that included two wines and "a velvety oyster soup . . . shad and cucumbers, then a young broiled turkey with corn fritters, followed by a canvas-back [duck] with currant jelly and a celery mayonnaise."

For young women amid such bounty, and amid a recently affluent and comfortable middle class, eating now carried new and powerful symbolic baggage. It was becoming an ambivalent act—not to mention potentially reputation-harming. Blame it on a synergy between Americans' pleasure-fearing puritanical roots, never far from the surface, and an increasingly rule-bound Victorian culture. The temptations of the table, and how—or whether—to give in to them, tapped into several late-nineteenth-century preoccupations. One was the confusing problem of class distinctions. In a society in which one could, as did Cornelius Vanderbilt, begin one's career at age sixteen with a hundred-dollar loan, and die, in 1877, the richest man in America, what should be the signposts of status? How was one to distinguish the truly refined from the simply bourgeois or nouveau riche?

During Mollie Fancher's girlhood, there was a a craze for etiquette books as manners, especially table manners, became one way to differentiate class levels. Rules proliferated, and so did tableware. The hands were never to touch food directly, so how on earth did one eat corn on the cob? A corn-scraper was invented, as were grape shears, asparagus tongs, orange spoons, cheese scoops, oyster forks, strawberry forks, pie forks . . . A written road map (with training available only to members of a leisured class) was necessary to negotiate one's place setting at a formal dinner party. And that was only the beginning. There was also to consider: How to serve oneself from a common dish, the exact angle at which to grasp one's fork (depending on what type of food was being eaten or cut), the precise way to break (never cut!) one's bread.

Proper behavior was by the late nineteenth century becoming so intricate that simple middle-class social occasions were conducted like royal audiences. In an 1878 article on New Year's Eve celebrations, Brooklyn's *Daily Union-Argus* spelled out the fancy footwork of "How to Make Formal Calls" for its regular-folk readers: "When a gentleman calls he should remain but a few moments. With hat in hand he enters the parlor, shakes hands with the lady of the house, bows to the persons who may be present, lingers and converses a few moments and then passes to the refreshment room. Returning he bows and retires to make way for others."

Rules of comportment for young ladies with aspirations to gentility were at least as deliberate, especially regarding their eating behavior. An insipid appetite was a proof of delicacy and elegance. Marion Harland sketched the late-Victorian ideal female: "She who brings up the tone of her nerves by a cup of coffee, and sustains the organ of which she is ashamed by a morsel of toast, lifted to listless lips by a dainty thumb and forefinger, and barely nibbles a strip of boiled ham; who carries a bon-bon box in her pocket into the school-room, and has a private bottle of olives in her desk, 'to relieve faintness,' is 'interesting' in the eyes of her little court—a soulful creature who looks as if she fed on air."

A young lady who admitted to a hearty appetite, on the other hand, would be, in the upper-class adolescent jargon of the 1880s, "not a bit nice," "quite too awfully vulgar, you know." She would be said to "eat like a ploughboy," and would likely be, wrote Harland, the object of covert sneers, or even overt jests. Think of Scarlett O'Hara, being laced into her corset and simultaneously stuffed full of food by her mammy, so that when she went to the barbecue she wouldn't "eat like a fieldhand and gobble like a hog"—because "young misses that eat heavy most generally don't ever catch husbands."

Even once they married and became matrons and mothers, Victorian ladies were expected to never quite be hungry. A turn-of-the-century article in *The Woman's Home Companion* described an interchange between a newly married couple. "I have been cross all day," said the husband as he arrived home. "I thought it was business worries. I know now that I was hungry. . . . I suppose you women don't know anything about that, eh?" "No," his wife replied. "I doubt if we do. I have often forgotten to eat until reminded by faintness and headache that it was past dinner or luncheon time."

When real ladies did confess to hunger, it was expected to be only for light, sweet, delicate morsels. A lecture-demonstration titled "Foods That Tickle the Feminine Palate" at the 1894 Food Fair in Boston presented three entrées featuring eggs and fish; then fudge, caramels, fruit salad with marshmallows, and an elaborate ice cream coupe. Mollie Fancher's feminine palate, likewise, on the few occasions when it could be tickled at all, preferred only the most insubstantial fare: crackers, spoonfuls of milk punch or wine, bits of fruit.

Conspicuously missing from the menu of Victorian women was meat, and the reasons for the prohibition extended beyond the physical. "No food (other than alcohol) caused Victorian women and girls greater moral anxiety than meat," writes the historian Joan Jacobs Brumberg. Meat was assumed to stimulate sexual development and activity—and sexuality, like class distinctions, ranked at the top of late-nineteenth-century obsessions. What Victorians feared, write the medical historians Walter Vandereycken and Ron Van Deth, was the "potentially dislocating power" of sexuality; in the era of the steam engine, "scientists knew how strong the driving force of repressed energy could be." Victorians fought that driving force by shutting down women's sensuality and establishing strict cultural taboos regarding female sexual desire. For a woman to enjoy a slab of roast beef was to suggest a baser nature that she was not supposed to acknowledge in herself. There was a slippery slope of debauchery: it might start with an apparently innocent filet of red meat, but such lusty fare would surely awaken other animal passions.

Any decent woman was expected to rise above all desires of the flesh, to define herself by the spirit rather than the innately sinful body. One (female) health specialist wrote severely, in 1852, of what she termed the low appetites and perverted passions (such as gluttony and intemperance) that arise when women satisfy their physical desires. Rather than be ruled by the demands of the body, women should work on improving their spiritual fortitude. "Let us remember that," she lectured, "when we cover our table with all the delicacies that money can procure, and expend time and thought on the subject of eating."

The particular result of Victorian young women's acceptance of the meat-as-sexuality restriction could easily have been predicted by a modern scientist. Take a sector of the population and remove from its diet a major food group, with all its specific nutrients, and what happens? In an era without one-a-day vitamins, many members of the deprived sector will develop a nutritional deficiency.

So it was that, beginning in the middle to late nineteenth century, a strange malady was noted to be striking teenage girls. Rarely seen before, it was called chlorosis, or sometimes the green sickness, because the skin of its victims could acquire a greenish tint. Chlorosis presented many different symptoms, but its most common signs were lack of energy, amenorrhea, weight loss, appetite disturbance, and what appeared to be melancholy or emotional upset. Medical historians now speculate that chlorosis was a type of anemia, probably attributable to a dietary deficiency of iron—that element found so abundantly in red meat. Chlorosis peaked in the 1870s and 1880s, with some doctors calling it an epidemic among adolescent girls. By the First World War it was thought to have vanished.

Except that, like hysteria, chlorosis didn't exactly vanish. It merely became understood as something else; it acquired a new name and a new identity. Many medical historians believe that it was absorbed into a diagnosis that was struggling to be born in the late nineteenth century, and that today is one of the most publicized emotional disturbances in Western society: anorexia nervosa. As time went on, as neurologists and psychologists began to compare notes, Mollie Fancher began to look more and more—among all her other distinctions—like one of the first notable victims of the disorder.

• • •

Chlorosis, like hysteria, was one of those vague conditions that became a catchall for symptoms—a diagnosis that could be applied to many kinds of "declines," some physical, some tending more to the emotional. One Victorian doctor, Edward Dixon (whose book about women's diseases carried under the title the telling line "To the pure all things are pure"), recounted a case of chlorosis that presented what he called a melancholy aspect. The young woman, who was a patient of one of Dixon's colleagues, was twenty-two years old, from an upper-middle-class New Jersey family, and had suffered a disappointment in love. Under the cloud of that heartbreak she gradually sank into what Dixon labeled a confirmed state of chlorosis.

Yet he described nothing specific beyond what might now be considered clinical depression and a resulting loss of appetite. She had existed on only a few teaspoonfuls of barley or milk a day for a period of months. Her doctors had tried every remedy they could find, both psychological (what Dixon termed "moral") and dietetic, to tempt her appetite and relieve her melancholy, but to no effect. Dixon, called in to consult, was no more successful. His elliptical account leaves the impression that she eventually died, though of what, precisely, is unclear; chlorosis was the diagnosis closest at hand. She was the victim, Dixon wrote, of a "disease that left no sign, save the extreme attenuation and unearthly paleness of a body."

Other contemporary descriptions of chlorosis go to the opposite extreme, detailing such a wealth of symptoms that the poor sufferer sounds as if she has a touch of everything: paleness, quickened pulse, darkened vision, "swimming in the head," vomiting, pain in the head and neck, constipation, shortness of breath, amenorrhea, faintness, stomach pains, capricious appetite, weakness, sensitivity to cold, dyspepsia. Despite this nastiness, chlorosis began by the late-Victorian period to carry with it a certain cachet. After all, paleness and faintness—just like the distaste for meat that prompted their appearance—had been romanticized into signs of a delicate nature that was almost too refined to support life. Walter Vandereycken and Ron Van Deth, specialists in the history of eating disorders, have described the special appeal imputed to these patients: "The chlorotic patient probably personified an aristocratic ideal of beauty, specifically with the pale complexion."

But another beauty ideal was evolving as chlorosis was becoming the sine qua non of Victorian adolescents: the aesthetic of slenderness. The eating behaviors of young women demonstrated their purity and high caste, and inevitably the body shape that resulted from such dainty appetites announced their refinement to the world. Not the utter skinniness aspired to by many young women a century later in the age of Twiggy and beyond—the quality that Marion Harland characterized, in her time, as "a slab-like leanness"—but certainly an absence of fatness. Harland wrote of the typical 1880s girl: "If plump, she berates herself as a criminal against refinement and aesthetic taste; and prays, in good or bad earnest, for a spell of illness to pull her down."

The mention of refinement and taste are dead giveaways: fatness and slenderness were becoming, just as eating had become, signals of class. Before, the leisured class was comfortably plump; now the Victorians were writing a new script, in which a heavy body meant that one's appetites were coarse and uncontrolled, and a willowy form conveyed a purity and elegance bespeaking higher origins. A health manual published in 1873 included the section "Horror of Fat": "No calamity is more dreaded than fat in an aspiring young lady," it read. "Consequently, on the presumption that partial starvation is the legitimate way of keeping it at bay . . . no efforts are left untried to preserve a slender form." This dread of fat becomes dangerous, the manual warned, "when it degenerates into an insane determination to be the shadow, rather than the substance, of a live woman."

Some modern historians, notably Nancy Theriot writing in *The Journal of Psychohistory*, take chlorosis beyond these fashionable ideas of delicacy and beauty. She interprets the incidence of chlorosis on a deeper and more psychological level, focusing on the new stresses being placed on young women in the late nineteenth century. Certainly, Theriot admits, "the chlorotic girl was the romantic heroine *par excellence*" at a moment when, according to personal letters of the time, "invalidism, pallor, small appetite, and a languid mode of speech and manner" were considered the height of female attractiveness. But she sees a more basic drive at work in Victorian teenagers' retreat into the weakness and dependency of chlorosis. The condition, she feels, was a response to the changing boundaries of female life in the 1870s and 1880s, when expectations and opportunities for women were shifting dramatically.

Middle-class girls like Mollie were inhabiting a world very different from that of their mothers. Vandereycken and Van Deth peg the 1870s as the moment when young middle-class women "began to seek a new self-image under the flag of intellectual self-fulfillment." Mollie's generation of women was the first to be allowed access to serious secondary education; like the country itself, young women were expanding their horizons. When they entered school, they stepped into a world in which they could not only learn Latin and history, but contemplate the possibilities of a life that reached beyond motherhood as well.

That new self-image, however, challenged another, even more powerful movement of the late nineteenth century. Vandereycken and Van Deth call it "the cult of true womanhood," in which motherhood was not just exalted but also newly defined as a profession—one that clashed with any other aspiration or vocation. The intimate, romanticized nuclear family was the new model of emotional life, courtesy of the ever-growing middle class (the result of the economic and industrial revolutions that had begun a century earlier). In the middle-class ideal, fathers provided material support while mothers, freed from farm labor, were expected to create and nurture a loving domestic circle. The mother was a family's moral and emotional bastion; she could not be spared from her family's side in order to enter the clamor of the marketplace.

With such cultural ambivalence about women's adult roles, it is not too surprising that schooling—especially in boarding schools, where girls lived away from the bosom of the family—was often blamed for the onset of girls' digestive difficulties and overly restrictive eating. Marion Harland criticized boarding schools' substandard fare, and described a young friend's recitation of the woes of eating at school. "We had apple-sauce, *sour!* ten times in one week, by actual count! And awfully stale, sawdusty bread every day, except Saturdays, when there were warm biscuits for tea. We were allowed but two apiece—they were not bigger than my watch! Mademoiselle announced that no young lady, *bien-elevée* [*sic*], would think of eating three. I was hungry for weeks at a time, having pledged my word to mamma that I would not buy cakes, nuts, and candy, which would have taken off the edge of appetite. The day scholars used to share their luncheons with us, and, when allowed to go shopping, I bought surreptitious buns and crackers." An advocate of improvements in the system of girls' schooling wrote in 1874 that "one great trouble with our American girls, and one which can be remedied by us, is not that their brains are over-worked, but that their bodies generally, including brain, are under-fed."

Even schoolgirls living at home were felt to suffer the nutritional consequences of the pressured scholarly life. A Victorian health expert described a hectic day for the average schoolgirl that evokes early newspaper accounts of Mollie's exhausting academic regimen at Brooklyn Heights Seminary. After an evening of study, the girl wakes in the morning, dresses and eats her breakfast, and hurries off to school. Often her toilette is performed hastily and breakfast swallowed quickly, "in defiance of the necessities of the stomach," out of her fear of being late. Once at school she sits confined in poorly ventilated rooms, eating unsuitable food, and worst of all, undergoing dangerous mental excitement. "Under such influences the child changes from a girl into a woman; such is the foundation laid for the important duties of adult life! If we were to sit down and carefully plan a system of education, which should injure the body, produce a premature and imperfect development of its powers, weaken the mind, and prepare the individual for future *uselessness,* we could hardly by any ingenuity construct a system more admirably calculated to produce these terrible results."

As the Victorian schoolgirl coped with these new stresses, her mother, at home, was living out a motherhood role of a single-minded intensity never before experienced. The new middle-class mothers— women who were adults by the 1840s, giving birth to children of Mollie Fancher's generation—defined a moral woman's life as completely focused on caretaking and child-rearing, and full of suffering and submission. They had little control over their fertility, they tolerated various "female complaints" that usually had no effective treatment, they not infrequently sickened and died from childbirth, and they found pride and meaning in self-sacrifice. "From their mothers' generation," Theriot writes of Mollie Fancher's generation, "daughters received the message that womanhood would bring suffering and self-denial and that submission to this fate was both expected and laudable."

While the worlds of mother and daughter were becoming increasingly polarized, parent and child had probably never been as close emotionally. The nuclear family was much more exclusive and privatized, and in this pressure cooker the differing scripts offered by society to mother and daughter must have generated tensions not unlike those perceived by contemporary adolescent girls. As in modern interpretations of anorexia, which suggest a fear of mature womanhood on the part of the teenage anorexic, the Victorian chlorotic girl may have been, in Theriot's words, performing "an exaggerated act of rebellion . . . a temporary refusal to accept the dictates of 'true womanhood' by rejecting maturity." The clever part, Theriot adds, is that the daughter could do this through chlorosis without openly challenging her mother—even, in fact, by imitating what were often her mother's own sickly behaviors.

The chlorotic girl—thin, wasted, tired, not menstruating, her secondary sexual characteristics (breast development, for instance) slowed by poor nutrition—could postpone deciding which type of female adulthood she was going to choose: a life of the mind out in the world, or that of a home-centered wife and mother. Her illness also brought her back to a more childish state within the family, with her mother and other family members nursing her back to health, sometimes putting her back in her childhood bed, pampering her, catering to her moods, tracking her digestive experiences as if she were a toddler.

It's impossible not to wonder whether Mollie Fancher was expressing some of this ambivalence about womanhood in her sickly teenage years. Many of the symptoms that led to the abandonment of her studies at the seminary suggest chlorosis: headaches, vomiting, dyspepsia, weakness, fainting spells, "wasting away." Mollie's own mother had been the model of long-suffering Victorian womanhood, devoting herself to a quickly growing family, enduring the loss of two children within one year, then wasting away herself before age thirty (and replaced by wife number two in little more than a year). Nothing in her mother's life presented Mollie with an appealing vision of the future. And the only alternative future within Mollie's immediate view was the womanhood represented by her aunt Susan: dependent on the generosity of relatives, sacrificing her own life plans and hopes of romance for the welfare of others, thanklessly raising children not her own.

Mollie, whether by fate in the form of an errant horsecar, or through the implacable demands of an unexpressed neurosis, by her late teens was opting out of the scenarios presented by her two female role models. She entered a twilight zone of childlike dependency and arrested development in which no decisions—whether about education, child-bearing, or submission to a husband—were necessary. This was a zone in which her body neither matured nor even functioned; in which she could truly rise above the carnal. In the view of Nancy Theriot, nineteenth-century chlorosis such as that experienced by Mollie offered at least a temporary escape from the fertile physical future (and its demands) represented by the girl's mother; similarly, modern physicians and therapists describe one unconscious result (or goal) of anorexia as preventing a girl from physically becoming a woman,

That mode of psychological thought would, of course, have been as alien to doctors in the 1870s as the workings of a computer word-processor to a nineteenth-century scrivener. Many steps, even leaps, of logic and insight lay yet to be imagined between the pale, drooping chlorotic girls of "capricious appetite" and the secretive self-starvers of modern anorexia. The first and most challenging leap was from the physical to the emotional. In the last quarter of the nineteenth century, the rift between anorexia as simple lack of appetite due to some physical malady yet unknown, and anorexia nervosa as a neurotic refusal to eat was wide indeed. It took an American, a Frenchman, and an Englishman, working separately, to close that gap—beginning about the time that Mollie Fancher decided to stop eating.

The first, little-noted baby step toward what became known in the 1870s as anorexia nervosa—a term that has survived remarkably intact to the present day—came in 1859, when Mollie was a still-healthy girl of thirteen. In that year an American doctor, William Stout Chipley, published an article in the *American Journal of Insanity* describing a condition he called "sitomania" (from the Greek *sitos,* meaning "grain")—although sometimes, he noted, "sitophobia" would more accurately describe the "intense dread of food" he would discuss.

Chipley, who was chief medical officer of the Eastern Lunatic Asylum of Kentucky, then the oldest and largest public insane asylum in the West, became a footnote in the study of anorexia nervosa, but an important one. The reason we don't call anorexia "sitomania" is that Chipley had figured out only part of the story. His sitomania was very broadly defined: it included essentially any kind of food refusal. Since he was an asylum director, most of his experience was with the flagrantly insane. One man whom Chipley described wouldn't eat because he was convinced he was dead, "and in conformity with what he supposed to be the customs of the dead, he refused to eat." A woman patient thought she was immortal and didn't need sustenance; another refused food because she believed a worm embedded in her scalp was making her ill. And then there were those who wouldn't eat because they were severely depressed (possessed by melancholy, as it was then called), suicidal, or suffering from the common delusion that their food was poisoned.

Among Chipley's descriptions of these cases, many of whom would now be classified as schizophrenic, a new and surprising type of self-starver appeared. These were young, upper-middle-class women, brought to the asylum by despairing and frightened parents. These patients refused to eat for reasons that seemed to Chipley to stem largely from "a morbid desire for notoriety." The doctor displayed a fair amount of disdain for such patients: they were high-born and accomplished, and didn't have the excuse of true insanity for their self-destructive behavior. Chipley's sympathies were with the desperate families of the starving young women, those parents of the bourgeoisie whose emotional lives were focused on their children's happiness.

"The intense anxiety of a loving father, the deep, indescribable agony of a devoted mother, the pallid cheeks and fast-falling tears of all who surround the couch"—these reactions seemed only to increase a starving girl's resolve, wrote Chipley. He saw this kind of sitomania as caused by a need for sympathy and attention: "The poor gratification of being pitied and talked of as suffering in a manner and to an extent which no other mortal ever endured, is the paltry reward that lures the victim on to ruin and the grave." Although in general he grasped only a fragment of what anorexia nervosa was later understood to mean, here Chipley was approaching one element that is now a cornerstone of anorexia nervosa theory. The family dynamic has come to be seen as central: the power play between parents and children, the arising issues of identity, dependence, and autonomy. When an anorexic teen is in conflict with parents who are powerful but also extremely invested in her well-being and survival, her wasted body is an astonishingly effective weapon.

Chipley, with a Victorian perspective and vocabulary, ascribed this self-centered and self-indulgent behavior to that plague of leisured women: hysteria. This would help explain its appearance in the upper social strata, whose members were not often driven to consult directors of public insane asylums on any affliction short of outright madness. And Chipley took his diagnosis one step further—partly because there was not yet the understanding of neurosis that described a territory beyond normal functioning but short of outright insanity. These self-starving young women, he felt, must be crazy. "Where shall we seek a solution of the problem involved in these cases, save in the morbid condition of the brain; and if this is their source, in what light are we to view these perverted actions but as evidences of insanity?"

Chipley discussed a representative case, of an unnamed Miss ——, that inevitably raises questions about Mollie's motivations some years later, as she lay surrounded by loving family and friends desperate to tempt her to a bite of food. Miss —— appeared to have all the advantages: wealth, social station, accommodating and refined manners, and an easygoing disposition that won her many friends. She also had, in classic Victorian style, a fashionably small appetite and occasional attacks of hysteria (Chipley did not give details of the attacks, which he termed moderate). On her return home from a prolonged period of travel, she seemed to be eating even less than before, and her friends became concerned. Miss ——, Chipley wrote, quickly perceived that the less she ate, the greater her friends' amazement and solicitude.

"The amount of food was diminished, until finally she would pass whole days together without tasting a single morsel. To an observing eye it was evident that she had no more exquisite pleasure than that derived from the remarks of those who daily and freely discussed the wonders of her case in her presence, and with marked ingenuity she would manage to introduce the topic whenever visitors called, if it was not alluded to by others, without delay. After a long struggle, in spite of every effort to restrain her friends, and to wean her from her folly, she died." An autopsy found no physical cause of death, only "an extraordinary diminution in the capacity of the stomach—an effect, doubtless, of the vicious habit that finally resulted in death." Miss —— had starved herself to death.

Chipley's depiction of the hysterical, upper-middle-class starving girl in search of attention occupies little more than two pages in a forty-two-page work. In 1859, food refusal was still largely about insanity, and its treatment was generally physical rather than psychological (although "persuasion" of various kinds sometimes worked, Chipley noted). Chipley himself, despite his insights into the psychological roots of food refusal, often resorted to physical methods of treatment, involving feeding tubes, spoons, and chisels to pry open unwilling lips. The true emotional subtleties of anorexia nervosa had yet to be revealed.

The greatest glory a nineteenth-century scientist or doctor could contemplate was the privilege of discovering—describing and naming—a "new" disease or syndrome. In all medical fields knowledge was exploding throughout the century: the microscopic world was being revealed and understood, and clinical doctors were finding more accurate and consistent ways of observing and categorizing illness. William Hammond had named a syndrome: athetosis, a brain disorder that causes slow, writhing movements of the hands and face. And George Beard, of course, laid firm claim to American Nervousness and neurasthenia. But the ownership of anorexia nervosa is something of a toss-up.

The "discovery" is usually ascribed not to William Chipley, whose observations did not add up to a full clinical picture of a specific ailment, but to an English physician, William Withey Gull. He first mentioned anorexia nervosa, briefly, and under another name (hysteric apepsia), in 1868, and then delivered an expansive address on the disorder in October 1873. Already in April of that year, a French doctor, Charles-Ernest Lasègue, had published a long article on what he called "hysterical anorexia" in *Archives Générales de Médecine.* The article was translated and reprinted in the British *Medical Times and Gazette* in September—one month before Gull's address on what he was by then calling "anorexia nervosa."

Lasègue had made no mention of Gull's one-sentence reference to apepsia in his article, and in fact he was probably unaware of the English citation. But Gull was certainly aware of Lasègue's work, and felt obliged to devote two paragraphs to it in his 1873 address. His mention amounted to an academic version of a territorial and defensive schoolyard boast: "I was here first! I was, I was!" Gull was very careful to give a chronology—when he became aware of Lasègue, when he conceived his own ideas. The first sentence of his speech cited his earlier address— in which, he said, "I referred to a peculiar form of disease occurring mostly in young women, and characterized by extreme emaciation." (Translation: "I thought of it first.") Later in the speech Gull announced that he saw Lasègue's paper "after these remarks were penned," and only because a colleague directed his attention to it in the *Medical Times.*

The medical historians Walter Vandereycken and Ron Van Deth find this account highly unlikely, for two reasons. First, English physicians were hardly unaware of what their French colleagues were working on, and enough of them were interested in this article to have it translated. Second, a physician of Gull's high standing was probably closely connected with members of the *Medical Times* editorial board, and was almost certain to read the publication, as it contained a broad range of medical news. The journal was a way of keeping abreast of new thinking and upcoming events, and it would be very strange if Gull did not read it frequently.

Gull clarified that it had been his idea to rename the syndrome anorexia, the term Lasègue had used: "In the [1868] address at Oxford," he said, "I used the term, apepsia hysterica, but before seeing Dr. Lasègue's paper, it had equally occurred to me that anorexia would be more correct." Having established his prior claim, Gull extended an olive branch: The discovery was probably simultaneous, further proof of its importance and relevance (although, of course, he did get there first). "It is plain that Dr. Lasègue and I have the same malady in mind, though the forms of our illustrations are different. Dr. Lasègue does not refer to my address at Oxford, and it is most likely he knew nothing of it. There is, therefore, the more value in his paper, as our observations have been made independently. We have both selected the same expression to characterize the malady."

And indeed, Gull did carry the day, whether through his greater assertiveness or because of his prominence in Victorian England (he was, among other things, physician extraordinary to Queen Victoria, who knighted him for curing her son Edward, Prince of Wales, of typhoid fever). In the end, though, Lasègue's paper is much more detailed and descriptive—and much more prescient of twentieth-century ideas of neurosis and of anorexia nervosa itself.

Lasègue was born in 1816, the same year as Gull, and although he rose to a high place in the French medical establishment, it was never quite as exalted as Gull's preeminence in England. Characterized as a neuropsychiatrist, in the very early days of the field, he was fascinated by various psychological conditions and published papers on hysteria, catalepsy, melancholy, delusions of persecution, kleptomania, and exhibitionism. When he wrote his anorexia paper he held the prestigious chair of clinical medicine at the Pitié hospital in Paris.

Lasègue's take on "hysterical anorexia" was oriented toward the psychological rather than the organic. He began by describing anorexia as a symptom of hysteria. Although there were numerous curious perversions of appetite attributed to hysteria, he wanted to talk about something very specific: a hysteria of the gastric center that was common enough, and consistent enough in its symptoms, to merit a full description. Lasègue was establishing a rationale for claiming anorexia as his own discovery, even going so far as to discuss why he chose the word "anorexia" over other possible terms, such as "hysterical inanition."

What Lasègue went on to describe sounds quite modern now, even down to his opinion that the stage of digestion least understood by physicians is the appetite for food—a statement plenty of modern researchers would agree with, as they continue the still-fruitless search for a behavioral or drug therapy to help obese people control their appetites. Lasègue culled his experience of anorexic patients into one representative case, that of a young woman between fifteen and twenty years old. He attributed the inception of this woman's anorexia to psychological factors, often relating to a real or imagined marriage prospect, or some other upset.

In Lasègue's representative case, an anorexic first feels symptoms resembling dyspepsia: uneasiness after eating, vague sensations of fullness, gastric pains. Her response is to diminish her eating to try to avoid these uncomfortable feelings—not an unreasonable solution—but in the hysteric the self-treatment begins to accelerate. She makes up new excuses for not eating. "At the end of some weeks," Lasègue wrote, "there is no longer a supposed temporary repugnance, but a refusal of food that may be indefinitely prolonged. The disease is now declared, and so surely will it pursue its course that it becomes easy to prognosticate the future."

That future, as detailed by Lasègue, creeps on the patient gradually and inexorably. Her repugnance for food progresses. She skips eating at certain meals, so that she is sustained by only breakfast or dinner. Then she becomes disgusted by particular types of food, whether bread, meat, or certain vegetables, and cuts them out of her diet. Strangely, for weeks or months as she whittles her food intake down, she appears healthy: sleeping well, not obviously emaciated, though ingesting less than an estimated one-tenth of her previous caloric intake. And even stranger, she seems to become more energetic than before: she feels more light and active, takes rides on horseback, receives and pays visits, and is able to pursue a fatiguing routine that normally would have exhausted her.

After several months of this behavior—and inevitably, several attempts by family members to cure her loss of appetite by various tonics and "gastric stimuli"—the disease enters a second stage. Parental anxiety accelerates, and with it come much stronger efforts at persuasion. "It is now that is developed that mental perversion," wrote Lasègue, "which by itself is almost characteristic and which justifies the name which I have proposed for want of a better—hysterical anorexia." This mental perversion proves extraordinarily stubborn. The family resorts to two alternating tactics—entreaties and threats—both of which serve only to strengthen the anorexic's resolve. Those around her become increasingly frantic. Delicacies are prepared and displayed to the patient; she is begged to eat even one more mouthful—as a favor, as a proof of affection for her parents and worried friends. She refuses.

Now the entire family is caught up in the perversion—in a way that only a middle-class family could afford to be. "The anorexia gradually becomes the sole object of preoccupation and conversation. The patient thus gets surrounded by a kind of atmosphere, from which there is no escape during the entire day." Her response is to dig her heels in further, to become even more convinced that she knows better than those around her what is good for her. The denials she issues sound notably like those of present-day anorexics, who stand before a mirror and insist they are not thin, and sit stoically before a plate of food and refuse to admit any sensation of hunger.

"The patient, when told that she cannot live upon an amount of food that would not support a young infant, replies that it furnishes sufficient nourishment for her," observed Lasègue. She adds that "she is neither changed nor thinner, and has never refused encountering any task or labour. She knows better than anyone what she requires, and, moreover, it would be impossible for her to tolerate a more abundant alimentation." What is most significant about the mental condition of the patient now is her quietude, even contentment, which seemed to Lasègue truly pathological. Not only does she not wish to recover, but she is not unhappy with her condition, despite the unpleasantness that accompanies it. Even hunger pangs have disappeared. The patient has an inexhaustible optimism that no amount of supplication or threat can alter. " 'I do not suffer, and must then be well,' is the monotonous formula," Lasègue wrote. "So often have I heard this phrase repeated by patients, that now it has come to represent for me a symptom—almost a sign."

What makes this condition so different from other kinds of loss of appetite, Lasègue deduced, is what goes on in the patient's mind—an intellectual perversion, he termed it. Without this, you had an ordinary disease that sooner or later would yield to the classic treatments. When the perversion was carried to its extreme, the result was "a dyspepsia bearing no resemblance to others."

Inexorably, the body suffers, and the disease enters what Lasègue characterized as the third stage. Again, the symptoms mirror precisely those of modern anorexia nervosa: menstruation ceases, thirst increases, the abdomen retracts and loses elasticity, constipation becomes obstinate, the skin is pale and dry, the pulse is quickened, the patient tires easily, and when she rises from resting often experiences vertigo. And finally, she becomes frightened. She looks at the sad and anxious faces around her, feels her weakness, and for the first time her indifference and her confidence are shaken. The moment has arrived when the physician has a chance to influence her; the patient is open to treatment, although she still tries to conceal her willingness. "The struggle thus established between the past and the present," Lasègue commented, "is a curious one to observe."

Even now, the cure is not quick or assured. Often the patient submits to treatment—that is, feeding—with a plan to avert the present danger and then return to her semi-starvation. Lasègue noted that he had seen patients ten years after he had initially treated them who still didn't eat like other people, and his observation has been ratified by years of twentieth-century research showing that anorexia nervosa is one of the most difficult psychological problems to resolve fully. "As a general rule," he concluded, "we must look forward to a change for the better only taking place slowly—by successive starts." Often the patient passes through periods of various appetite disturbances, and strange cravings, on her way back to health—a health that might never be complete.

Take away the Victorian idea of hysteria that accompanies Lasègue's diagnosis, and add the twentieth-century concept of thinness-as-beauty, and what remains is an accurate description of modern-day anorexia nervosa. The *Diagnostic and Statistical Manual of Mental Disorders* (*DSM-IV*), the Bible of psychological diagnoses, describes in the anorexic a reduction in total food intake or a limiting of food to only a few types; increased or excessive exercise; denial of the malnourished state; typical onset in middle to late adolescence (often associated with a stressful life event); such physical symptoms as amenorrhea, constipation, abdominal pain, lethargy, emaciation, dry skin, and dehydration. The disease also appears to be far more prevalent in industrialized societies, in which there is an abundance of food.

The Family Mental Health Encyclopedia is more specific about the psychological landscape of anorexia, especially as it involves the family, in a description that recalls Lasègue's writings: "Anorexia nervosa appears to be caused primarily by an interaction of psychosocial factors. Some of these factors are overcontrolling parents, a strong-willed adolescent, an upwardly mobile family, and a culture that overvalues a

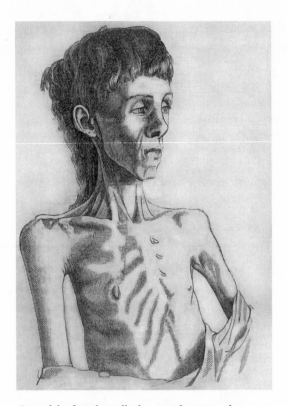

One of the first clinically diagnosed victims of anorexia nervosa, 1887. This young woman was a patient of William Withey Gull, the English doctor credited with defining the disease in 1873. (PHOTOGRAPH BY R. D. RUBIC OF AN 1888 ILLUSTRATION IN *THE LANCET.* THE NEW YORK ACADEMY OF MEDICINE LIBRARY)

thin female body. When the adolescent female diets to an extreme, parents often react with stern lectures and warnings. The issue becomes, 'Who is in control?' A battle of wills ensues. Not eating becomes a symbol of the adolescent's ability to exercise autonomy."

In his representative case, Lasègue continually emphasized the interplay between the anxious family and the anorexic girl. The morbid condition of the anorexic girl and the preoccupations of those who surrounded her, he wrote, were intimately connected, "and we should acquire an erroneous idea of the disease by confining ourselves to an examination of the patient." That in itself was an extraordinarily sophisticated psychological idea, pointing the way toward the family-systems theories that would be developed in the next century.

Sir William Gull, in his 1873 speech and article on the newly named anorexia nervosa, also mentioned family influence, although not nearly as extensively as Lasègue (he pointed out that relatives and friends were the least effective attendants for the anorexic). And he appeared to take a psychological stance at times—writing that the lack of appetite was due to a morbid mental state, that mental states might destroy appetite, and that young women at these susceptible ages (from sixteen to twenty-three, in his estimation) were prone to "mental perversity." But he could not completely free himself from the shackles of nineteenth-century assumptions of a physical basis for every condition, even a condition of mental state; later in his article he maintained that the disease was the result of a disturbance of "nerve force." Lasègue, whose voice as the prescient definer of early anorexia nervosa has been largely lost to history, was by far the more psychological thinker.

Was Mollie Fancher anorexic? Diagnoses more than a century after the fact can be dicey, especially when descriptive clues—what did she actually eat? who fed her?—are hard to come by. The answer may also depend on which definition of anorexia is applied to her case, the Victorian or the twenty-first-century. There is an argument to be made that Mollie was one of the first prominent victims of the new disease anorexia nervosa, at least as it was defined in the 1870s. She was seventeen when she first developed symptoms, within the age range proposed by both Lasègue and Gull—and this, coincidentally, just as they were forming the basis for their definitions of anorexia nervosa in the mid-1860s. Mollie's aunt Susan described her symptoms at the time; they match Lasègue's in particular, beginning with "sickness at the stomach, sinking, fainting feelings," and then growing more severe.

Mollie was forced to leave her classes at the seminary when she "vomited her food, and could keep scarcely anything on her stomach." Both Lasègue and Gull mention vomiting as a common early sign of anorexia. Mollie was described at that time also as having "wasted away and become weak." If "wasted away" is taken to mean that she lost weight and became emaciated, that sounds even more like a physical symptom of Victorian anorexia. Her physical state once she was bedridden after the horsecar accident appears even more to betray the effects of anorexia: the sunken abdomen described by Dr. West, the vomiting of the tiniest morsel placed in her mouth.

Then there is the question of Mollie's mental and emotional state as she neared graduation from the seminary. All accounts of anorexia nervosa, even latter-day, mention the possibility of precipitating events: emotional upsets that may trigger the neurotic refusal of sustenance. Lasègue's Victorian example is a "real or imagined marriage project"— marriage being the inevitable choice of a future life for most nineteenth-century girls. Mollie herself had become engaged to marry, shortly before the horsecar accident. She was about to enter adult life, emerging from a rigorous course of education that may have instilled new ideas of venturing beyond marriage and children. In addition, her disrupted family life may have given her uncertainty about the idea of rearing children and handing her life over to a husband. The effects of that early life, infused as it was with loss after loss, may have been catching up to her, imposing a delayed reaction. Mollie's inability to keep her food down may have expressed an inability to get on with things, to be strong enough to finish growing into adulthood. Then too, like Chipley's sitophobes, Mollie had attained notoriety and attention— more than most young women of the era could imagine—for her alleged fasting, and this could have been a powerful incentive to continue to resist feeding.

In short, Mollie's condition comes close enough to Victorian anorexia nervosa to merit the term, but with a few key distinctions. Her case was much murkier than that of the average troubled Victorian girl, as it included her possible physical damage from the accident; the extreme psychiatric symptoms of hysteria, multiple personality, and claims to clairvoyance; the potential for deception about what she was actually eating; and not least, her fame. Mollie's case diverged from the prototype of Victorian anorexia nervosa when it failed to follow the prescribed path of either eventual death or eventual recovery. She became a seemingly permanent anorexic, perhaps largely because of the untold benefits—including stardom—that came with the role.

Mollie's diagnosis under modern guidelines for anorexia nervosa is clearer: she would not meet the standards, because she lacked (as did the Victorian culture at large) an obsession with thinness. Anorexia as we know it now, though it shares many physical and psychological symptoms with the Victorian variety, has as its focus and goal the drive to lose weight, to be extremely thin. In the process of doing that, the anorexic loses all perspective on body shape and size, so that soon even emaciation isn't thin enough. The unattainably lean ideal of female beauty was in its infancy in the 1870s; until it flowered in the next century, anorexia nervosa would remain focused on the matters of control, attention, family dynamics, and "mental perversion."

Mollie was thus emblematic of other neurotic girls of her era, and also a harbinger of the wave of modern-day fasters to come a century later. But her condition also harked back to a much more primitive brand of self-denial. Until nineteenth-century scientists such as Lasègue and Gull classified refusal to eat as a medical condition, "living on air" had been seen not as a neurosis but as a miracle. Self-starvation had belonged to the saintly and the mystical, and it even had its own name: anorexia mirabilis. There were still many believers who would rather have seen Mollie Fancher as a fasting saint than as a flawed, confused, even deceptive girl, many who preferred a religious interpretation over a newfangled medicalized diagnosis.

One way to get at the truth of who Mollie was lay in the physical reality of starvation, considered without reference to either theology or medical hypothesis: What would someone look like, and act like, if she was really existing day after day, week after week, without sustenance? How long could humans live without food, in the real world of scientific experimentation? Today the answers to these questions leave little room for doubt, but Victorian physicians and philosophers were still probing for the limits. When they found those limits, they saw something that looked quite different from Mollie Fancher.

CHAPTER SEVEN

❧

Pure Hunger

I declare that I have used no deception, and that for six years I have taken nothing but once, the inside of a few black currants; for the last four years and a half nothing at all.

—Affidavit by Ann Moore, "The Fasting Woman of Tutbury," 1813

Death from long-lasting hunger is like a candle burning out slowly.

—*Hunger Disease: Studies by the Jewish Physicians in the Warsaw Ghetto,* 1946

STARVATION IS a quiet and relatively painless way to die, though on the face of it, dying of hunger sounds horrific. What could be worse than a ravening, desperate emptiness without end—our most powerful animal craving left unsatisfied? History is filled with evidence of hunger's ability to override our very humanity, to make killers and devouring cannibals of us: the Donner party trapped in the snow-clogged passes of the Sierra, the whalemen of the wrecked *Essex* adrift in the Pacific for three months, plane-crash survivors in the Andes.

When an adult human stops eating, or eats far less than his or her daily requirements, the body begins slowly to consume itself, in a kind of self-cannibalization. And yet, strangely, this process fairly quickly loses the capacity to cause pain. After a few days sensations of hunger fade away, and are revived only by eating. This may happen because the feeling humans know as hunger is at least partly the result of digestive acids bouncing around in an empty stomach, and after a period of starvation such acids decrease. The stomach goes into stand-by mode.

Appetite also appears to be regulated at least partially by a clever neurotransmitter in the brain called neuropeptide Y. Under normal conditions—a meal every few hours—levels of neuropeptide rise at a modest rate when an animal starts to eat, until chemical signals of satiety kick in. Then neuropeptide Y levels decline, and the animal starts to feel satisfied and soon stops eating. Starvation, or even semi-starvation, throws off this logical system. In the absence of adequate food, neuropeptide Y levels dip lower and lower. Since the neuro-transmitter seems to encourage eating, low levels may tell the body the opposite: not to bother to eat. But when the animal encounters food again, neuropeptide Y springs into overdrive. It rises precipitously with the first feeding—and keeps going. It overpowers satiety signals and urges the animal to overeat, and to choose predominantly carbohydrates, the type of food most quickly converted to energy. A laboratory rat that has been starved will eat its first meal, and then, neuropeptide Y soaring, eat another one right after.

The disappearance of hunger (and its rabid reappearance in the presence of food) makes evolutionary sense: if there's nothing available to eat, there's no advantage to feeling hungry. While there may be no physical experience of hunger in a starving person, the brain will take over for the stomach. Hunger sensations go away, but the mind be-comes obsessed with thoughts of obtaining food. It's just one way in which the human body is marvelously built to survive starvation. When deprived of food, the body becomes extremely efficient at using nutrients. An intricate internal catch-22, bemoaned by modern-day dieters, exists, purely for sustaining the body through famine. The body wants to hold on to fat and preserve weight. The smaller the rations it is provided, the more efficient the body becomes; the less you eat, the less you need.

The mechanism for this efficiency involves a set of hormones and transmitters. Normal eating triggers the release of insulin from the pancreas to the liver, telling the liver to convert its thyroid hormones to the active form, T-3. A rise in insulin also tells the hypothalamus, in the brain, to increase the production and turnover of neurepinephrine, the major transmitter for the sympathetic nervous system, which controls automatic functions such as blood pressure and heart rate. When neurepinephrine increases sharply, an animal goes into fight-or-flight mode: heart racing, blood pumping, ready for action. Together, T-3 and neurepinephrine are the major control mechanism for basic metabolism—how many calories an animal needs to burn in order to produce energy to live. When very little food is coming in, not much insulin is being released. Consequently, T-3 and neurepinephrine levels decrease, bringing the metabolic rate down with them. A slower metabolism means an animal needs fewer calories in order to function; its body is making the greatest use of available resources.

At the beginning of a period of food deprivation, this method works well, and a hungry animal, human or otherwise, functions at almost the same intensity as the well-fed. The starving body carefully wrings the last bit of energy from every morsel, and uses fats stored on the body as well. The stomach empties more slowly, so that the body holds on to the feeling of fullness as long as possible. But given enough time—and the amount of time it takes to expire of starvation varies widely from creature to creature—the body slowly shuts down. First it ignores the most expendable items: skin gets dry, hair stops growing, extremities feel cold. It feeds heart and brain the best it can until the last. In humans, starving to death is effectively like becoming an old person in fast-forward mode. And in complete refutation of the claims about fasting girls who looked rosy-cheeked and blooming, it is not an invisible process. A starving person is a physical wreck, a hollowed-out husk.

The best evidence we have of how starvation works comes from grim sources; scientists can't put humans in a lab and observe them starving to death. But in the midst of the misery of the Warsaw ghetto in 1942, that was in effect what happened, and the result was one of the richest and most wrenching sources of clinical information about the wasting body. In 1940 the Nazis sealed off the Jewish section of Warsaw, intending to starve to death the several hundred thousand inhabitants. A group of Jewish physicians, themselves condemned to the same fate as their patients, decided to study the effects of hunger as scientifically and comprehensively as they could, under virtually impossible conditions. The details of the study were discussed in clandestine meetings, some of the necessary equipment was smuggled into the ghetto, and the operation had to be kept secret from the Nazis, who wanted none of their actions reported to the outside world. The final manuscript detailing the findings had to be smuggled out and buried until it could be revealed after the war.

The ghetto doctors selected patients who were suffering only from hunger and not from the many infectious diseases that made the rounds of the ghetto, and systematically measured metabolism, circulatory changes, blood volume, arterial and venous pressure, and changes in pulse, body temperature, skin, eyes. They were helpless to save these suffering patients; they were barely surviving themselves. After watching their subjects die they performed autopsies to document further the ravages of starvation. Of the twenty-eight physicians involved, eight survived the war—one only by a year.

The organizer of the project, Dr. Israel Milejkowski, head of the department of public health in the ghetto, committed suicide in 1943, after deportations had carried off the ghetto's surviving inhabitants. Before he died, he wrote an introduction to the study, calling the work "an unfinished symphony full of meaning." Milejkowski's last words addressed his lost colleagues directly: "You by your work could give the henchman the answer 'Non omnis moriar,' 'I shall not wholly die.' "

The starving process in Warsaw was lengthy. Inhabitants were consuming, on average, 800 calories per day—a third to a quarter of what their bodies normally required. The Warsaw doctors described three stages of emaciation. At first, as the body consumed all available stores, surplus fat disappeared. Often the patients actually looked better, or at least younger, at this stage—as if, the doctors commented, they had been away for a "reducing cure." Next came a stage in which patients appeared old and withered, followed by the terminal stage of complete emaciation.

Starvation begins with the specific—sharp hunger and thirst, a dry mouth, an obsession with food—and gives way to the general, the systemic decline of a body. As the "aging" process speeds up, the body slows down, trying desperately to suck every ounce of energy from each sparse calorie ingested. Metabolism decreases markedly, heart rate and blood pressure drop, rate of respiration and volume of air intake also decrease. Even when stressed, the starving body refuses to expend any extra energy—Warsaw patients showed no increase in pulse or blood pressure after doing sit-ups or other activities. The body temperature drops, and extremities in particular are always cold, as the circulatory system practices triage and services the most vital areas first. Women lose their menstrual cycles and men become impotent, the body in its wisdom refusing to add hungry mouths to the famine.

Meanwhile, the starving body, like the portrait of Dorian Gray, exhibits to the world the effects of this hidden withering. The patient complains of aches and pains in various joints and bones, feels exhausted, and wants only to lie motionless under blankets. Wrote the Warsaw doctors: "One of the patients said, 'Our strength is vanishing like a melting wax candle.' Active, busy, energetic people are changed into apathetic, sleeping beings, always in bed." The skin grows pale, whitish, and is chapped, dry, and prematurely wrinkled. It becomes so thin and parchmentlike, with no fat beneath the surface, that a scratch with a fingernail produces a mark that remains for hours. Sweat glands atrophy, and palms and fingertips are never moist. If the skin is pulled into a fold with the fingers, the fold remains rather than subsiding back into the skin.

Beneath the skin's surface the body often becomes bloated, or subject to what is known as hunger edema. Edema is the cause of the telltale swollen stomachs or extremities seen in photographs of famine victims around the world. There are two biochemical reasons for hunger edema. The first is that a starving person has become functionally hypothyroid: the thyroid hormone, in the absence of the insulin that would be released with eating, is not being converted to T-3 (its active form). Hypothyroid people don't excrete salt and water adequately, and this makes them bloat. Their capillaries also become more permeable, and blood leaks into the surrounding tissue. When that blood disperses, the body senses that its blood volume is dehydrating, and in an effort to rehydrate it releases a hormone that causes even more salt and water retention.

The other reason for edema is that starving people have low levels of the critical chemicals dopamine and neurepinephrine. Well-nourished bodies release these when they are seated or standing, and these chemicals in turn tell neurotransmitters in the sympathetic nervous system to make the small arteries constrict. Arterial constriction prevents the approximately five cubic feet of blood volume in the body from simply pushing down, with gravity, into the very thin capillaries and from there into the tissues. In the absence of dopamine and neurepinephrine, the capillaries leak blood, and this contributes to the hypothyroid effect. Without knowing the chemical underpinnings, the Warsaw doctors noted that edema was worse in the lower extremities, and that it lessened when people lay down; when the body is horizontal, pressure of the blood volume is more evenly distributed.

In other ways, the starving person continues to "age." Hair falls out, even from armpits and genitals. Muscles weaken and atrophy, and the starving person falls often. Bones are weak and thin, easily broken and very slow to heal. The eyes show premature changes in the lenses similar to those seen in senile cataracts. The voice becomes weak and hoarse.

When the end comes, it resembles most closely that of a ninety-year-old from whose body life simply slips away (a reason why many euthanasia advocates support starvation as one of the better methods). "Passage from life to death is slow and gradual, like death from physiological old age," the Warsaw doctors wrote. "There is nothing violent, no dyspnea [difficult respiration], no pain, no obvious changes in breathing or circulation. Vital functions subside simultaneously. Pulse rate and respiratory rate get slower and it becomes more and more difficult to reach the patient's awareness, until life is gone. People fall asleep in bed or on the street and are dead in the morning."

The Warsaw material has provided us with the most complete record of the physical effects of starvation on humans. But what goes on inside the mind of a starving person? Another wartime study found the answer almost by accident. In 1944–1945, Dr. Ancel Keys, a specialist in nutrition and the inventor of the K ration, led a carefully controlled yearlong study of starvation at the University of Minnesota Laboratory of Physiological Hygiene. It was hoped that the results would help relief workers in rehabilitating war refugees and concentration camp victims. The study participants were thirty-two conscientious objectors eager to contribute humanely to the war effort. By the experiment's end, much of their enthusiasm had vanished.

Over a six-month semi-starvation period, they were required to lose an average of twenty-five percent of their body weight. If weight loss slowed, bread and potatoes were cut back; if they lost weight too quickly, those foods were increased. The daily intake averaged 1,570 calories—almost twice what the Warsaw inhabitants had eaten. They were also required to exercise daily, a task that became increasingly difficult as the weight loss continued.

Even eating twice the Warsaw rations, the men exhibited physical symptoms identical to those of the ghetto inhabitants: their movements slowed, they felt weak and cold, their skin was dry, their hair fell out, they had edema. And the psychological changes were dramatic.

These were people being studied in a safe vacuum, not in the hell of war; they were not on the verge of extermination by a hate-filled army. These were idealistic volunteers who felt they were doing something morally worthy—and who had the comfortable knowledge that after the experiment they could live on steak and eggs if they liked. Yet they discovered lurking behind their previously well-fed humanity a core of animalistic urges.

The men became apathetic and depressed, and frustrated with their inability to concentrate or perform tasks in their usual manner. Six of the thirty-two were eventually diagnosed with severe "character neurosis," two of them bordering on psychosis. Socially, they ceased to care much about others; they grew intensely selfish and self-absorbed. Personal grooming and hygiene deteriorated, and the men were moody and irritable with one another. The lively and cooperative group spirit that had developed in the three-month control phase of the experiment evaporated. Most participants lost interest in group activities or decisions, saying it was too much trouble to deal with others; some men became scapegoats or targets of aggression for the rest of the group.

Food—one's own food—became the only thing that mattered. When the men did talk to one another, it was almost always about eating, hunger, weight loss, foods they dreamt of eating. They grew more obsessed with the subject of food, collecting recipes, studying cookbooks, drawing up menus. As time went on, they stretched their meals out longer and longer, sometimes taking two hours to eat small dinners. Keys's research has been cited often in recent years for this reason: The behavioral changes in the men mirror the actions of present-day dieters, and especially of anorexics.

Self-starvers are notorious for thinking about food constantly, planning meals, making food for others, being obsessive about food even as they deny themselves the pleasure of eating it. The anorexic's will is controlling what she eats, but the primitive, unreasoning part of her brain continually pushes her toward survival: Think about food, it insists.

Hunt and gather and cook, whatever it takes—just eat. The similarity between modern anorexic thought patterns and those demonstrated by Keys's semi-starved subjects has led many clinicians to believe that the characteristic obsessions and behaviors of anorexia nervosa are as much the result of starvation as the cause of it. The starving mind kicks in with everything it's got, in an effort to stay alive.

Certainly by the scientific standards of twentieth-century research Mollie Fancher was not fasting or starving. Her hair was not falling out; in various photographs taken in the first decade and a half of her invalidism, when claims were made of a twelve-year fast, her body did not appear emaciated. By all reports she did not obsess about food— she appeared simply to have no interest in it. Her cheeks remained full, not sunken; she looked quite beautiful.

There is much that is not known about Mollie's condition, both because of the limitations of Victorian medical knowledge and because of the private nature of her debility. It is possible that some of Mollie's visions—of the dead, of wandering about among them in heaven, perhaps even the multiple personalities—were induced partly by semi-starvation. Many modern anorexics speak of almost hallucinatory sensations, of heightened sensory effects that led them to seek out quiet, darkened places (just as Mollie's room was habitually shaded from bright light). Her metabolism, heart rate, and respiration may indeed have been slow; she certainly spent all her time curled up under blankets. Her mood is difficult to assess: many people spoke of her cheerfulness, yet there were said to be moments of despair, times when she voiced the desire to join her dead mother and friends and be relieved of her suffering, even though, she once said to Dailey, "that relief is only to be found in utter annihilation." But it doesn't take starvation to depress someone who is permanently bedridden, subject to the contractures and other horrors that Mollie's body reportedly endured.

Some things about Mollie's experience, however, are clear—even from the standpoint of Victorian medicine, and on the basis of today's body of knowledge. If she had indeed been fasting, living without food, she would have died in fairly short order. If she was living on greatly reduced calories, even as few as the 800 meted out to the Warsaw ghetto inhabitants, she would have appeared withered and ill. Eventually—sooner than a dozen years—she would have died, from the effects of such an inadequate diet on her internal organs.

For the Victorians who witnessed, and wondered at, Mollie's drama, the most interesting question—and the one apparently most amenable to an answer—was not what effects semi-starvation had, but how long humans could live entirely without food. Yet answering that definitively was as difficult then as it is now. Previous nutritional status, amount of stored body fat, even gender play a role (women appear to survive longer both because they have more body fat and because their metabolism is able to slow down even more than men's).

In early 1881, the Englishman L. S. Forbes Winslow published a book titled *Fasting and Feeding Psychologically Considered.* He was prompted, he wrote, by "the widespread interest in this subject, excited by recent successful and unsuccessful attempts to sustain life under abnormal conditions." Winslow's book was a compilation of tales of starvation and near-starvation. In all of them, it is evident that starvation cannot be understood without taking dehydration into account. A group of four trapped coal miners, for instance, survived twenty-five days on no food, but they had water that trickled from an underground spring. Three Italian women were reported to have survived on melted snow for thirty-seven days after being trapped by an avalanche.

When Winslow moved on to the cases of "total abstraction of food," the impossibility of living very long without nutritive substances was incontrovertible. He told the tale of a Yorkshire man who in 1795 developed an obstruction in the esophagus that made it difficult to swallow food. The man, who was tall and "naturally corpulent" at 240 pounds, shrank to 179 pounds while still able to squeeze in a few liquids. Eventually the obstruction, which proved to be a growing tumor, closed off the tube. Twenty-four days later, sustained only by enemas of broth and egg yolk, he was down to 149 pounds. On the thirty-second day of total fasting his pulse became weak and rapid and his eyes crossed; the next day he was delirious and restless, alternately burning-hot and clammy. Finally, after thirty-six days without any nutrition, the man's breathing became labored and his pulse feeble, and he died in his bed. Before his death the man complained very little of hunger, or even of thirst.

The length of time a human could live without food, Winslow concluded after many case histories, "must always be an undecided matter. The varying need of different physiques imports an uncertainty into any consideration of the kind that will prevent a definite statement of a time within which all must succumb." The window of death, according to the evidence he presented, opened anywhere from thirty-some days to sixty-one, in the case of a shipwrecked seaman. In April 1881, a few months after Winslow's book appeared, an Iowa City woman died of starvation after a nearly seven-week fast, succumbing at forty-seven days—in the middle of the window of survival. A fifty-two-year-old spinster aunt suffering from years of "nervous disease" and "neuralgic pains," Miss Hattie Duell had simply decided to give up. She stopped speaking (communicating only by means of a slate and pencil) and turned away all food.

Miss Duell's slow-motion suicide, as reported in *The New York Times,* fit all descriptions since produced of death by starvation. She consented to sip a little water each day, as her brother-in-law had told her that she might otherwise suffer fever and delirium, but steadfastly refused all food. After thirty-four days she was "wasted to a skeleton, her nose was thin and pinched, her cheeks were hollow, and her skin was an unusually dark color." But Duell assured her friends that she was suffering no pain whatsoever. By the fortieth day she was in a coma most of the time. Her pulse went up and down over the next few days as she sank further, making it known to the last that she wanted no food. The autopsy found "not a drop of blood in the body, which weighed only 45 pounds." Her stomach was found to be empty.

Hattie Duell's story confirmed Winslow's evidence, as well as that of other observers such as William Hammond, who found that absolute fasting could in most cases not be survived beyond forty or fifty days—and that as the final days approached, the fasting person visibly declined into a helplessly feeble state. There could be no stronger refutation of claims like Mollie's, of existing in an apparently healthy condition for years without food. Yet immediately after coming to that conclusion, Winslow entered other, less concrete ideas into evidence—ideas, he wrote, that "require to be taken with more than a single *granum salis,* but they deserve some notice." Those ideas help demonstrate how a sizable number of people could believe that Mollie's claim might be true.

The first idea—and this was one that Winslow found himself espousing—was that the air itself could help support life; that one could indeed "feed on air." "There can be no question," Winslow wrote, "but that there is always floating in the atmosphere an amount of matter, organic and inorganic, sufficient to go some way towards restoring the small loss undergone by a fasting body in repose." He quoted a Dr. Schmidtmann, who had treated a sixteen-year-old girl in 1798. The girl was reported to have lived for ten months with neither food nor drink, while bedridden with a complaint that sounds suspiciously like hysteria (convulsions, loss of the sense of feeling, comas or trances). "Though she had not taken the least nourishment during all this time," Winslow recounted, "Dr. Schmidtmann found her, to his utmost astonishment, fresh and blooming."

The tale of the girl's fasting spread, and to establish the truth of the matter, six men were appointed to watch her day and night. This they did for two weeks, and then gave evidence under oath that she had neither taken any sustenance nor produced any excrement. Dr. Schmidt-mann decided, after much thought, that "she drew, by resorption, such elementary particles from the atmosphere as were sufficient for the nutrition of the body, and that the excretions were likewise replaced by the skin." Winslow's and Schmidtmann's theories exhibit a patina of science, at least a groping toward some form of logic within the confines of nineteenth-century thought. But Winslow followed up with a series of outlandish tales, told (after the grain-of-salt comment) without a trace of irony—as if to demonstrate that the Victorian scientific mind was not quite ready to give up all belief in the fantastic.

Thus, said Winslow, "Toubertus relates that a woman lived in good health three years without either food or drink; and that he saw another who lived to her tenth year without food or drink. . . . Albertus Krantzius says that a hermit in the mountains in the canton of Schwitz lived twenty years without food. . . . Citois gives the history of a girl at Confoulens, in Poitou, who lived three years without food."

One story in particular in Winslow's narrative gets at an idea about fasting that reaches back into the mists of medievalism—and that begins to explain the special appeal of Mollie Fancher's case. The story involved a woman who had fasted a "most supernatural" length of time, who was reported to have lasted for seven and a half years without any food or liquid, except a little of the latter to moisten her lips. After that period, it was said, she existed on a fragment of bread and a glass of water a day. She was said to be very mild and even-tempered, wrote Winslow, as well as religious and "very fervent in prayer—the natural effect of the state of her body, long unembarrassed with the grossness of food, and a constant alienation of thought from all worldly affairs."

Before the unfamiliar ideas about the psychological meaning of food refusal that were introduced by Lasègue and Gull, living without food had long been thought to be connected not to the imperfect and mortal (not to mention neurotic) self, but to the divine. Fasting was the ultimate way to free oneself from carnal needs and desires, to prepare for visions and trances: Moses fasted forty days before receiving the Ten Commandments, Jesus forty days before his enlightenment. Medieval saints (most of them women) fasted to demonstrate their purity, their holiness—and if their fasting appeared to continue far beyond normal human bounds, it was proof of God's grace. So when Mollie Fancher informed her worried attendants in 1866, as they attempted to coerce her to eat, that she "received nourishment from a source of which [they] were ignorant," that idea resonated with her Victorian audience—even as it ran headlong into the brand-new thinking about anorexia nervosa.

Mollie Fancher probably didn't have precisely this image in mind when she turned away anxious offers of juice or crackers with talk of spiritual sustenance, but the basic idea behind religious fasting is the eternal battle between good and evil. The body, naturally, with its unthinking needs and desires, represents the ever-present potential for sin and depravity. To rise above those needs, to refuse to partake of them, releases the pure soul from its carnal prison. In the Gnostic era of early Christianity (in the first few centuries after Christ), asceticism was practiced by hermits who left civilization to live in huts or caves, subsist on bread and water, and contemplate the end of the world. These hermits were mostly male. In Europe from the thirteenth to the seventeenth centuries, it was prolonged religious fasting among women that became popular to the point of being a fad.

The undisputed queen of fasting saints, as these women were known, was Saint Catherine of Siena. Modern scholars of psychology have found her fascinating: although her self-abnegating life in a dusty medieval Italian town could not be further from that of a twenty-first-century urban young woman, and although she claimed only the most overtly religious basis for her refusal to eat, many aspects of her history and behavior are markedly similar to present-day anorexia nervosa.

Self-hatred, perfectionism, struggles with a controlling mother, daily self-induced vomiting, fear of becoming a mature woman, refusal to maintain anywhere near a normal body weight—Catherine would have made an easy diagnosis in a modern shrink's office.

Catherine's life is well documented; she left behind letters and other writings, and her confessor, Raymond of Capua, wrote her biography soon after her death. She was born in 1347, the twenty-third or twenty-fourth of twenty-five children of the same mother. Her relationship with her mother was peculiarly intense. Catherine was the only child of the twenty-five to be breastfed by her rather than sent to a wet nurse. Catherine's mother reportedly told Raymond more than once that Catherine was her favorite child. When she was twelve, her mother began to groom her for marriage, pressuring her to look as pretty as possible with an eye to attracting the most eligible and successful mate. Catherine resisted almost hysterically, and later confessed tearfully to Raymond her abhorrence of receiving any male attention.

When she was fifteen, her most beloved older sister died in childbirth, and the loss appears to have intensified Catherine's resolve not to marry. She began keeping to herself, turning away from the outside world, devoting much of her time to prayer—and eating less and less. Her goal now was to devote her life to God, and she begged her parents to allow her to become a nun. She began to flagellate herself regularly, and hacked off her hair to make herself unattractive. Finally her parents consented to her joining an order that allowed her to live at home rather than in a convent.

Now, living in her little room in her parents' home, officially released from any womanly obligations, Catherine could indulge fully in her inexplicable desire to deprive and punish herself physically. She permitted herself very little sleep, and when she did, it was on a bed of sharp sticks, her body wrapped in a tight iron chain. She lived on as little food as possible, and made herself vomit daily by scratching her throat with twigs. Her confessor could not persuade her to stop; she told him that it helped expiate her sins. Later, in her writings, she explained: "They (sinners) vomit forth the corruption of their sins and so receive the gift of grace." Meanwhile, the food she took in dwindled further. She reduced her intake to uncooked vegetables and bread, then almost exclusively to the sacrament (the wafer and wine taken at Holy Communion). When Raymond repeated to Catherine her family's pleas that she eat more so that she wouldn't die of starvation, she replied, "What does mealtime mean to me? I have food to eat of which they [her family] know nothing"—that is, she lived on the sustenance of her spiritual life. Five hundred years later, Mollie Fancher unwittingly echoed Saint Catherine when she spoke of receiving nourishment from other than natural sources.

Catherine explained to her confessor that food itself was not a pleasure but a torture to her. "It was a greater suffering for her to take food than it is for a starving man to be deprived of it," Raymond recounted. "This was one of the very reasons why she took food at all—to mortify herself and make her emaciated body suffer." Many modern anorexics share that horror of food; the very act of eating is painful and frightening because it violates their internal admonition against it, and to give in and eat is to suffer. They have trained themselves, in the words of one modern psychiatrist, to experience their hunger itself, rather than their food, as pleasant and desirable. Catherine's words also call to mind Mollie Fancher's rejection of food as painful to her. Mollie described for Abram Dailey her method of resisting nourishment during the early years of spasms and trances: "It was forced into my mouth, and I kept it there until I got the opportunity, and then I rejected it. My doctor thought I was insane, but, as a matter of fact, I was never more rational in my life. I found every remedy increased my sufferings, and I begged to be let alone."

Mollie and Saint Catherine shared another conviction, one expressed by modern anorexics as well: that they did perfectly well without food, thank you; that in fact food might kill them. On one occasion

when Raymond was urging her with particular vehemence to eat, Catherine said to him, "Why do you not forbid me to take food? You have seen for yourself time and time again that this [taking food] is what is putting me to death, and if fasting were having that effect, by your own admission you would forbid it." Mollie insisted to her caregivers that their efforts to feed her were not only useless but even counterproductive and dangerous to her. Instead, she felt, "my spasms and trances were essential to my living; but this my physicians did not know. . . . When they stop I shall surely die." The modern anorexic is likely to protest that she has never been healthier, that she is not hungry—even as her body withers away. According to Hilde Bruch, a preeminent twentieth-century specialist in eating disorders, the anorexic's mantra is the sullen statement "I do not need to eat."

But whether food made Saint Catherine suffer or not, what made her long so much for the opportunity to mortify herself in every way possible? She appeared both to feel inherently unworthy and to be aiming for a state of what she termed perfection—rather a lofty goal, and one cited often by latter-day anorexics. They wish to be perfect in everything they do, including in controlling their appetites. "I thought it was just wonderful," one of Bruch's anorexic patients told her after her recovery, "that I was molding myself into that wonderful ascetic pure image." Many anorexics confess their conviction that only then—when they are perfect, and pure—will they be loved. For Catherine, it was God's love that was sought, and perfection in her asceticism that would lead her there. Nothing was to be loved but God—not food, not physical comfort, certainly not oneself. "Make a supreme effort to root out that self-love from your heart and to plant in its place this holy self-hatred," she wrote. "This is the royal road by which we turn our back on mediocrity, and which leads us without fail to the summit of perfection." That road led, for Catherine, to her death at age thirty-three from malnutrition.

Hundreds of religious women followed her example in the next several hundred years, perhaps inspired by Raymond of Capua's biography as well as by her own fervent writings. The Church may have contributed to the practice of this "holy anorexia" by rewarding with sainthood many women who fasted to death. That changed in the Renaissance, for a very practical reason. The Church was threatened by the rise of heretical cults that suggested that any individual could develop a personal relationship with God. The Church responded by putting the priest firmly back in charge as messenger between man and God. Starving saints like Catherine, who described visions of direct contact with God and claimed that her vomiting and hunger "paid Him an infinite debt," were out of style.

The practices of self-flagellating, self-starving religious women of the Middle Ages seem at least as remote from the modern world as the trances and contractures of nineteenth-century hysterics. Yet in his authoritative book *Holy Anorexia,* the historian Rudolph Bell theorizes that the holy anorexic and the modern anorexic, though externally different, are psychologically similar, each pursuing her objective of self-starvation with fanatical energy. The underlying drive, all these centuries later, has remained the same: "Whether anorexia is holy or nervous depends on the culture in which a young woman strives to gain control of her life." The girl in question battens on to a highly valued societal goal—physical health, thinness, and self-control in the twenty-first century; spiritual health, fasting, and self-denial in medieval Christian culture—and takes those objectives to dangerous levels. The disease, Bell feels, pursues a similar psychological path in both types of anorexia, from the original insecurity ("I am no one / I am a worthless, debased sinner") to the absolute certainty and power that come with self-denial. "To obliterate every human feeling of pain, fatigue, sexual desire, and hunger is to be master of oneself"—a heady accomplishment, and one of which every anorexic, whether holy or modern neurotic, would likely feel openly proud.

Other historians, notably Joan Jacobs Brumberg, have seen fasting saints and modern anorexics as linked more fundamentally by the fact of their gender than by their pursuit of cultural goals. Why is it, she asks in her 1988 book *Fasting Girls,* that the fasting saints were exclusively women? And why are most present-day victims of anorexia nervosa young women? Because of the social and cultural systems of these women's respective eras. These systems, she writes, "encourage or promote control of appetite in women, but for different reasons and purposes."

The two pivotal periods for female self-starving were the Middle Ages and the postindustrial age, according to Brumberg, and each offered cultural incentives for fasting. In the former era, not eating was linked to piety and spirituality; in the latter, to new social rules regarding class, gender, and family structure established in the nineteenth century. The modern anorexic continues this tradition of using food as symbolism. Though their experience of self-starvation is the same, Brumberg believes that the medieval holy woman's experience of penitential fervor essentially differs from the modern woman's search for autonomy, physical purity, and perfection through anorexia nervosa.

The distinctions between Bell's and Brumberg's arguments are difficult to tease apart. Both play on the cultural contexts of the medieval and postindustrial eras, and the powerful effects of society's values and expectations on striving young women. Even if the two phenomena—holy anorexia and anorexia nervosa—were the same in essence, they would be understood differently in their times. One reason that we now define anorexia as a nervous or medical condition, Bell believes, is that we live in a time of scientific rationalism, when it is assumed that illnesses such as this can be treated or cured, that all one needs is to find the right therapy. Medieval people were much less secure in their physical world, and less assured of their ability to shape events or change outcomes. In dealing with a woman who refused food to the point of dying of starvation, her medieval peers probably wondered what other forces were at work, forces larger than mere human ideas or psyches. Perhaps it was the hand or word of God; perhaps the work of the devil.

Although anorexia mirabilis as an overtly saintly phenomenon trailed off in the seventeenth century, a less formal connection between fasting and the miraculous persisted into the Victorian era. Living without food was just too magical a notion, too suggestive of the construct most people entertained of the body and the soul—the one mortal, hungry, and inherently sinful; the other ethereal, immortal, pure, closer to God than to the animals. In this philosophy, someone who was herself closer to God, who was more soul than body, might be able to break the rules of ordinary life.

In his 1694 medical text *Phthisiologia: Or, a Treatise of Consumptions,* one Richard Morton, an English specialist in consumptive, or "wasting," diseases, described "a Nervous Consumption" caused by "Sadness, and anxious Cares." Though the disorder occupied only three pages in this largely forgotten magnum opus devoted primarily to tuberculosis, some aspects of Morton's detailed picture of "Mr. *Duke's* daughter in *St. Mary Axe,* in the year 1684, and the Eighteenth Year of her Age" appear modern:

[She] fell into a total suppression of her Monthly Courses from a multitude of Cares and Passions of her Mind, but without any Symptom of the Green-Sickness following upon it. From which time her Appetite began to abate, and her Digestion to be bad; her Flesh also began to be flaccid and loose, and her looks pale. . . . She wholly neglected the care of her self for two full Years, till at last being brought to the last degree of a *Marasmus,* or Consumption, and thereupon subject to frequent Fainting Fits, she apply'd her self to me for Advice.

I do not remember that I did ever in all my Practice see one, that was conversant with the Living so much wasted with the greatest degree of a Consumption (like a Skeleton only clad with skin) yet there was no Fever, but on the contrary a coldness of the whole Body; no Cough, or difficulty of Breathing, nor an appearance of any other Distemper of the Lungs, or of any other Entrail. . . . Only her Appetite was diminished, and her Digestion uneasie, with Fainting Fits, which did frequently return upon her.

Morton, bemused at this illness that mimicked some aspects of consumption but without other telltale symptoms, such as cough, tried various medicines and tonics, to no avail. The girl tired of the useless treatments, and "beg'd that the whole Affair might be committed again to Nature, whereupon consuming [wasting away] every day more and more, she was after three Months taken with a Fainting Fit, and dyed."

This mention slipped quietly into the backwater of medical diagnosis. Two hundred years passed between Morton's description of an anorexia-like illness and William Gull's and Charles-Ernest Lasègue's full-fledged introduction of the real anorexia nervosa. During that time, female fasting underwent a gradual transition. The era of the fasting saints may have been over, but that didn't mean women stopped starving themselves—or even that they stopped claiming a mystical source for their survival without food. As the medieval holy anorexics gradually metamorphosed into the nineteenth century's fasting girls, a subtle change occurred: living without food became less of a solemn proof of piety and much more of a public spectacle.

The first step along that route came with the advent of the "miraculous fasting maids" in early-seventeenth-century Europe. Though mainly Catholic, they were cut from a different cloth from that of all-suffering, intensely religious saints like Catherine of Siena. These young women were of humble birth, and tended to be of a delicate sensibility rather than harshly ascetic. Of one such young woman, according to Joan Jacobs Brumberg, it was said that she "din'd on a rose and supt on a tulip"; another was said to live only by scent, not taste, inhaling the "smell of a rose." They were just as virginal and pure as the fasting saints, but softer, more feminine.

There was another major distinction between the miraculous maids and the fasting saints, a distinction that reflected the emerging rationalism of the Enlightenment, and that was only to intensify as the world moved toward the scientific transformations of the nineteenth century. Instead of simply accepting a young woman's word that she didn't eat, the people around her—clergymen, civil magistrates, physicians, even occasionally dukes and kings—began to investigate. No longer was it automatically assumed that a miracle was taking place; skepticism had crept in alongside religious fervor. Although most people still believed that miraculous fasting was possible—that is, that certain people specially chosen by God could live through divine grace rather than by the normal laws of nature—the possibility of fraud and deception had entered the equation. Perhaps some of these girls were simply pulling the wool over everyone's eyes for the sake of fame or, occasionally, money. Amid the new faith in the knowability of all things, teams of local authorities were often summoned to test a reputed miraculous maid with as scrupulous and scientific a method as possible.

Brumberg tells of one miraculous case, in France in the year 1600, that achieved so much renown that it caught the attention of King Henry IV. He promptly dispatched his top physician, Jacob Viverius, to see if the girl, Jane Balan, survived "by deceit or not." Balan, the fourteen-year-old daughter of a locksmith, claimed to have abstained from both food and drink for almost three years. Viverius, accompanied by other observers, described the girl's desiccated form: "The inferior part of her belly is in such manner grown lean, and dried up in her, as down from her sides, and so along her navel, there remaineth nothing of the belly she had before. . . . [There is] a Cartilage or gristle, hanging pointed down from the thorax, or sternum, after the manner of an eaves of a penthouse." Beyond this corporeal evidence, the clearest sign of complete fasting, Viverius felt, would be a lack of any excrement, and in some unnamed manner he determined that Balan indeed neither urinated nor defecated. He designated her a "miraculous maid" whose life without sustenance was an act of God. The Balan case was significant because the investigation of Jane's truthfulness was led by a doctor rather than a clergyman—an important step in the long process of shifting authority from the Church to scientists and philosophers. That shift, in which human health and behavior became defined in medical rather than spiritual terms, was still evolving more than 250 years later, when Mollie Fancher's story reached the newspapers.

Later in the century that opened with Jane Balan's case, the story of a young Englishwoman represented the next stage in the evolution away from magical and religious interpretations of fasting. Martha Taylor, dubbed "The Derbyshire Damsel," became something of a celebrity in 1668 through her claims of existing on virtually nothing—only the very occasional "juice of a roasted raisin" or a few drops of syrup of stewed prunes. Two religious pamphlets helped spread her fame, calling her a wonder of the world and a miracle sent by God as an exhortation to sinners. Her face was said to be fresh and lively—unlikely if she was starving—but the rest of the description fits that of a severely undernourished person. Her body was shrunken "into the ghastliness of a skeleton," the lower part "languid, and unapt for motion," and her skin was dry, with a "prurignous scurf." She spent her days in bed.

Taylor's case was so well known, attracting a constant stream of visitors to the family's small home in the village of Bakewell, that it inspired a ground-breaking written critique. John Reynolds, a doctor with connections to London's Royal Society of Physicians, published his *Discourse on Prodigious Abstinence* about Martha Taylor in 1669. In it he attempted to debunk miraculous maids in general and, more important, provide a scientific rationale in place of their spiritual claims (as curious as his medical explanation may sound to modern ears). To dispatch the maids, Reynolds used every logical argument he could find, including the fact that Taylor, like many fasting maids, was an improbable target for God's grace. She was not particularly devout or learned, and her self-denial, unlike that of miraculous biblical fasters, served no discernible purpose. It was time, Reynolds wrote, to release the notion of long-term spiritual fasting from its "supernatural asylum."

Reynolds was convinced that Taylor's inability or unwillingness to eat was an illness, although he could not say what kind. But he did offer an elaborate physical explication of how someone might live without eating, based on the new theory of fermentation. This held that the major organs of the body were filled with particles that could ferment, like grapes transforming into wine, and move into the bloodstream. Reynolds took the extra step of proposing that such fermentation could enrich the blood enough that new food was not necessary, especially if excretory functions were reduced and blood elements consequently retained in the body. Absurd though that sounds now, it was a firm, medically minded step away from the idea of surviving on spiritual sustenance directly from God.

Reynolds did make one physical observation that would withstand the test of time. He noted that this rejection of food appeared to be especially an adolescent affliction—an idea that would later be confirmed both by the Victorian limners of anorexia nervosa and by modern specialists in eating disorders. "Most of these damsels fall to this abstinence between the ages of fourteen and twenty years," he wrote, "when the seed hath so fermented the blood." The reasons later devised for this female, teenage susceptibility have ranged far from blood fermentation—into the psychological territory of fear of maturation, struggle for autonomy, relentless perfectionism—but the connection had been made.

Not surprisingly, as fasting became something more of this world than the next, other more worldly elements entered the picture—in particular, the potential for profit and the lust for fame. One of the most famous early-nineteenth-century cases of food abstinence, that of the Englishwoman Ann Moore, "The Fasting Woman of Tutbury," displayed both elements in abundance. Moore, whose reputed fasting spanned the years 1807 to 1813, stood on the dividing line between miraculous maids and fasting girls. She claimed to be religious, and was careful always to have her Bible placed prominently near or on her bed. According to a pamphlet published after her unmasking in 1813, she declared outright "that her case is a miracle wrought immediately by the power of God, an interference of Divine Providence on her behalf, by which she is kept alive, without either eating or drinking." But Moore's life history told a tale that wasn't quite as righteous. She had married at twenty-seven but had soon separated from her husband; at the time of her fast she was forty-six and had been living in adultery with another man, by whom she had had two children, then in their teens. She was clever enough to try to make use of her disreputable past by speaking of her fast as a sign of God's forgiveness, and of her redemption.

What Ann Moore shared with many of the fasting girls who followed her was a very secular interest in celebrity and in money. According to the 1813 pamphlet, it was Moore herself who offered to submit to observation, sometime after she first attracted attention by declaring that she lived without food. In September 1808 she was moved to the house of the town grocer (an ironic choice, it would seem), and a very public test was established. All inhabitants of the town were invited to work a shift on watch. To assure medical veracity, a physician, Robert Taylor, oversaw the investigation. A total of 117 people observed Moore over the course of the trial.

As word of the fasting test spread throughout Staffordshire, obscure little Tutbury was having its moment of celebrity thanks to Ann Moore—and she was being enriched for her labors. Accounts vary of how much money she took in from visitors, and no one recorded what she charged for the privilege of seeing her, but apparently she gained at least several hundred pounds sterling. After sixteen days Moore had not been seen to consume anything but a little water (on the first three days), and was declared to be a genuine faster. Robert Taylor published his findings, and many more publications followed, increasing the steady stream of visitors to Moore's bedside. At the least she was taking in very little food; one account described her as "extremely emaciated." Her case excited popular wonder, and a great deal of scientific pontificating as well: What could be keeping her alive?

Finally, in 1813, her critics roused themselves once again. Enough was enough. To the forward-thinking, it was outrageous—a caving in to superstitious ignorance—to allow anyone to continue to assert that she had lived six years without food. Another test was demanded. This one would be much more scientifically rigorous, although it was overseen, interestingly, not by a doctor but by a well-known clergyman, Legh Richmond. Moore was placed on a special bed under which a "weighing machine" could be installed, and an authorized person was in her room at all times.

This test, predictably, proved quite a contrast to the first. At the end of seven days without any nutriment, Moore was clearly suffering. She began to show the signs of true starvation. A pamphlet published after the event, *A Full Exposure of Ann Moore,* related the ghoulish details: "A fever arising from abstinence, kept continually increasing. Parched with thirst, she requested the watch to give her cloths dipped in vinegar and water, which they did, and with these she kept wetting her mouth and tongue. . . . On the eighth day, she was exceedingly distressed. Her pulse had increased until it amounted to 145 in a minute. On the ninth day, she insisted the watch [be] given up, declaring that she was very ill, and that her daughter must be sent for. She was now greatly reduced, and her voice very feeble."

The watch committee, fearing she would die at any moment, called off the vigil. Moore still insisted that she had not taken any food for six years, and even asked to sign a solemn oath to that effect, but shortly thereafter she was firmly and forever exposed. One of the watchers found her bed linens, which she had hidden in her room. On them, according to *A Full Exposure,* was "the deep stain of urine, and, as some suppose, of excrement. The blanket, also, on which she sat, was wet through to the bed." Moore, "overwhelmed with confusion," signed a document of confession: "I, Ann Moore, of Tutbury, humbly asking pardon of all persons whom I have attempted to deceive and impose upon, and above all, with the most unfeigned sorrow and contrition, imploring the Divine mercy and forgiveness of that God whom I have so greatly offended, do most solemnly declare, that I have occasionally taken sustenance for the last six years. Witness my hand this fourth day of May, 1813." The mechanism of Moore's deception soon became public knowledge: her daughter had secretly fed her by washing her face with towels made wet with milk or gravy, and by passing food to her mouth-to-mouth during kisses. Early one morning soon after her debacle, Moore left town. An eyewitness account described her sitting in an open cart along with several pieces of furniture, taunted by a crowd of onlookers.

Ann Moore may have been finished, but her fame spread even further after her fast was exposed. The story now had an ending—an ending full of drama and morality, a triumph of truth over the most shameless mendacity. Books and pamphlets about the massive fraud she had perpetrated spread even to America, and a wax image of Moore was exhibited at a Boston museum. Throughout the rest of the century, according to Joan Jacobs Brumberg, Moore was seen as a symbol of female deceit, "decried by everyone as a fraud and cited in medical books as evidence of the scurrilous nature of religious fasting claims." Here, finally, was a clear victory for medicine and science over mysticism and blind faith.

And yet, because of the very nature of the beast, that victory could never be unequivocal. It had indeed been shown that this particular woman had lied; that she did need to eat in order to live. But that fact did not perforce prove no one could ever accomplish what Ann Moore claimed to have done. It is always more difficult to prove a negative than a positive—to prove, in this case, that no one can exist without food—because there is that little nibble of doubt, of uncertainty. There remained the tantalizing question: What if? Perhaps, somewhere, there lived a woman who survived on miracles rather than on bread. To the nineteenth-century mind, which still entertained fantasies of divine powers overcoming mundane physical laws, the case was not yet decided.

That became clear in 1869, when the Sarah Jacob disaster demonstrated how many people were willing to believe in the impossible—and how high the stakes of belief and disbelief could go. The Jacob case, the story of the Welsh Fasting Girl told so frequently by William Hammond in making his anti-fasting argument, became a cautionary tale that hung over the Mollie Fancher frenzy like a shroud. Sarah Jacob was the perfect pattern of the late-nineteenth-century starving girl-wonder: young, pretty, visited at her bedside by hundreds of curious and admiring strangers, willing to accept monetary gifts for her fame, adorned with a vague aura of religiosity. Once again, it seemed possible that miraculous fasting could be true, that medical materialism was perhaps too literal—particularly after an initial period of observation, from March 22 to April 5, 1869, appeared to prove that Sarah Jacob was genuinely fasting.

That was when Sarah hit the big time. Stories were published about her reputed feats. Visitors crowded into the town of Carmarthenshire, following local boys whose hats sported "To the Fasting Girl" signs to the thatch-roofed Jacob farmhouse. There they would offer gifts and money, and observe little Sarah in her bed. The scene was described by Robert Fowler, a member of the Royal College of Surgeons, who visited in the summer of 1869 and published an account of his medical opinion, *A Complete History of the Welsh Fasting Girl,* in 1871: "The child was lying on a bed, decorated as a bride, having around her head a wreath of flowers, from which was suspended a smart ribbon the ends of which were joined by a small bunch of flowers, after the present fashion of ladies' bonnet-strings. Before her, at proper reading distance was an open Welsh book supported by two other books upon her body." Sarah Jacob was then either twelve or fourteen, depending on the source, and her fast was said to have lasted a year and a half. Yet when Fowler examined her he heard some gurgling from her intestines, a sign that her digestive system was in fact being used; and she was described by visitors as appearing well nourished.

In some ways Sarah Jacob was a younger, simpler precursor to the complex Mollie Fancher. Her case, like Mollie's, pitted believers (led by her staunchest supporter, the local Anglican vicar, the Reverend Evan Jones) against the newly powerful medical establishment. As with Mollie, Sarah's claims prompted serious discussion in the press and medical journals; and like Mollie, she was characterized by many doctors as a hysteric, subject to "a diseased volition" that prompted her to simulate fasting. Emotions ran almost as high about her case as about Mollie's.

Sarah Jacob's story, however, was cut short—both by the arrogance of the physicians around her, and by some obscure convergence of stubbornness and delusion in her and her parents. She submitted to a second watch eight months after the first, in December 1869; and this one was, unfortunately for Sarah, much more scientific. Four nurses were sent from Guy's Hospital in London, and the conditions for the watch were determined with a committee of local folk. The farmhouse was checked for hidden food, and Sarah's younger sister was no longer allowed to sleep with her. The nurses sat by her candlelit bedside night and day, in shifts. Within the first day and a half, evidence of excrement was found on her nightclothes.

The watch continued, with Sarah's parents refusing any physical examination of their daughter. After six days, the nurses appealed to the local doctors and to the Jacob family to call off the watch, to allow Sarah to obtain food in whatever occult manner she had before. The girl was visibly failing, growing weak and cold. The family refused indignantly, insisting that Sarah needed no food; and Sarah, presumably caught up in her miraculous identity, did not ask for any. Finally her sister was put back into her bed to help warm her cold body, but to no avail. Sarah Jacob died eight days after the watch had begun. Doctors later surmised that she had been surreptitiously supplied with bits of food, possibly by her sister or her parents, who slept in the same room with the girls.

The medical community reacted with horror: How could doctors, nurses, and family members have stood by while Sarah died? Their inaction was a testament to the compelling pull of atavistic belief; had she been thought to be ill, rather than possibly miraculous, she would have been force-fed long before death was imminent.

The power of the self-delusion that propelled Sarah toward death from starvation inevitably raises the question of how Mollie Fancher obtained the food that she must have had to survive—and of whether she would have stuck to her story as obstinately as Sarah did, if Hammond had had his way with a test of her fasting. Surely Aunt Susan must have been the primary source of nutrition for the bedridden Mollie. One wonders if the pleasures of being noted, written about, marveled over, were just too irresistible amid the daily dreariness of the sickroom. Did Mollie and Aunt Susan discuss her eating? Was there any planning involved, or just a tacit understanding that Mollie's ingestion was never to be mentioned?

On these questions, Aunt Susan's diary, usually so detailed, is silent. But Mollie apparently had enough self-knowledge to understand that to accept Dr. Hammond's challenge, to submit to a watch, would be to sign either her confession, like Ann Moore, or, like Sarah Jacob, her own death warrant.

In the epilogue to Rudolph Bell's *Holy Anorexia,* the clinical psychologist William Davis presents a compelling argument for the connection between anorexia mirabilis and anorexia nervosa. The problem, he points out, is that while victims of the two types of anorexias share many features—including weight loss in excess of twenty-five percent of normal body weight, physical symptoms of starvation, denial of their nutritional needs, and resistance to external efforts to get them to eat—one element diverges widely: motivation. Modern anorexia nervosa is strongly tied to a dread of fatness and a powerful desire for thinness. The fasting saints, on the other hand, pursued purity, holiness, an intense relationship with their God.

At first glance, the two goals could not seem further apart: the one focused on worldly, external judgments of appearance, the other turned inward to timeless spiritual values. And yet, Davis says, merely substitute the word "holiness" for "thinness" when characterizing anorexia nervosa and you are left with the bare bones of the same phenomenon— the same state of mind, the same psychopathology. So, for instance, if one describes current anorexia nervosa clinically as "a distorted, implacable attitude towards *eating, food or weight* that overrides hunger, admonitions, reassurance, and threats," one can translate that into anorexia mirabilis simply by saying "a distorted, implacable attitude toward *holiness* that overrides hunger, admonitions, reassurance, and threats." In Davis's words, while a modern anorexic takes "apparent enjoyment in *losing weight* with overt manifestation that food refusal is a pleasurable indulgence," a holy anorexic takes "apparent enjoyment in *gaining holiness* with overt manifestation that food refusal is a pleasurable indulgence."

The underlying mechanism is the same: the use of appetite and eating (or more precisely, the denial of those) to gain entrance to a state of existence that is highly valued. That last point is a key to why the connection between the two anorexias may be initially difficult to see from the twenty-first century. Holiness is not something most people think about from day to day; it's certainly not a way for a woman to gain prominence or respect from society. But in the Middle Ages it was exactly that—an ideal state, as thinness is today. "In medieval Italy holiness was held in the highest regard," Davis writes. "Women were presented with specific models of holiness toward which they could aspire. Struggling to live up to them could provide new and enhanced experiences of self-esteem." Young women today are also presented with specific models—not of holiness but of slenderness and, implicitly, self-control. Looking like these models—and in this case they are, literally, models, in magazines, films, TV shows—dangles this same promise of self-esteem.

With both types of anorexia, however, that promise is (and was) rarely fulfilled. Another element they share is an unremitting and unforgiving perfectionism, so that anorexics are never content with their thinness or holiness. This is one reason why fasting saints like Catherine of Siena so often died of starvation, and why anorexia nervosa has the highest death rate of any psychiatric illness: the anorexic is never pure enough, thin enough, holy enough. "[Both types of anorexics] constantly experience themselves to be in grave danger of losing control over their fanatically pursued aims, and so are forever watchful and self-critical," observes Davis. "Their thoughts are obsessively focused upon holiness or thinness, so much so that there is little time or energy for anything else." Happiness is not the point; rather, the only way to feel at all comfortable is to remove oneself from ordinary life, with its messy desires and needs.

The late-Victorian era provided the logical turning point, the bridge between mirabilis and nervosa. Holiness and religious faith in general were in steep decline, thrown into disarray and doubt by the mind-numbing advances of science. Waiting to replace religious belief was a growing trust in human capabilities, and a concurrent focus on human potential and achievement. Perhaps humans could become their own gods, in a way—could cure disease, control their own fate, rule their own bodies and minds.

CHAPTER EIGHT

From Soul to Mind

And so, dear Miss Fancher, I hope it will be a joy and a comfort to you, to realize that your life has not been fruitless. That you have been highly privileged by Providence in helping us to strike a telling blow at the wretched Sadduceeism of our age, towards which the physical sciences seem to be leading those who ignore such facts as your case exhibits.

—Letter from Epes Sargent, Spiritualist, to Mollie Fancher, January 8, 1879

The world has never been able to get away from the inexplicable and the unseen.

—Elizabeth Stuart Phelps, in *The Forum,* June 1886

B Y EARLY DECEMBER 1878, Mollie Fancher was on her way to becoming an urban legend in New York. On the first Sunday of the month, the Reverend Dr. Hugh Carpenter discussed her case from the pulpit of the Bedford Avenue Congregational Church, saying that "prodigies in human nature are nothing new" and that "the mystery of the connection between mind and matter has not yet been fathomed." When a contortionist named Charles Warren demonstrated his amazing talent of disjointing various parts of his body at Rush Medical College, he was playfully referred to in *The World* as "a husband for Miss Fancher." Even thirdhand anecdotes about her were finding their way into the newspapers.

One such tale, which appeared in the *Brooklyn Daily Union-Argus,* held that two ladies who called to see Miss Mollie Fancher were met by a young man requesting five dollars for admission. The report did not surface anywhere else, and it goes against the accounts of Mollie's friends that she never attempted to profit from her fame. In his biography of Mollie, Abram Dailey emphasized her "excessive sensitiveness to all notoriety," as well as her desire to keep all knowledge of herself from the public (a desire frustrated as early as 1866, with the first *Daily Eagle* article). Dailey also insisted that Mollie had never made a penny from her gifts (although he tells of her commissions for wax work and embroidery). But the rest of the *Union-Argus* story has a ring of authenticity: if the ladies brought a letter of introduction from someone known and approved by "Miss Fancher's friends," the paper reported, the money would not be required until they were about to leave. And further, the publicity about the Fancher case had brought "large numbers of people" to Mollie's door (Dailey's total estimate for 1866 to 1894, based on Mollie's visitors' book, was between seventy-five and one hundred thousand), and charging admission was an effort to stanch the tide.

An invasion of curiosity-seekers would not be surprising, when one considers that new, titillating details about Mollie's story were every day delighting readers of New York's *Times, Herald, World, Tribune, Star,* and *Evening Post,* and Brooklyn's *Eagle, Times,* and *Union-Argus,* not to mention the enterprising New York *Sun.* It was the *Sun* that, in the last week of November, had put first William Hammond, then George Beard, on record in the Fancher affair. Its reporter had haunted the doorstep of Professor Charles West, and pried commentary out of "the reticent Dr. Parkhurst." Now the paper sent its inquisitor to another scholar, Joseph Rodes Buchanan, the chair of physiology and anthropology at the Eclectic Medical College in New York, and in so doing opened another flank in the Fancher battle.

Professor Buchanan aspired to the distinction that his archenemy Beard had achieved with neurasthenia: identifying and naming his own medical condition. But Buchanan's ambitions were even grander. He wanted to establish a new branch of science that would explain the workings of the entire universe. It is a measure of his success—or more precisely, his lack of it—that his word to describe this science, "psychometry," today exists only as an obscure detail from the history of crackpot theories of the nineteenth century.

Buchanan came up with the term in 1842, calling it "the most pregnant and important word that has been added to the English language." The *Oxford English Dictionary*, which attributes to Buchanan the first official usage, defines *psychometry* as "the (alleged) faculty of divining, from physical contact or proximity only, the qualities or properties of an object, or of persons or things that have been in contact with it."

Buchanan considered that special seeing or divining only the beginning, an entry to the meaning of all things. He had coined the term from the Greek *psyche* (soul) and *metron* (measure), because, he explained, just as the barometer measured the weight (*baro*) of the atmosphere, the psychometer measured the soul. In this case, however, the object measured (the soul) and the measuring instrument (the soul) were the same "psychic element." The study of psychometry, Buchanan believed, would elucidate everything from medicine, physiology, biography, history, paleontology, philosophy, anthropology, geology, and astronomy to theology and "supernal life and destiny." His discovery, he wrote in 1854, constituted the dawn of a new era of science, philosophy, and social progress; psychometry would be more important to human enlightenment than all the arts and sciences that had come before. In the art of self-importance, Buchanan made Hammond and Beard look like amateurs.

The *Sun* reporter who sought him out in the first week of December 1878 reminded readers that Professor Buchanan had studied the nervous system for forty years, and had made "many marvellous experiments" (which the reporter left unnamed). Just as the interview started, the reporter recounted, the two were interrupted by a visit from a woman to Buchanan's office. This unidentified woman, whose name, the reporter said, was "known to the readers of *The Sun* as that of an independent thinker," was introduced to him as a member of the New York Psychometric Society (which appeared to organize upper-crust séance soirées exclusively for "ladies who possess this marvellous power of psychometry"). The reporter asked to see a demonstration of her psychometric abilities, and she assented. He handed her a note (presumably folded) from a personal friend of his. Holding it in her right hand, she described the friend who had written the note, said the reporter, "as freely and judiciously as though she had personally known him." Her amazing ability, the professor proclaimed, was common among the members of the Society. Any of them could have done as well with such a test.

The episode is almost identical to tales of Mollie Fancher's many feats of clairvoyance: Henry Parkhurst's newspaper story of handing her a sealed envelope and hearing her accurately describe its contents; Abram Dailey's anecdotes in his 1894 book: "Sometimes I have carried to [Mollie] a photograph of someone whom she knew before the accident. She always saw and recognized it before it was taken from my pocket." Mollie's purported ability to "read" by touch while blind also corresponds to Buchanan's descriptions of psychometry. "I took her a book one day," Dailey recalled, "and she drew her thumb rapidly over the title page and began to laugh. Of course I asked the cause of her merriment, and she answered that . . . a very dear friend had two years before given her the same book; and with that she gave me a running sketch of its contents in a highly intelligent and surprisingly accurate manner."

Mollie Fancher's case, Buchanan told the *Sun* reporter, was not new or wondrous, either in her clairvoyance or in her fasting. There were many authentic instances on record of long-lasting abstinence. The only reason for the uproar about Mollie was the ignorance and arrogance of the mainstream medical profession, which wanted to hear nothing that went against its own "infallible dogmas." The key to Mollie's abstinence, Buchanan felt, was the separation of her body and soul—a concept foreign to most doctors, who could "tolerate no other conception of man than that of a mere animal. They refuse to recognize the soul as an entity, or even an object of scientific investigation." Once her soul was freed from her animal nature, she would (in some unspecified way) no longer need human sustenance.

Buchanan's explanation of the symbiotic relationship between Mollie's fasting and her spirituality—how the one made possible and sanctified the other—recalls anorexia mirabilis, with a gloss of nineteenth-century pseudorationalism. "When the close connection of soul and body is disturbed," he told the *Sun,* "their powers may be separated—the body lying as if inanimate, while its vital principle, which is spiritual, acts independently of the body, as it must when the body has been destroyed by death." This way station between life and death is where fasting and clairvoyance meet, where the soul, for once, rules its carnal shell rather than the other way around.

Buchanan's explanation is convoluted at best, but it boils down to this: In the usual state of affairs, with body and soul tightly knit together, the body rules. Its fleshly appetites mask the more delicate spiritual impulses; all is hunger and satiation, pleasure and pain. The animal that lurks within us all has no interest in its own soul, or in the spiritual world beyond this corporeal one. (One senses Victorian moral judgments lurking here.) But the balance between physical and spiritual could be shifted, according to Buchanan, and one way to do that was through denying the body—effectively the argument used by Catherine of Siena and other fasting saints centuries earlier. Once the actions and base appetites of the body were partially suspended, the soul could be emancipated. Trance, somnolence, catalepsy, or ecstasy could follow.

Buchanan's guidelines for reaching this otherworldly state were tough: even one's hunger had to be on the saintly side. "If fasting excites hunger it only develops animality," he told the *Sun* reporter, "but if it suppresses appetite then it is favorable to religious ecstasy, clairvoyance, and spiritual communion." Those are words to warm a saint's heart—and Mollie appears to have gained Buchanan's full spiritual approval. Her fasting had quieted the animal functions in her brain and given her, he said, "an exalted character—a degree of angelic purity, elevation or sentiment, and clearness of perception similar to that of the disembodied soul after a virtuous life." For all his efforts to sound scientific, Buchanan here evokes Romantic poets earlier in the century, for instance Wordsworth, in "Lines Composed a Few Miles Above Tintern Abbey," celebrating "that serene and blessed mood" in which "the motion of our human blood / Almost suspended, we are laid asleep / In body, and become a living soul."

Despite Buchanan's scientific pretensions (he loved throwing around terms like "basilar convolutions" and "septum lucidum"), he came no closer than the most extreme religious apologist to explaining how a human being could live more than a dozen years without food. But that wasn't his primary motivation for inviting himself into the Mollie Fancher affair. Buchanan had grander ends in mind: the promotion of his beloved psychometry, and the chance to thrash the more legitimate scientific figures who stood against him and his ideas (including, most emphatically, Hammond and Beard). The *Sun* reporter, recognizing good copy when he saw it, gave him full rein.

The medical profession, obsessed with its "stupid mechanical materialism," constituted the most ignorant part of society, Buchanan informed the reporter. The teachers in the most fashionable medical schools cultivated ignorance as a fine art, tossing out any testimony, facts, or statistics that went against their ingrained ideas. Likening them to spirited mules, Buchanan seemed to shock even himself: "Excuse the coarseness of the metaphor," he said, "for a coarse illustration is necessary for a coarse subject. Common courtesy and common sense are equally disregarded by medical skepticism."

The medical profession, Buchanan insisted, was populated largely by "old fogies" who could not adopt "modern ideas." This was a curious turnaround: a believer in mysteries and spiritual essences was painting himself as more modern than a doctor who saw humans as machines. Buchanan went on to make this odd comparison: "To ask one of these skeptics [the "materialist" doctors], who considers mind a secretion of the brain, as bile is a secretion of the liver, his opinion of Miss Fancher's case, would be as profitable as to ask a description of the climate of Cuba from one of the learned monks in the days of Columbus, who denied the existence of the western hemisphere." The metaphor is ironic; Buchanan is associating modern doctors with medieval religious figures, while advocates of the soul like him are compared to the great explorers and discoverers of new worlds.

For all the confusion and bombast of his ideas, however, at a meeting of the Brooklyn Spiritualist Society on December 28, 1878, Buchanan came closer than anyone else connected with the Fancher case to interpreting the hoopla around her. Reporters from the major newspapers showed up at Everett Hall on Fulton Street to hear his announced lecture, "Mind, Soul, Spirit; or the Case of Miss Fancher and Its Relations to Science and Christianity." Most of the papers found the lecture newsworthy enough to report on it the next day; some, such as the *Tribune,* even put the story on the front page. *The New York Times* was considerably more jaded in its coverage. The subhead under a headline of "Psychometry in Brooklyn" read: "Dr. J. R. Buchanan Speaks Before Some Spiritualists—A Little About Miss Mollie Fancher and a Great Deal About Dr. Buchanan." According to the *Times,* Buchanan moved from Mollie's story into a general dissertation on Spiritualism, supplemented by blasts at the "educated ignorance" of physicians like Hammond and Beard.

But among Buchanan's various epithets and calls to have bigoted and narrow-minded people like Dr. Hammond "placed in asylums for disordered intellects," one sentence specifically leapt out at every reporter in attendance and made its way into every article (although with slightly varied wordings). Early in his speech, he declared grandly: "The case of Miss Fancher stands in the very center of the conflicting forces of the present century—on one side of which are arrayed reason, religion, and morality, and on the other side materialism and the material theories of the medical colleges." Hammond and Beard were quintessential materialist physicians, seeking a physiological explanation for every affliction, and rejecting any evidence that was not observable (preferably by experts). Buchanan and other thinkers saw a universe of possibilities beyond the physical.

Many would argue that the word "reason" in Buchanan's stated schism rightly belongs on the other shore, that religion and reason are different in kind—one requiring faith, the other logic. Certainly Hammond and Beard would see it that way. But to Buchanan, as to many other believers in the "unseen," nothing was more reasonable than to believe the accounts of so many eyewitnesses: there was indeed a spirit world.

However fuzzy Buchanan's thinking, in this statement he recognized with surprising sharpness the context of Mollie's story. The late nineteenth century was dominated by a conflict between the hard evidence of the mind and the senses, and the enduring testimony of the heart and the emotions—between science and faith. And Mollie Fancher stood at the center of that conflict, appearing at one moment to be the epitome of hysterical conversion disorder, a scientific diagnosis, and at the next to be living proof of the existence of a soul that could survive starvation and "see" without eyesight. She could be one of the first victims of the new, scientifically described disease known as anorexia nervosa—or one in a long line of spiritually gifted miraculous fasters in the tradition of anorexia mirabilis. When the Spiritualists arrived on the scene at the end of December, that dual reality became even more muddled—to some extent because both sides were trying to appropriate the same language. Both coveted the new argot of scientific rationality, but each had its own, quite different understanding of "psychology," a word whose meaning was soon to change dramatically.

Buchanan's unhesitating juxtaposition of reason and religion made perfect sense to the Spiritualists in his audience that night. Those two forces, after all, together formed the raison d'être of Spiritualism, the "scientific religion." Spiritualism seemed a contradiction in terms, combining a superstitious, almost childlike belief in spirit communication with a dogged determination to prove itself real by the laws of nineteenth-century empirical science. Spiritualists wanted to create the first religion whose tenets required not blind faith (which had not been holding up very well under the onslaught of the scientific revolution), but only intelligent thought and a mind open to new evidence. To this end, they sprinkled their philosophy with scientific terminology; they spoke of "searching for objective proof" and "critical analysis of results."

For a movement with such intellectual aspirations, Spiritualism had an unprepossessing start as a practical joke between two mischievous sisters. In the early spring of 1848, Margaret and Kate Fox, thirteen and eleven years old, heard mysterious rapping sounds in the upstairs bedroom of their family's modest cottage in the town of Hydesville, New York. Their parents were convinced that the sounds came from otherworldly spirits—especially when the rappings appeared to respond intelligently to questions—and that the girls somehow functioned as mediums between the spirit world and the corporeal one, since the rappings occurred only in the girls' presence. Neighbors were called in to witness the miracle, as the rapping spirit gave people's ages, confirmed that it was the ghost of a murdered man, and correctly answered queries about neighborhood children. A pamphlet was written about the amazing Fox Sisters, newspapers picked up the story, and visitors besieged the Fox home.

The family moved to Rochester, where their fame grew. By the next year Margaret and another sister, Leah, who had discovered her own mediumistic powers, gave a public demonstration of their communications to an excited crowd at Corinthian Hall, the largest public hall in Rochester. Many came to see the sisters unmasked as frauds, but no one could detect any deception in their communication with the spirits. By the end of the evening, excitement and controversy had reached such a pitch that a riot broke out at the hall, complete with shouting, firecrackers, and finally, a visit from the police. Spiritualism was launched. Forty years later, in 1888, Margaret confessed that she and her sisters had produced the rappings by cracking their toe joints against any available hard surface.

The Fox sisters moved their show to Manhattan's Barnum Hotel in 1850, befriended by two very prominent supporters who did much to advance their credibility: Judge John Worth Edmonds, a respected member of the New York State Court of Appeals, and Horace Greeley, founder and editor of the *New-York Tribune*. Not coincidentally, both had recently lost loved ones: Edmonds his wife, and Greeley his son— and thus the possibility of being in touch with the spirits of the departed was especially appealing for both men. The Foxes held regular séances at the hotel, acting as mediums for paying customers, and Greeley gave them favorable mentions in his paper. Trances, séances, hypnotism, mesmerism—all of these altered states of consciousness, which presumably put one in touch with another, parallel world, were decidedly in fashion.

Soon the Spiritualism craze expanded from public halls and paid mediums to the more refined province of exclusive drawing rooms and ladies who dabbled in clairvoyance. "The spiritualistic *séance*," wrote Elizabeth Stuart Phelps in the *Forum* magazine in June 1886, "has risen from the bottom to the top. It floats upon the smooth surface of society easily." What Phelps called silken society began to seek out the esoteric as it would seek a new waltz or an original dinner-card; a live Theosophist (believer in a mystical discipline sometimes called Esoteric Buddhism) became just the thing to wake up a sleepy drawing room. Certain mediums had their brief moments of fame; they came into vogue, like bonnets, and were donned or doffed as the season or style decreed. Phelps described dinner-party conversations about summoning family ghosts, or arranging to meet distant friends in dreams, or trying to journey into the realm of the spirits.

Mediumship had become a profession, with individual practitioners setting up their own shops, sometimes even advertising their services, as did Miss Fanny M. Hancox in *The Brooklyn Daily Times* in 1866, under the simple headline "Clairvoyancy!" In the ad, sandwiched between notices for boardinghouse rooms and the Williamsburgh City Fire Insurance Company, Miss Hancox begged leave to announce to her friends of Williamsburgh and its vicinity that she had taken rooms at the Wall House, corner of Fourth and South Fifth streets. This she had done for the purpose of "giving clairvoyantly, medical and business communications, on Wednesdays and Thursdays of each week. Office hours from 10 A.M. till 6 P.M."

Spirit communications, often purportedly from famous personages, were presented in lectures, or even published, as evidence of the continuing nature of the soul. A reporter for the *New York Herald* gave an account in 1866 of attending a Spiritualist lecture that promised to describe the entrance of a recently deceased local hero, General Scott, into the spirit land, welcomed by the shades of Lincoln, Washington, the Duke of Wellington, Napoleon, and many others. The reporter described enduring that same evening an excruciatingly bad poem that the lecturing medium claimed had been dictated to her by a spirit. That same year, Brooklyn's *Daily Times* offered a review of a new publication, from the city's Spiritualist Society, that included a poem from the spirit of John Wilkes Booth, Lincoln's assassin. Through a medium named Joseph Styler, Booth was said to have begun: "Oh God! what fiery waves of hell / Across my burdened conscience roll! / What agonies, what tortures dwell / Within the chambers of my soul!"

But if silly tales and sensationalistic shows, complete with table-raising and flickering candles, were all that Spiritualism consisted of, it would not have the place in nineteenth-century cultural and religious history that it occupies. In sheer numbers it demanded attention; Elizabeth Stuart Phelps quoted estimates of an army of believers in the United States numbering between two and ten million. And it also took on a philosophical aura. "The thing has overflowed the culvert of superstition," Phelps wrote in 1886. "It has gone above the level of what we call a craze or a fashion. It has reached the dignity of an intellectual current."

Spiritualism owed that dignity largely to its most serious followers' insistence that psychic phenomena be studied as scientifically as possible. No longer was it a sign of culture or sophistication to ignore the inexplicable. Ghosts were being invited not only into the drawing room, but into the library as well. "Mesmeric miracles and clairvoyant marvels and the problems of the trance," wrote Phelps, "are not henceforth to be left to the 'Banner of Light' [a popular Spiritualist publication], they are straightway tabulated and dispatched to the learned societies for psychical research."

It was this tinge of respectability that most irked scientists such as Hammond and Beard. They had both been openly at war with Spiritualism for at least a decade when Mollie Fancher reached the front page in 1878. The source of their animosity was both philosophical and very practical: this was a turf war between the newly established specialty of neurology, the science of the mind, and Spiritualism, the science of the soul. Whoever won could claim mental phenomena like somnambulism and trance for their own side. The implication for materialist thinkers was chilling; if they lost, they felt, the world would have taken a step back toward superstition and magical thinking. The forces of rationality and science would have that much further to go to reach their rightful ascendancy. Beard and Hammond could sense their side losing ground; séances were becoming so popular that many people were more inclined to think of somnambulistic trances like Mollie's as supernatural events rather than as medical manifestations arising from, say, hysteria.

Hammond aimed his first blow at Spiritualism in his 1871 book *The Physics and Physiology of Spiritualism*. Characteristically combining scientific reasoning with personal insult (and in a manner that reveals his casual nineteenth-century racism), he wrote: "[Spiritualists'] minds are decidedly fetish-worshipping in character, and are scarcely, in this respect, of a more elevated type than that of the Congo negro who endows the rocks and trees with higher mental attributes than he claims for himself."

To debunk the Spiritualists fully, Hammond felt that he and other scientists had to do two things: discredit the Spiritualists' claims to clairvoyance, and establish their own scientific definition of the conditions the Spiritualists considered mystical. As far as the latter, Hammond devised his answer to Spiritualism's supernatural trances: he categorized all such phenomena, including catalepsy (rigid trance), ecstasy (fit or trance in which the patient appeared delusional or "transported"), and all types of hysteria, as cerebrospinal disorders, sometimes treatable by a remedy as mundane as bromide of potassium.

Hammond, in company with many nineteenth-century physicians, believed that the spinal cord was the source of countless unexplained physical symptoms. In somnambulism, for example, he hypothesized in an 1869 medical article, "the action of the encephalic ganglia [nerve tissue in the brain] is so materially lessened that the spinal cord becomes able to control and direct the body in its movements." Hammond based this theory partly on observations of decapitated frogs in which it appeared to him that the spinal cord might act with volition or "intellection." Thus, he felt, the spinal cord and sympathetic nervous system were capable of "originating certain kinds of mental influence, which, when the brain is quiescent, may be wonderfully intensified." That was the explanation for the phenomena that people mistakenly took for Spiritualism, Hammond insisted: those stray bits of mental power that could come from the nerves, while appearing to come from some greater source outside the body.

Beard was focusing on placing trance, in particular, firmly in the real, materialist world and establishing it as a way to explore the mind and how it functioned rather than as a way to explore the spirit world. In articles like "Current Delusions Relating to Hypnotism (Artificial Trance)," published in *The Alienist and Neurologist* in 1882, and in his 1881 book *Nature and Phenomena of Trance,* he defined trance not as a mystical separation of body and mind but as a straightforward condition of the nervous system. It was, he wrote, a concentration of nervous force in one direction, which necessarily suspended nervous force in other directions.

Beard presented a real-world analogy for this state: a gas-lit chandelier. When all burners were lighted, that was a normal waking state. When all were turned down low, that was ordinary sleep. When all burners were turned out entirely and permanently, that was death. And when all but one burner were turned out completely, that was trance—"and that one [burner], as often happens, flames all the more brightly from the increased pressure," Beard explained. That flaring burner would account for the hypersensitivity of the senses that he believed was mistaken for Spiritualistic phenomena like mind-reading and clairvoyance.

In "trance seeing," Beard wrote, "the subject sees when the eyes are closed and thoroughly bandaged, by holding the object near to the forehead"—exactly the sort of psychometric skill mentioned by Buchanan, as well as the method used in many successful clairvoyance

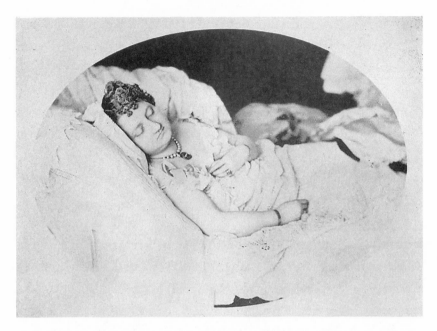

Mollie Fancher, looking remarkably well fed, in a trance in 1887, nine years after the media circus that made her famous. The trance state was a source of argument between scientists and Spiritualists: Was it a physical condition, or a mystical experience? (FROM *MOLLIE FANCHER, THE BROOKLYN ENIGMA*)

tests described by Spiritualists defending their beliefs. Beard accounted for trance seeing with a rationale that strove to be scientific, but in the end sounded as convoluted as one of Buchanan's theories. What happened, according to Beard, was an exaltation of the "general sense" (which he did not define) to such a degree that it filled in for the "special sense" of seeing—all the special senses (presumably the standard five) being but evolutions of this mysterious general sense.

Both Beard and Hammond had a preternaturally modern sensibility about the power of public opinion, especially when it came to Spiritualism, and both used the popular press, not just medical journals, to hammer home their ideas. Their bylines had graced anti-Spiritualist screeds in the *New York Daily Graphic, North American Review, The*

Atlantic Monthly, and other publications. Mollie Fancher, once she was established in the newspapers as a public figure, promised to deliver an even greater audience. She was a ready-made, headline-grabbing fount of publicity, and Hammond and Beard did not hesitate to partake. Hence Beard's skeptical article in *The Medical Record,* portions of which were reprinted in New York papers, about the "medical lessons" of Mollie's case, and, most dramatically, Hammond's public challenge in November 1878 (delivered, naturally, through the newspapers) that her clairvoyance and fasting be tested.

From the Spiritualists' point of view, such challenges could not be ignored. Hammond's and Beard's staunch refusals to believe in Mollie unless her claims were scientifically validated infuriated the Spiritualists—perhaps to some extent because they highlighted the weakest point of their "scientific" theology. The essence of scientific proof is logic and consistency, and the notion that a clairvoyant could sometimes fail defied both. If it is scientifically true that souls live on after death, and that the living are able to contact them, one should presumably be able to put someone into a laboratory situation and measure every blip of the spiritual encounter. And similarly, the encounter should occur predictably, like clockwork—or, to use the analogy many Spiritualists seemed to prefer, like the earth orbiting the sun. Defenders of psychic phenomena grasped at reasons for the unpredictability of clairvoyance—that it couldn't happen under pressure, for instance, or when being performed for personal gain. But they must have known that that failure was a central flaw, a point of entry for doubters.

The next Spiritualist to spring to Mollie's defense brought to the knotty problem of proving the unprovable the most impressive intellectual credentials yet to grace that side—and a wicked wit to boot. When the controversy over her case came to dominate the New York newspapers at the end of 1878, Epes Sargent was living in Boston, near where his family had been based for six generations. His bloodlines

could be traced directly back to William Sargent, who had received a grant of land in Gloucester, Massachusetts, in 1678; his ancestors included the early colonial governors John Winthrop and Joseph Dudley. Sargent showed an affinity for language and poetry at a young age, and by his teen years he was contributing to the *Literary Journal* at Boston Latin School. He went on to be a sometime newspaperman and magazine journalist and essayist, as well as a playwright and poet, and became a household name in the 1860s for writing several series of school readers. In his fifties Sargent began to explore Spiritualism, and he applied his formidable philosophical and literary skills to spreading its gospel. By the time of his defense of Mollie Fancher, he had published two books on Spiritualism, and he would write another, *The Scientific Basis of Spiritualism,* before his death in 1880.

Sargent was a combatant worthy of Hammond and Beard, both in brainpower and in audacity. On December 23, 1878, he wrote an intricately argued letter to the editor of *The Sun,* which ran to two and a half columns. He plucked out and quoted Beard's most inflammatory and personal statement against Mollie: his claim that "unsought-for evidence" had been brought to him that she lied and used trickery. Beard, Sargent implied, was hiding behind his pronouncements about science in order to publish what amounted to libel against a lady prostrated by disease. Sargent illustrated his contention by translating Beard's statement into libel against an anonymous "Dr. Blank," presumably a stand-in for Beard himself: "It is very much as if one were to publish a paragraph like this. 'Unsought-for evidence has been brought me from various quarters, by most honorable and trustworthy persons, that Dr. Blank is a forger, a thief and a murderer.' "

Beard had emphasized the importance of expertise in determining the validity of Fancher's claims, and in his letter, Sargent launched into an exploration of what made an expert or a non-expert, and what distinguished deductive from inductive reasoning. In the process he exposed Beard's essential tautology: that he was right because he was right, and smart into the bargain. "Having claimed that in the whole world at this time there are only seven or eight experts of the kind needed [to prove or disprove Mollie's gifts]," Sargent wrote, "he gives us very clearly to infer that Dr. Beard is one of those seven or eight highly gifted persons, nay, the very Corypheus of the band." But what was his expertness based upon? Sargent asked. "On his estimate of his own remarkable cleverness at 'deductive reasoning.' Great as a physician, it seems he is greater as a metaphysician."

Sargent's analysis got at the heart of the general public's lurking mistrust of the new and rapid ascendance of science, a mistrust that facilitated belief in Spiritualism—and in Mollie's abilities. The scientific establishment, after all, had not always been infallible, or wise, or openminded; it had often ignored what seemed improbable or upsetting. Its mistakes offered an excuse to explore other belief systems. "Deductive reasoning may err, as well as intuitive judgment," Sargent wrote. "It was deductive reasoning that led Bacon, Melanchthon, Luther and other learned men to reject the Copernican system. Deductive reasoning opposed the introduction of gas, the system of cheap postage and ocean steamship navigation. . . . It has stood in the way of many great inventions and wise reforms."

Beard's emphasis on experts touched an emotional core of resistance that still exists today, manifested for example by the growing popularity of alternative medical treatments that are scorned by mainstream, and expert, physicians. People are inclined to believe the evidence before their eyes, and Beard mocked that belief. Most people also instinctively resist being thought of as chemical formulas or mere machines, a favorite formulation of Victorian physicians. Scientists such as Hammond and Beard were thrilled to be finding what appeared to be the measurable, biological keys to finally unlock the mysteries of human illness and dysfunction; the average nineteenth-century citizen was less convinced that everything about a human being could be explained biologically. Sargent expressed this skepticism with dry irony when he wrote: "Thought is now merely a product of the movement of certain kaleidoscopic molecules in the brain. And if I think differently from Dr. Beard he must not blame me, since it is merely because the molecules in my brain get disposed, or shaken up, differently from those of his own."

Human testimony (such as anecdotes about Mollie Fancher's fasting and her clairvoyant sight of distant happenings) was, in Beard's view, simply the result of a physical event in the human brain, a product that could be studied only by physicians devoted to understanding how the brain worked; philosophers, theologians, and other thinkers could have no legitimate part to play in judging it. Sargent ruthlessly used Beard's logic against him. If only brain experts were capable of judging evidence reliably, then all kinds of other evidence and philosophies might be discarded—those minor brain-events from Aristotle, Locke, Hume, Kant, Hegel, and so on. Those must be displaced as rubbish, "to make room for the writings of Drs. Beard and Hammond!"

And why stop there? If Beard was such an expert in judging products of the human brain, why should he not judge other products as well, and for the same reason? Why could he not lay down for everyone laws of taste in poetry, painting, music, and general literature? Were they not all, equally with human testimony, products of the human brain, and did not their scientific study belong to one who devoted himself to the study of the human brain in health and disease? Beard's claims and beliefs, Sargent implied, rested on a view of himself as a scientific sun around which other, lesser minds orbited.

By the end of his lengthy letter, Sargent had wound himself up to a pitch of personal antagonism toward Hammond and especially Beard that matched anything those two doctors had meted out. His choice of words was scorching: "Unless the Fancher case is overturned by something very different from the impotent and unscientific antagonism of Dr. Beard, its well attested facts must be a valuable contribution to the enlarged science of psychology."

Despite Sargent's elegant and pointed arguments, however, which ran oratorical and syllogistic circles around Beard's and Hammond's pronouncements, and despite his description of numerous incidents of demonstrated clairvoyance as "testimony," he was left with the same old problem. Why couldn't Mollie's genuineness be put to the test? Sargent's only defense was to point out how fundamentally unamenable clairvoyance was to the rules of the scientific method. "You might as well expect the needle to point true while you are agitating the compass as expect to elicit clairvoyance under the stress and excitement of an anxious motive," he contended, "or under the disturbance produced by the simple presence of an uncongenial person, aggressively disposed."

To the modern eye, Mollie's reluctance to subject herself to testing seems obvious: she had nothing to gain from submitting to a test of either her second sight or her fasting. If she were indeed as uninterested in publicity as she claimed, why should she bother to prove herself to people whose opinions were meaningless to her? In any case, even if she succeeded in demonstrating clairvoyance, there would still be people who remained unconvinced. And if she failed, the phenomenon of Mollie Fancher would be over—she would be branded a deliberate fraud. To test the fasting instead of the clairvoyance would be not only humiliating but excruciating as well. No matter what Mollie's level of denial in terms of her eating, some part of her must have recognized that she would first go through a hell of starvation, then inevitably be exposed.

What neither Sargent nor his opponents knew was that the question of clairvoyance and its credibility would be the least significant or lasting effect of Mollie Fancher's case, and of Spiritualism in general. Neurologists such as Beard and Hammond, and Spiritualists such as Sargent were focused on understanding the workings of the mind—in effect trying to redefine psychology, which we now know as the study of the mind and its various emotions, impulses, drives, and desires.

The two factions were simply tackling the problem of psychology from opposite corners. While neurologists were determined to define mental states as completely subject to the physical condition, Spiritualists and early psychical researchers rejected the materialist approach and concentrated solely on the workings of the mind, which they preferred to think of as the soul, in its various states of consciousness. In a sense, both sides would eventually win.

In the late nineteenth century, Spiritualists, philosophers, scientists, and "psychometrists" alike discussed with utter earnestness the properties and the meaning of the soul. Did it exist, how was it distinguished from the body or mind, did it survive after death? These questions were drawing-room material, not to mention the subject of books, articles, and public lectures. Fascination with the soul was a driving force in Mollie's fame, in the 1870s and later, in the early 1890s, when Abram Dailey wrote the story of her life.

Dailey, who was himself not a clergyman but a surrogate court judge, gave as his purpose in writing *Mollie Fancher, the Brooklyn Enigma* the possibility that "new lessons will be learned of the strange and mystic relations of mind and soul to the houses we live in—these bodies of ours." On page three of his book, Dailey outlined the conundrums of the soul that his fellow citizens were struggling with in what he called "the most remarkable era of human existence," and that he felt Mollie's story might help to elucidate: "Why we think, and how we think, involves mysterious operations of our minds imperfectly understood in any respect. Who has been able to tell us what is the mind, and what is its relation to the soul? Do they exist conjointly, or are they separate forces and powers, but having relations to each other? . . . Has the soul a particular place where it abides, until released or forced out by some destructive event, or disarrangement of the mechanism so strangely placed and operating within?"

Mankind had, of course, speculated and theorized about the soul and its possible immortality in a sacred and spiritual context for eons. But this public and often secular inquiry was a new development, brought about, in large part, by the shattering effect of the scientific revelations of Charles Darwin. Although there were other world-shaking ideas and philosophies on the rise, nothing approached Darwin's theory of natural selection in its ability to induce a society-wide identity crisis. The Harvard biologist Ernst Mayr wrote of *On the Origin of Species,* Darwin's first presentation of his ideas, that it "ushered in a new era in our thinking about the nature of man. The intellectual revolution it caused and the impact it had on man's concept of himself and the world were greater than those caused by the works of Copernicus, Newton, and the great physicists of more recent times." Darwin's ideas necessitated not only a scientific rethinking but a very personal questioning of man's role in nature.

Darwin himself was almost horrified by the ideas he introduced to the world. It took him twenty years to produce his *Origin of Species,* twenty years in which he suffered many afflictions that appeared hypochondriacal in nature and that slowed his work considerably. Darwin's list of symptoms sounds much like Beard's outline of neurasthenia: fatigue and languorousness that at times kept him in bed, trembling, swimming in the head, boils on the skin, vomiting, depression, a general feeling of being unwell. His physical and emotional state was tied closely to those around him; he often suffered breakdowns toward the end of his beloved wife's many pregnancies, and his own health deteriorated along with that of his dying father. Darwin attempted several treatments of the time, including electricity and a water cure at a sanatorium—an unpleasant regimen of cold-water scrubs, cold foot-baths, and cold compresses worn all day long. Nothing produced a permanent remission, and biographers have suggested that a precipitating factor in Darwin's ailments was his almost existential anxiety about the implications of his work.

Darwin was a perfectionist, who could easily have kept working on his sprawling manuscript a few more decades before publishing it. But another scientist, Alfred Russel Wallace, had come to the concept of survival of the fittest independently, and was about to publish his own strikingly similar theory of evolution. Spurred by competitive and proprietary fervor, Darwin boiled his work down to a reasonable book length. *On the Origin of Species* was published by John Murray of Albemarle Street, London, on November 24, 1859. Rumors of its publication and its shocking ideas had leaked out, and the first edition of 1,250 copies sold out that very day.

The public reaction was immediate and powerful. Most people had a hard time with the idea of apelike ancestors, and newspapers and magazines delighted in running cartoons of long-tailed monkeys sitting in trees, their monkey heads replaced with Darwin's heavy-browed, balding head. If Darwin's ideas were true, they destroyed the basis of the Bible's presentation of human history, of a universe only a few thousand years old, and of man and woman—and the rest of the natural world—created whole and immutable in one weeklong burst of godly genius. But in fact, Darwin had tried hard to keep God in the picture even as he outlined the ruthless system of survival of the fittest. Near the end of his book he spoke of natural selection as "the laws impressed on matter by the Creator," and he concluded by musing on the "grandeur in this view of life, with its several powers, having been originally breathed into a few forms or into one"—phrasing that implied a deity-like force breathing life into being.

No one was fooled. Something about Darwin's theory powerfully suggested a godless universe. The idea of evolution had been bouncing around for much of the nineteenth century, but it was the concept of natural selection that raised searing doubts in the minds of Victorian readers. Before Darwin, the religious view of the world had posited some sort of design in nature, and if there was a design, there also existed some sort of purpose and a designer, namely God. Evolution could be part of the grand design. But natural selection, with its paradigm of strength always conquering weakness, did away with any need for a personal director or creator or loving presence; it simply rolled on its way, impersonal, perhaps even meaningless. Darwin's theories raised the prospect of a frightening void, a chasm of empty, random existence. His was a picture not of the meek inheriting the earth—the essence of Christian belief in justice, forgiveness, and love for one's fellow man—but of the strongest, and perhaps most brutal, triumphing over the weak in an amoral universe.

A decade or two did bring some perspective. By the time Mollie Fancher's case put questions of the soul on the front page of New York newspapers, philosophers were more calmly sorting out and theorizing over some of the vexing questions raised by ideas of evolution and natural selection. In "Darwinism and Divinity," an article published in *The Popular Science Monthly* in 1872, the British philosopher and critic Leslie Stephen (father of Virginia Woolf) described theologians' gradual coming to terms with at least the outlines of Darwin's ideas. Stephen's reassuring thesis was this: Darwinism would change religion, but not destroy it or produce the moral chaos some critics feared, because mankind had inherent spiritual needs that would not disappear.

Yet he acknowledged that Darwinian thought raised interesting questions about the nature of the soul. "Does not the new theory," Stephen wrote, "make it difficult to believe in immortal souls?" Here he got into points that, while perhaps absurd to modern minds, were seriously troubling and perplexing to Victorian ones: Do animals have souls? Does an elephant have a soul? Does a dog? How about a monkey? If we believe that the difference between men and apes is only of degree, of time and evolution, he posited, "can we continue to hold that monkeys will disappear at their death like a bubble, and that men will rise from their ashes?"

Stephen foresaw the same future for the soul that he did for religion in general—namely, that new scientific ideas such as Darwinism would alter how humans defined the nature of the soul, but could never destroy a belief in its existence. Stephen's argument for continuing to trust in the reality of the soul came to rest, in the end, on simple, almost blind, faith—perhaps not too surprising an attitude to find in an Anglican priest, as Stephen was at the time (he renounced his ordination three years later, and declared himself an agnostic). Just keep believing, he seemed to say, because you know in your gut that mankind has an ineffable spiritual essence. "Whatever reasons may be drawn from our consciousness," he urged, "for the belief that man is not merely a cunning bit of chemistry—a product of so much oxygen, hydrogen, and carbon—must remain in full force."

Here he hit on the deepest fear underlying much Victorian hand-wringing about the nature, existence, and immortality of the soul—the kind of fear that prompted such excitement and furor over a case like Mollie Fancher's. Again and again, thinkers in the second half of the nineteenth century brought up a painful question: Are human personality and individuality merely a matter of how particular molecules and chemicals have been arranged? Is that all the essence we have? Does the "soul" boil down to a chemical formula?

Elizabeth Stuart Phelps, in attempting to explain the appeal of Spiritualism in an age of science, wrote in 1886: "We learned that we were not men, but protoplasm. We learned that we were not spirits, but chemical combinations. We learned that the Drama of Hamlet and the Ode to Immortality were secretions of the gray matter of the brain. We learned that guilt was nothing but the law of heredity. We learned that one's prehistoric amoeba (if anybody) should be blamed for one's private vices." Her ideas echo Epes Sargent's sardonic comment that thought is merely the movement of molecules in the brain, and differences of opinion merely the result of those molecules' being shaken up differently.

These concepts were upsetting, to say the least, and many people searched for other philosophies that would help them cope with the new images of the universe that science was unveiling. This era of great scientific progress saw the rise of several new religions: not only Spiritualism, but Mormonism and Christian Science as well. The intense anxiety Victorians were experiencing about where science would take humankind, emotionally and spiritually—the fear of being merely a "cunning bit of chemistry"—was, in Leslie Stephen's view, "the penalty we pay for progress." The realization that there would be such a high price of admission to the modern age was painful, especially so because most people had believed that scientific progress would demand no spiritual cost at all. In fact, it had been widely thought that science would prove to strengthen religion rather than destroy it.

Living as we do in a culture that seems in many ways profoundly secular (despite the traditions of "In God We Trust" and "God Bless America"), it's easy to forget that in the nineteenth century almost everything was viewed through a religious lens. This held true despite the damning philosophical proclamations of revolutionaries such as Engels and Marx (among the latter's most famous words were written when he was twenty-five, in 1844: "Religion is the sigh of the oppressed creature, the heart of a heartless world, and the soul of soulless conditions. It is the opium of the people"). Even those who were beginning to doubt, who had been infected with some of the relentless questioning of eighteenth-century philosophers including Hume and Kant, clung on an instinctual level to the assumption, or the hope, of a God in the universe.

Kant, Hume, and other thinkers established the theoretical base later built on by such scientists as Darwin and his friend and inspiration, Charles Lyell (author of *Principles of Geology,* which advanced the concept that the earth was far more ancient than anyone had imagined). Kant and Hume asked the unanswerable: How do we know there is a God? Could humans have made all this up merely to feel better about their lives, and to comfort themselves with a conviction that there actually is order and meaning in the universe? Perhaps, suggested Hume, "matter may contain the source, or spring, of order originally, within itself, as well as the mind does," rather than spring from a larger intelligence like God. Who could prove otherwise?

Hume's frightening idea of humans adrift in a lonely, purposeless universe whose rules they had to divine on their own was written eighty years before Darwin's *Origin of Species* appeared. But its logical and disturbing guesswork was prophetic; it laid the foundation, writes A. N. Wilson, "for the devastations caused in the Victorian Age by 'science.'" Hume's disquieting thoughts, adds Wilson, which removed "any philosophical *necessity* for believing in God," lacked just two elements: any physical, evidentiary backup, and a large audience. A small, educated class read Hume, Kant, and other philosophers; when Darwin and other scientists supplied the missing physical evidence in the next century, their ideas were debated in popular magazines and discussed at the dinner table by members of a much larger, educated middle class.

The "devastations" wrought by science sneaked up on Victorians, in part because science and religion had been, until this time, fairly inseparable; they had shared the same universe. So, for instance, Mollie Fancher's defenders felt no sense of contradiction in stating, as did Professor Buchanan, that her soul could be "an object of scientific investigation"; or in urging, as did Professor West, that a "commission of the scientific men of the country" look into her miraculous fasting and clairvoyance so that "the entire scientific world should know all about her."

Science would, it was believed, through diligent investigation of what had always been merely theoretical hunches, pinpoint where and what the soul was, and prove the reality of God's design; it offered, in other words, a real hope for revealing the meaning of life itself. At mid-century, writes the psychologist Edward Reed, "to be pro-science was most assuredly not to be antireligious or to denigrate religion in any way." And among all the sciences, psychology ruled, because in the mid–nineteenth century it was still defined as the "science of the soul." The human animal was envisioned as a microcosm of the universe, with the soul as its organizing agent. The soul was the metaphorical

God of each individual human, its grand designer holding together all sensations and ideas, the essence that breathed immortal life into its being. Psychology was the study of that essence; there was something almost divine about its mission.

But slowly, over the course of the nineteenth century, that definition of psychology was transformed. It came to be less about the spiritual mysteries of the soul (which, when solved, would reveal God and His design), and more about a secular world of the mind, of mental illness and treatment—a change of identity and intent that went far beyond semantics. Neurologists such as Hammond and Beard illuminated a step along the path to that new psychology, although, true to form, they both felt they were shining a light on the final and correct interpretation.

What the neurologists did was to take psychology out of the realm of the soul and define it in secular terms—but then they planted it firmly in the body. Beard's pithy definition of psychology was "physiology out of sight": anything happening in the mind, including trances and hysteria, was the result of changes in the state of the body. Hammond too saw psychology as so fundamentally physical that "as long as psychology was expounded by teachers who had never even seen a human brain, much less a spinal-cord or sympathetic nerve, who knew absolutely nothing of nervous physiology . . . it was not to be expected that the true science of mind could make much progress."

Rooted though they were in their materialist philosophy, Hammond and Beard and their late-nineteenth-century colleagues began to venture into territory that would be fully explored and claimed by the thinkers who followed them. Beard in particular, with his gift for peering inside the American psyche, toward the end of his abbreviated career edged closer to the modern concept of psychology. One historian has offered as the general twentieth-century view of Beard that he was "a pioneer in the study of the neuroses, a forerunner of Freud and modern psychological medicine." As a doctor in the 1890s, Freud had indeed studied and admired Beard's ideas about the connection between neurosis and the stresses of modern life, leading some scholars to speculate about the debt that Freud's *Civilization and Its Discontents* may owe to Beard's American Nervousness theory.

In a larger sense, what the physically based neurologists shared with the psychological thinkers who came after was the basic and secular idea that the human mind was something that could be studied, controlled, treated, even cured—by experts. Rather than about understanding divinity or the meaning of life, modern psychology was (and is) about understanding and treating individuals, allowing them to master their own lives, to become, in a manner of speaking, their own divinities. The way of the future was reflected in the name that graced Freud's newly defined specialty: psychiatry. Psychiatrists would not just study and demystify the mind, as psychologists did, but would, as clinical doctors, devote their careers to treating the emotional and behavioral maladies that arose from the disordered mind.

Oddly, during this crucial period of flux, the Spiritualists, though still hewing to the old-fashioned definition of psychology as the study of the soul, unwittingly came closer to one central Freudian idea than did materialist neurologists such as Hammond. The "supernormal" powers of the mind that Spiritualists and psychic researchers were striving to understand (the ability to vanish into a trance or amnesiac "other state," for example) were effectively the same mental terrain that Freud was exploring in the 1890s—terrain he called the unconscious. Epes Sargent referred to this mental territory when he claimed that Mollie Fancher's case would be a valuable addition to the "enlarged science of psychology." Freud and the Spiritualists shared a conviction that the answer to the mind's mysteries would be found in the depths of the mind itself, not in the mechanics of the body.

When the new psychology ceased to be about the soul, it forecast the collapse of any hope that science and religion would have the same end point; their estrangement persists to this day. When Mollie Fancher's story prompted renewed speculation about the survival of the soul, it was already starting to seem like the last gasp, the beginning of the end. One could believe either that Fancher was a psychological case-study of a sick mind, or that she was a living soul beyond natural laws, a proof of immortality and a spirit life beyond. In Mollie's case, as in the world evolving outside her bedroom, it appeared—Spiritualists' hopes notwithstanding—that science and religion could no longer occupy a common ground.

CHAPTER NINE

"A Mystery to This Day"

Medical theories as to body tissue and the food necessary to sustain it are trembling in the balance.

—*The New York Times,* July 10, 1880

THE LAST NIGHT OF 1878 was calm and clear, with no breath yet of the biting Arctic storm that would reach New York and Brooklyn the next day. As winds and snow accelerated toward the East Coast, however, it appeared to those within the Fancher household that their personal storm might at last be about to pass. William Hammond's public challenge to Mollie would expire at midnight, and her answer, of course, remained a definitive no. Hammond would claim victory, but without Mollie's overt and demonstrable failure at either fasting or clairvoyance, the outcome was more of a draw.

The most recent newspaper articles had been in Mollie's corner: Epes Sargent's defense, Joseph Buchanan's rationales, even unexpected support from Andrew Jackson Davis, the éminence grise of Spiritualism. Davis, known as "The Poughkeepsie Seer," was famous as a self-proclaimed prophet and the author of more than thirty books on the nature of Spiritualism. Sought out by a New York *Sun* reporter at his home in New Jersey for commentary on Mollie's case, he gave a long interview that was published on December 30. In it, he stated that

Mollie's fast most likely involved "nerve and cellular tissue feeding, which makes the use of food by mastication almost entirely unnecessary." Davis deemed the condition that had been claimed for her "not only possible, but even probable," and said he firmly believed that "Miss Fancher is on the borderland of the other world very many times."

Mollie was said to be an avid reader (in her peculiar, blind-but-seeing method), not just of books but of newspapers as well. It's easy to imagine that on December 31, 1878, friends called at 160 Gates Avenue to wish her the best for the New Year, and that recent newspaper articles may have provided subjects for discussion. Despite Mollie's reported aversion to publicity, she was quite sociable, welcoming the regular visits of her devoted intimate friends as well as hundreds of curious strangers—men and women alike, whom Abram Dailey described as "distinguished in the various arts, sciences, and learned professions; as well as in the financial, commercial and social world."

Visits to her bedside could be gay and were often invested with drama—a cross between an interview with a delicate celebrity and an audience with the oracle at Delphi. The set never varied. Mollie lay back, day and night, in the bed she had occupied since the horsecar accident in 1865. The coverlet and pillows, in classic Victorian style, were white linen, edged with elaborate lace, supplemented with filigreed antimacassars, bolsters, and throw pillows. Her nightgowns were usually white or pastel, and were designed and embroidered by Mollie herself. She loved pets; there were usually one or two birds hopping and singing in cages, and she had a cat she named Sarah Bernhardt. Like most middle-class rooms of the nineteenth century, her bedchamber was overfilled. Every surface was covered with bric-a-brac, every stool and table draped with fringed cloth.

Next to her bed were two pieces of furniture suited to Mollie's invalid state. One was a low chair with a side arm, and a seat that could be lifted to reveal a compartment underneath. This was the usual visitor's seat; it also held books and papers Mollie could reach without help. Against the wall was a specially designed combination bureau-and-cabinet, with curtained shelves instead of drawers, and a canopied top that served as a decorative storage area for her various implements and sewing materials. The unoccupied side of her bed was a space for writing, needlework, or waxwork. The room was Mollie's little kingdom, her Proustian refuge. One visitor called it "both prison-house and shrine."

From this shrine Mollie held court, often displaying an assertive sense of humor surprising in one whose entire adult life had been spent in one room. A male friend who considered himself a wit once attempted to tease her about her second sight and spiritual visitations.

"When you are away on any of your occult perambulations, do you ever come across *me*?" he asked.

"Oh yes, frequently!" Mollie replied.

"Well, that's interesting," he said. "Do you ever see anybody around me?"

"Very often," Mollie told him.

"Indeed! Can you give me any idea what they look like?"

"Creditors," Mollie shot back.

Mollie Fancher may not have minded being a celebrity quite as much as she protested. One close friend, Sarah Townsend, who took care of her when Aunt Susan was away, told of fending off an agent from P. T. Barnum's circus. Having read of Mollie's fasting and clair-voyance, he came hoping to convince her to exhibit herself in one of Barnum's sideshows. Townsend met him on the doorstep and wouldn't let him set foot inside the house. "I talked to the agent at the street door," she recounted later, "and felt very indignant and angry." When she finally shut the door on him and went upstairs, Mollie reported that she had "heard," clairvoyantly, the entire conversation. And she was not angry, but laughing. "Just think of it!" she said. "Imagine me exhibiting myself for twenty-five cents. I am glad you were so firm with him. Had you not been here he would have certainly got in somehow or other."

Sarah's husband, Thomas, told an equally revealing story. On one occasion Mollie's reaction to pain was tested by applying heat to her skin. Not only did she apparently not feel it, but her skin did not even redden or burn. When asked by one doctor to what she attributed the oddities of her existence, Mollie laughed and replied, "I don't know what they can base my complaint upon. I have broken the backbone of science and all the 'ologies!"

In her own private way, without ever admitting a newspaper reporter into her presence, Mollie may have been just as stubborn and proud as Hammond or Beard or Sargent or Buchanan about the meaning, and the interpretation, of her experiences. Her response to the doctor reveals her understanding of how much was riding on her case—that it might well have the power to change how others thought about new scientific assumptions. It also suggests a certain delight in that power. There is a hint of gloating, of taunting, in her jaunty abbreviation " 'ologies"—one might just throw psychology and neurology and theology and what have you into one big grab-bag and shake them into submission. Mollie's statement about breaking the backbone of science, made several years before her 1878 celebrity, presages Beard's angry, almost bitter pronouncement that if her story was true, "then all science goes for naught." Mollie recognized as well as did Beard and his cohorts that her claims held a particular resonance.

The flipside of Mollie's egoism and teasing wit was her occasional gloominess—especially, as she explained to one visitor, when the day was gray and rainy. "No person has gone through so much suffering with greater patience and resignation than Miss Fancher," wrote Abram Dailey. "It is not wonderful that at times she is depressed." She could easily be brought to tears while speaking of her pains, and of her loved ones who had died, whom she could see only in her spiritual wanderings. Mollie often mentioned her mother as the one named person with whom she conversed in the spirit life. Again and again she described viscerally and longingly what small comfort it was to see her mother and friends in the noncorporeal spirit world. "I want to feel the material touch of their hands," she told Dailey, "to hear their voices, and experience the impression of their kiss upon my lips as of yore." It is possible to hear the yearning of the eight-year-old for her lost mother in the words of the adult and invalid Mollie.

That last evening of 1878 may have provided some solace for the Mollie who felt afflicted and bereft. She was likely joined by friends who drank a cup of tea or glass of sherry to toast the New Year—friends who could share her delight, as Hammond's challenge expired, in having proved the 'ologies wrong. While the temperature fell outside, and bells rang out, and the snows headed down out of the Arctic, Mollie felt safe and protected in her cocoon.

Then, as now, New Year's Eve was a night for parties and celebration, even rowdiness. At the stroke of midnight churches chimed, steam whistles shrieked, and the streets were full of revelers who welcomed 1879 in different styles. *The Brooklyn Daily Eagle* described "pious Methodists . . . thoughtfully pursuing their homeward ways from solemn watch meetings," in which the turn of the year was celebrated with prayers and sermons. "Gay and festive youths, uproarious in their mirth," made the avenues echo. And for the upper crust, it was a night of grand galas. Some three hundred couples attended the sixth annual ball of the James C. Gallagher Association at the Assembly Rooms on Washington Street, in a gallery decorated with flags and bunting. At the same time, the Eagle Association ball was taking place in Gallatin Hall on Fulton Street, and members of the Welcome Social entertained their friends at a dance at Stella Hall on Bedford Avenue, in a ballroom decorated with flags and evergreens. The Daughters of Israel held their fifth annual fête at Novelty Hall on Fulton Street.

The parties and revelry were a prelude to the true focus of celebrations in New York: what one paper called the "good old Knicker-bocker custom" of making social calls on New Year's Day. Up and down Gates Avenue, and every other street of Brooklyn, families—modest and prominent alike—opened their doors to callers. Men donned their silk hats and gloves, women their best bonnets, to stroll and drop in on friends. Visiting hours began as early as nine or ten in the morning and continued into the evening. Such popular figures as the charismatic minister Henry Ward Beecher, whose door held a sign reading "Enter Without Ringing" from eleven a.m. to six p.m., received hundreds of callers (Beecher's count for January 1 of that year was 1,139). His wife helped him welcome guests, wearing what the *Eagle* judged "a tasteful costume of dark purple silk, trimmed with lace, and a lace headdress of very becoming style."

The following day, *The Brooklyn Daily Times* reported on unfortunate fallout from the Knickerbocker custom. "Her Last Call" told readers about Mrs. Nancy Collins, aged seventy-five, who paid a New Year's visit to her friend Mrs. Wood. A few minutes into the visit she fell forward from her chair, and died—from natural causes, it was assumed. And in "One Call Too Many," the paper gave three times as much space to the unsavory case of Edward and Lizzie Heins. Mr. Heins became angry with his wife when he had to go looking for her on New Year's Day at the houses of her friends; he found her at 199 Washington Street, too drunk to stand up. When he tried to drag her home, Mrs. Heins hit him on the the head with an umbrella. He finally prevailed, and when they got home he "threw her around a little to keep her quiet" (his words). Her version, the paper said, was that he "kicked and beat her, and abused her most terribly."

By January 2, the storm had arrived in earnest, delighting the men whose livelihood came from cutting ice in the frozen rivers and selling it to restaurants and brewers, but distressing most other merchants and businessmen. The combination of wind-driven snow and frigid temperatures, as low as three degrees below zero, brought railroad travel to a virtual standstill. Trains out of Buffalo were stopped by snowdrifts of six to eight feet. When the storm reached New York City, and water froze overnight in the pipes of train steam engines, service on the elevated was slowed and complaints were heard from commuters accustomed to the convenience of the new rapid transit.

The East River ferries continued to run, however, helped by the rapid current, which kept chunks of floating ice from accumulating into a solid, impassable block. Dockings were dodgy, as the ferries fought the winds and the ice floes that gathered in the relatively calm waters of the slips. The Brooklyn Bridge, partially built, would begin to take over for the ferries when it opened in 1883, but in 1879 it towered uselessly over a portion of the river. On January 3 and 4, the whistling of fierce winds through the network of the bridge produced a strange, discordant music. The wind ripped down telegraph wires strung throughout the city, disrupting a method of communication that had recently and quickly become a necessity of business life. Partly as a result of storms like this, Western Union within a few years buried its lines under the streets.

As Brooklyn residents sat in their homes, sequestered by the weather, they had plenty to gossip about. The New Year brought fresh fashion reports, to the effect that this year's fans would be of brocade, to match the latest style in dress material; gilded combs and shoe buckles were projected to be the rage. A mania for Scotch plaid was spreading, and gentlemen's neckties and handkerchiefs were being made in silk tartans. If a lady wanted to carry an up-to-date muff in the winter of 1879, it had to be of medium size, and finished without tassels or bows at the ends. The fashionable kid gloves for full dress reached to the elbow, demanded exactly nine buttons, and were finished with a pleating of Breton lace.

On a more serious note, a debate about rapid transit in Brooklyn, specifically elevated trains, was in full swing. Almost everyone was in agreement that rapid transit was a dire necessity in the fast-growing city—especially given the success of trains in Manhattan. When the Brooklyn City Railroad Company switched in 1858 from omnibuses pulled by horses to horsecars that ran on tracks, the cars carried more than 7.7 million passengers per year. By 1878, that one company alone carried 20 million per year—and with the other horsecar companies the total number of passengers was at least four times that figure. Yet neither residents nor tradesmen wanted the elevated trains to run down their own street. Merchants especially worried that the elevated would slow their trade, because it was noisy and would obscure storefronts, and because it would whisk local customers into Manhattan to do their shopping. Myrtle Avenue residents thought the trains would be just fine on Atlantic Avenue; Fulton Street people agreed. Many thought no decision should be made until the Brooklyn Bridge was finished.

There was also great excitement over the thirty-one-year-old Thomas Edison, who had become world-renowned more than a year before by inventing the phonograph (whereby, gushed the London *Times,* "articulate speech can be stored up for an unlimited period and given forth at any time at the will of the possessor"). Now Edison was claiming to be moments away from producing an electric incandescent light that could be used indoors, in homes and businesses. Inventors had been toying with electric lighting for decades, but had come no closer than the so-called arc light, which produced a light so blinding it was suitable only for such grand spaces as streets, public halls, and large stores. Near the end of 1878, Edison said he had solved the problems of dividing the electrical current and transmitting electricity over distance, and that within weeks he would be able to demonstrate his new system: underground wires would bring electricity into buildings, where existing gas burners and chandeliers would be used as fixtures for electric lights, which would be not only bright but inexpensive.

Edison's invention would not be complete until the end of 1879, but the prospect itself was breathtaking. The gas companies, predictably, were horrified as their stocks fell and their future hung in the balance, and in January 1879, as the world waited for Edison's first lamp, officers of gas companies spoke out. Burr Wakeman, president of the Harlem Gaslight Company, proclaimed that the highest scientific authorities had found, in their own experiments, that electric light for use in both houses and retail spaces was "not practicable. For great spaces in the open air and for vast interiors, it is, of course, very serviceable, but there its usefulness must stop." Some worried that the powerful lights might be "very trying to the eyes," perhaps causing cataracts or other serious damage.

While Brooklyn buzzed about Edison, residents might also have indulged in discussing the offbeat and the shocking. There was the story of the St. Benoit Twins, one-year-olds who were separate individuals above the waist and one female child below. One could sleep while the other was awake; one liked sweet things, the other sour. The *Eagle* called the Siamese twins alternately "they" and "it," and explained: "Let the reader notice that the plural and singular are badly mixed, but when nature takes it into her head to produce such an anomalous being, even the rules of grammar must give way."

For the truly shocking rather than freakish, nothing beat the case of Kate Cobb. The story of her trial became the next Mollie Fancher–style event—an unfolding drama that demanded daily newspaper coverage, editorials, and letters to the editor. In the way of all media stories, Mollie's had, for the moment, played itself out. Mollie would rise again, but in early 1879 it was Kate Cobb's turn.

The trial of Cobb and her alleged lover, Wesley Bishop, for the murder of her husband and his wife, began on December 31 in Norwich, Connecticut. The story of their crime had it all: illicit passion, local scandal, death by poisoning, and finally, betrayal of each other. The Cobbs and the Bishops had been friends together, though Wesley Bishop, a grocer's clerk, was a step or two lower on the social scale. After his wife died, in what was presumed a natural death, Wesley and Kate were seen to be openly friendly—too friendly. Neighbors remarked on their daily visits to each other, their exchanging of notes; the lovers were anything but discreet. Then Mr. Cobb died, and a post-mortem was performed. It found enough arsenic in his sytem to have killed him twenty times over. Mrs. Bishop's body was exhumed and found also to be infused with arsenic.

Wesley Bishop now showed his true character: he claimed that everything had been Kate Cobb's idea, that she had planned the murders. She scornfully denied the charges, and pleaded innocent. The public was transfixed with one question above all: What did an educated, high-toned woman like Kate Cobb see in a lower-class weakling like Bishop? For the newspapers it was a psychological puzzle, a case study of human impulses. The story, editorialized the *Eagle,* "exemplifies the strength of the unnatural passion that a woman of powerful intellect can have for a weak, uneducated man." Kate Cobb was so "bright, spirited and handsome, and the man for whom she braved so much and sinned so greatly is a creature so cowardly and weak" that their inequality protected them from a public assignment of guilt: most people who knew of them couldn't believe there was anything indecent between them.

Attempting to dress up sensationalism in a proper wrapping, the *Eagle* stated that "the story is worth the telling only in that it illustrates once more the mighty power of that form of insanity known as love. For its sake, this wife and mother willfully played the part of paramour and then became a murderess." The tale could almost qualify as an academic exercise in the new field of psychology, according to the paper. Its editorial closed with an oblique reference to the Mollie Fancher case: "Experts who are noting the phenomen[on] of mind reading and giving explanation of the clairvoyant power would do well to exercise their knowledge in the case of this woman [Cobb] and tell us what condition of mind she was in when she deliberately murdered her husband and forgot her children for the sake of a man who had killed his wife in order to possess himself of her."

The trial was riveting. Newspaper descriptions were not only phys-ically detailed but filled with emotion—especially when the newspaper involved was *The Sun*. As Wesley Bishop took the stand on January 7, wrote a reporter, he "turned his cold and chalky-hued face" toward the judge. Mrs. Cobb then came in on the arm of a jailer: "Her long black veil nearly swept the floor. She took her accustomed seat and fixed her piercing black eyes, with an expression of bitter and revengeful ani-mosity, on the face of the witness." A few more days into the trial, ac-cording to *The Sun,* the question on everyone's lips was, "Will they hang her?" The paper's opinion: "The prisoner herself is the furthest possible remove from the cold-blooded murderess that she is accused of being. There is nothing in her looks of the woman who craves noto-riety and glories in unnatural crime."

On January 11 came the dramatic high point of the trial, the ap-pearance of Kate Cobb's ten-year-old daughter, Adele, who testified about a cup that may or may not have been given to Kate Cobb by Bishop, and that may have later held the poisoned tea. Adele's testi-mony was expected to contradict her grandmother's, and implicate her mother further. *The Sun* milked the scene for everything it was worth. Entering the courtroom with a sheriff, Adele was "a bonnie wee thing, with her long golden hair pushed back over her face by a black circu-lar comb, golden ear-drops, and a hat of lustrous blue silk and white lace perched on top of her ringlets. The tiny white lace scarf about her throat was tied with just the least suspicion of jauntiness." By the end of her testimony, Adele reportedly had everyone in tears: the judge, the prosecutor, the defense counsel, and of course, Kate Cobb herself.

When she left the stand, Adele trotted unhesitatingly to the silent figure in black, "whose life she had been helping to swear away." Cobb caught the girl up in her arms, raised her on her lap, pressed her to her breast, and smoothed back her hair with trembling hands. The coun-sel for the defendant rose to demand in a tremulous voice that the evidence to which Adele had just testified be ruled inadmissible; tears coursed down his furrowed cheeks. His request was denied.

What Kate Cobb's story lacked in the metaphysical depth that suffused Mollie Fancher's, it made up for in pure theater. And it had one important element that Mollie's, so far, lacked: an ending. The jurors needed only seven hours to decide that Cobb was guilty of murder in the second degree. She bent her head and wept as the jurors filed out past her chair, on their way to determine whether she should be hanged. Almost all of them, *The Sun* reported, looked at Kate with pity. Her mother sat nearby "in a frenzy of grief." Cobb was sentenced to a life term in Wethersfield Prison in Connecticut, and by January 18, the matter had come to a satisfying close. (Wesley Bishop's fate would be decided in the spring, but that promised far less drama, since he had already confessed; the only question remaining was whether he would face prison or the gallows.)

Although no one had seen Kate Cobb put arsenic in her husband's tea and hand the cup to him, evidence had been presented and a group of people had decided that it added up to murder. Similarly, no one saw Mollie eat, but evidence had been presented on both sides: the historically proven impossibility of maintaining life without food, versus her friends' insistence that she was unable to swallow or keep anything in her stomach, that she must live on spiritual sustenance. Without a scientific test like that proposed by Hammond, there could be no definitive verdict. Even from the vantage point of today, with our more precise knowledge of the limits of human starvation and our certainty that Mollie must have taken in food, there is no way of knowing what or how she ate, or even whether she was an outright liar or simply under the spell of neurotic self-delusion and denial. She is a mystery, with clues but no irrefutable proof.

There is an advantage to such a mystery, a story without an ending. The case is never quite closed. There is always the possibility of a breakthrough, a new answer, definitive proof of guilt or innocence. In

Mollie's case, her story remained dormant for a year and a half—until it sprang to life again in the guise of an argumentative doctor named Henry Tanner.

A year had elapsed since the expiration of Hammond's challenge to Mollie Fancher when Dr. Tanner stepped onto the New York stage, ready to play the next role in the fasting drama. He had been following Mollie's story from his home in Minnesota, then still considered part of the faraway West. Hammond and his ideas about fasting were all wrong, Dr. Tanner felt, and he was just the man to prove it—and to bear the standard for Mollie.

Henry S. Tanner was, by all reports, an eccentric and obsessive man, given to enthusiasms that quickly turned into causes. In 1880, when he came to New York to take on Dr. Hammond, he was fifty-four, gray-haired, short and tending to stout, with a full, round face. The primary elements of his personality, as soon became evident, appeared to be a need for attention, an obstinacy and an arrogance about his views, and a propensity for flirting with the ladies. Two doctors with whom he practiced in Minneapolis characterized him as "an honest enthusiast; a little crazy, but not in the least a fraud; with an inordinate craving for notoriety, a strong will, and a phlegmatic habit of body, which enables him to reduce the activity of his vital actions at will."

Tanner had come to America from England at age sixteen, and at twenty-eight married a woman who was as interested in medicine as he was. They graduated together from the Eclectic Medical Institute in Cincinnati, and practiced medicine in several Ohio towns, eventually specializing in electrothermal baths. According to friends, Mrs. Tanner helped keep her husband's feet on the ground while he toyed with various newfangled medical theories. Unfortunately for his marriage, once Tanner got an idea, he wanted everyone around him to agree.

This generated some marital strife when Tanner took up the theory that the secret of health and happiness was to eat as little food as possible. Mrs. Tanner emphatically disagreed. She was described as "a good feeder, fond of that which, with most of the remainder of mankind, goes to make up all that is pleasant in life—good living." When her husband tried to enforce his ascetic ideas on her, she decided to have no more of them, or of him. She separated from him in 1877, and this, his friends believed, probably opened the way to his later fame. Freed from her rational influence, Tanner moved to Minneapolis, where he surrendered himself to his theories and experimented with his stomach.

Most of his experiments involved fasting. In Minneapolis, *The New York Times* wrote, Tanner "made his great discovery that he could gain a larger share of the notoriety for which his soul thirsted by denying himself food than by running electro-thermal baths or practicing eccentric medicine." His first long fast lasted forty-two days, and was performed under the watch of his medical partners, Drs. Moyer and Putnam. Although he was briefly a sensation, the notice Tanner achieved for his feat was apparently less than entirely positive. "In general," reported the *Times,* "he was regarded as a mildly aggressive nuisance, who bored the public too much with his stomach and the newspapers too much with his theories."

That changed when Tanner decided to accept Hammond's challenge to Mollie Fancher to fast while under strict scrutiny. His own goals, Tanner insisted, were altruistic: both to defend Mollie's name against the doctors who accused her of being a fraud, and to offer himself in the interests of science, in order to enhance man's knowledge of the human body under starvation conditions. But he admitted to some personal interest in the outcome as well; Hammond's denunciation of Mollie's fasting had thrown discredit on Tanner's own claim to have survived for forty-two days without food. Quite frankly, he wanted revenge.

But Hammond showed a great deal of reluctance to take Tanner up on his proposal. Perhaps he recognized in the determined doctor from Minneapolis a will and a self-confidence close to his own in strength, or perhaps he felt the outcome of the various physiological and theological debates about Mollie Fancher had been less than satisfactory. Whatever the reason, he steadfastly ignored Tanner's letters proposing the public fast. Tanner then wrote to Joseph Buchanan, asking him to intervene; Hammond ignored also the psychometrist's attempts at contact. Finally, Tanner made his counterchallenge through the newspapers. When a reporter from *The New York Times* knocked on Hammond's door on December 30, 1879, Hammond at last consented to respond— and what he said marked something of a retreat.

Hammond told the reporter that his challenge to Mollie had been primarily about her clairvoyance, not her fasting. As far as fasting itself, he played quite a different tune from the one of the year before. "I never claimed, under any circumstances, that it was impossible for a human being to live without food for thirty days," he said. "As to denying anything in nature outside of mathematics, I certainly mean to be more cautious than even to deny the possibility of a man's living a whole year without food, no matter how improbable such a thing is."

Then he accepted Tanner's proposition, but with a caveat that would become crucial to the outcome of the fast: Tanner must agree to be supervised to a "reasonable" degree. Everyone involved with the case, as might be expected, had a slightly different definition of "reasonable." Hammond wanted Tanner to carry out his experiment at the Medical College of the University of the City of New York, where he would assure comfortable lodging for Tanner, and a team of medical students to carry out the constant monitoring. Yet when the two men met in New York in May 1880, that plan fell through. Tanner proposed that the experiment be performed before members of Hammond's Neurological Society, but the two stubborn doctors were unable to agree to the conditions of the test. Finally Tanner, determined to carry out his fast before returning to Minneapolis, rented Clarendon Hall on East Thirteenth Street in Manhattan, gathered a group of doctors to watch his every move, and at noon on June 28 settled down for his forty days and nights.

Within a few days, the newspapers recognized what a gold mine had opened for them. The Tanner story promised ghoulish detail, potential death or insanity, and plenty of infighting among New York doctors about the validity of what Tanner was attempting. The possibility of fraud formed a constant backdrop to daily stories. It was carefully explained that the fasting doctor occupied a railed-off section of the hall that contained only a narrow iron cot, a small writing stand without a drawer, and a rocking chair. Tables and chairs nearby accommodated a team of watching physicians as well as reporters, who were constantly in attendance. Before the fast began, Tanner stripped to the skin and his clothes were thoroughly searched. Once it started no one was allowed to shake hands with him or give him anything, even a letter, that was not first checked by his watchers. When he bought an evening paper, *The New York Times* reported, the paper boy was not allowed to hand it to him; "it was examined as closely as though it were possible to conceal a good-sized ham in its folds."

One of the first physicians to speak publicly about the spectacle being presented at Clarendon Hall was, not surprisingly, William Hammond. A *Times* reporter sat down with him in his office on July 3 for a long conversation about the fasting experiment. Hammond's remarks began in a friendly vein but soon became barbed. "I would not throw the least discredit on Dr. Tanner," he said. "I think he honestly believes that he can do what he has attempted. It is a pity, though, that he is not in the hands of the regular physicians. I offered him a room in my house to try the experiment, but he declined the offer. Had he accepted he would have been under the charge of regular members of the profession, and some scientific results might have flowed from the trial." As it was, Hammond sighed, "the test is not placed absolutely beyond fraud, and therefore it is worth nothing in a scientific point of view. It is entirely thrown away."

The reporter pressed Hammond: Did he think it was possible for Dr. Tanner to obtain food, under the watchful conditions at Clarendon Hall? "It is very possible to cheat in this business," Hammond replied. But, as with his comments about Mollie, he left the doctor an out—the possibility of self-delusion. "I don't mean to insinuate that Dr. Tanner is cheating. I have come to the conclusion that he is an honest man who deceives himself more than he does others." As to whether Tanner would succeed, Hammond was adamant: "Not the least chance in the world!" If he kept on losing weight at his present rate (ten pounds in six days), he would either die or go insane within a week. Hammond's opinions had plenty of adherents, as to both the probability of fraud and the foregone conclusion of utter, and quick, failure on Tanner's part. The first twenty of Tanner's allotted days were, in fact, accompanied by a more or less constant chorus of dire predictions of imminent death or madness.

The newspapers settled into a routine of detailed dispatches from the front lines at Clarendon Hall. Every day New Yorkers could catch up on Tanner's vital statistics of the day before: his pulse, body temperature, frequency of naps, mood (often nervous or irritable); the number of times he rinsed his mouth; the state of his tongue (at the end of seven days, slightly coated but not yet giving off "starvation odor"); his looks (at seven days, hollow-eyed, with ever deeper lines on his once smooth face).

At ten days, *New York Times* editors articulated what Tanner and Hammond had not: that this experiment was about that ever-present question of soul and body. "The whole world is interested in knowing whether the soul is independent of bodily functions, and would be grateful for experimental evidence on that point," an editorial commented on July 8. The editorial further speculated on whether the doctors in charge of watching Tanner, and possibly even Dr. Hammond himself as the indirect instigator, would be in danger of being named accessories to willful murder if Tanner were to expire. The importance

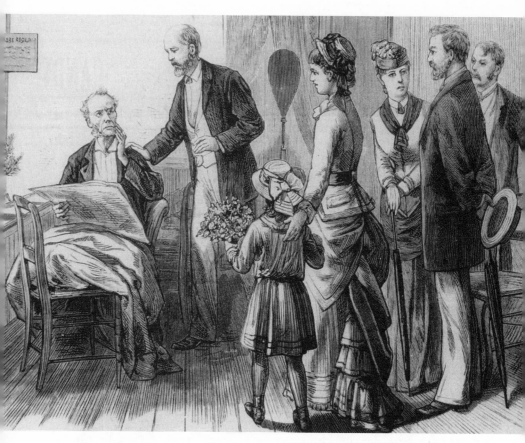

Henry Tanner during his forty-day public fast in support of Mollie Fancher, in an engraving that appeared in Frank Leslie's Illustrated Newspaper. *The excruciating experience turned into a sideshow: a New York impresario even offered Tanner $1,200 to finish his fast at his theater.* (COLLECTION OF THE NEW-YORK HISTORICAL SOCIETY)

of the question of whether the soul is independent of the body might be a defense, the editors wrote, but would any jury really buy the argument of "homicide in the pursuit of scientific knowledge"?

Two days later, a pair of doctors on the watch committee did in fact withdraw out of fear of a "fatal conclusion" to the fast. Tanner at that point was still attempting to do without water as well as food (he eventually took small amounts of water). He was emaciated and haggard, with eyes sunk deep in their sockets and exhibiting an unnerving bright glitter. "A timid person would hardly care to be shut up alone with that glittering eye for company," wrote a *Times* reporter. Predictions of Tanner's demise began in earnest. The "starvation odor," it was said, would indicate that the end was near. The monitoring doctors discussed their options, and decided that if, after a warning from them of approaching death, Tanner still refused sustenance, they would force something down his throat. They would do this, said one doctor, "just as I would force the knife from a man whom I found trying to cut his throat. We don't intend to let [Tanner] commit suicide under our eyes."

At day thirteen, one doctor stated, "In my opinion, Dr. Tanner cannot continue this fast five days longer and live." Another physician, who had declined to be a watcher of what he felt was an "immoral exhibition," predicted on day fourteen that the experiment could not continue beyond the fifteenth day. "Dr. Tanner is insane on the subject of fasting," he added, "and I am sorry that my profession has not raised its voice against this crime of permitting a man to die by starvation." Two days later, Dr. Maurice Miller, one of the watchers, said, "He is failing very, very fast. He will never see another Sunday unless he gives up the fight soon." The inaccuracy of these predictions became part of the story; *The New York Times* headlined a July 13 article "Wanting a New Prophet: Somebody to Truly Fix the Day of Tanner's Death," but two days later announced: "Tanner Declines to Die."

Tanner did decline, most emphatically. He soldiered on, sometimes cranky, always tired, often cold, the glitter in his eyes replaced by a dull, leaden stare. Yet never for a moment did he lose his confidence that he would complete the fast. By day seventeen, even the doubting Dr. Miller told a reporter that he would "speculate no more on this remarkable case. I'll give him till he dies or upsets all our theories of vital chemistry." By then, Tanner had begun to take some water daily, and the hydration acted on him like a tonic. At last, by the middle phase of his experiment, he was able to enjoy the fame he had always craved.

Hundreds of people were visiting Clarendon Hall daily; Tanner had instituted an admission fee of twenty-five cents on the tenth day of the fast to discourage the most unsavory of these (and to put cash in his pocket, and help defray the costs of renting the hall). By mid-July the story of his ongoing fast had crossed the Atlantic, and English and French doctors debated whether its result would be scientifically valid, and how long he could possibly continue. Tanner received a trans-atlantic cable from one prominent English physician, J. Marion Sims, urging him on. "Your experiment watched here with great interest by scientists, ridiculed by fools," Sims wrote. "Courage, brave fellow, hold on."

The dramatic value of the show at Clarendon Hall was recognized by the proprietor of a New York theater, who offered Tanner $1,200 to spend the last two weeks of his fast there instead of the hall, promising perfect light, ventilation, and spring water. The curator of a museum in Maine wrote to ask Tanner what he would charge to promise his body to the museum so that he could be stuffed for the edification of future generations. Tanner also had the satisfaction of learning that the citizens of his former burg of Minneapolis had become as fascinated with him as the New Yorkers who gaped at him daily. And when a *Times* correspondent dug up the information that Tanner had had a wife—who, when he tried to convert her to his ascetic ways, "left him to get three square meals a day"—it put Tanner on the front page, a distinction the paper usually reserved for national and international news, or local disasters like train wrecks. The details of Tanner's personal history had become news fodder, as if he were a candidate for public office.

Bags of fan mail, along with notes from a few lunatics, arrived at Clarendon Hall every day, and gifts flowed in from all directions. Soon the hall resembled a curiosity shop filled with goods: a glass globe with two singing crickets, Indian clubs, dumbbells, books, embroidered pillows, a music box, and flowers of every description. A Canadian admirer sent an elaborately decorated enameled bonbon box, not more than a finger in length. Inside were a minute vial containing some fifty drops of Holland gin, another vial labeled "Claret," two tiny crackers accommodating dainty morsels of smoked beef, and at the bottom a dozen bonbons the size of dried peas, nestled into the velvet lining of the box. These fairy-sized delicacies were accompanied by miniature gold-bordered cups and saucers, and a microscopic silver spoon. Tanner laughed heartily when he saw it. He also laughed when a large envelope was opened to reveal a piece of roast beef; he ordered it thrown out the window to the crowd that steadily occupied the opposite side of Thirteenth Street. Many correspondents sent poetry or doggerel rhymes to amuse the starving doctor. One letter contained a marriage proposal from a Philadelphia girl—if he survived the experiment.

One reason the news about Tanner's ex-wife reached the front page was that the doctor had presented himself as a bachelor—and had exhibited, even at low moments of his fast, a talent with the ladies. Many of his gifts, in fact, and all the flowers and bouquets, were from female admirers. The papers made frequent mention of his female visitors, and finally the *Times* was explicit. "The Doctor's strongest likings seem to be for ladies, music, and flowers," wrote a reporter in the July 18 edition, "and certainly nobody can find fault with his taste. He listens eagerly to the music, smells at the bouquets as long as there is anything left of them, and pays great attention to the ladies. However irritable he may be, whenever a lady comes around he is all smiles."

Tanner took walks up and down the hall with his admirers and lectured them on living on only two meals a day. There was a piano in the gallery of the hall, and Tanner was often serenaded. One young woman in particular, Henrietta Maurer, performed for him often, and groups of singers came to entertain him. At times almost a party atmosphere prevailed in Clarendon Hall. Seldom were there fewer than several dozen visitors, and things always became more lively when bags of mail arrived, or when songs were heard. One afternoon a gentleman played the piano while a woman sang "Comin' Thro' the Rye." The doctor sat

This editorial cartoon caricaturing Henry Tanner's forty-day fast ran in Frank Leslie's Illustrated Newspaper *on August 21, 1880, over the caption: "A possible phase of the fasting business."* (COLLECTION OF THE NEW-YORK HISTORICAL SOCIETY)

on his cot, feet wrapped in a blanket for warmth on the mid-July day, and when the singer stopped he called out, "That's the best kind of rye—give us some more of it." The woman then sang "Way Down Upon the Swanee River," and Tanner clapped. "Can't you all sing together once?" he shouted at the other visitors. "Or shall I come over and help you?"

The one fly in Tanner's ointment was the stubborn reluctance of Hammond and other prominent doctors to recognize or even believe his achievement. The very energy that he displayed with his guests at mid-fast made some doctors more suspicious that he was receiving food. Thirteen days into the fast, the president of the New York Neurological Society, Landon Carter Gray, felt compelled to write a lengthy letter to the *Times* protesting that the Society denied any connection with Tanner's experiment; any members who had volunteered as watchers were acting on their own initiative.

The letter harshly criticized the conditions of the watch on Tanner. Gray asserted that "any person well versed in sleight of hand could feed himself or be fed with ease as the watch is now being conducted." His conclusion was even blunter: "I do not mean to express any opinion whatsoever as to Dr. Tanner's uprightness, but the gentleman must remember that, hard as it may seem, a necessary assumption at the outset of his self-imposed test is that he will cheat at every turn."

The acrimony about the merits of Tanner's fast was to some extent a new battle in an ongoing war that plagued the medical profession in the late nineteenth century: the war of "regulars" versus "Eclectics." The regular doctors were the mainstream of the profession (including neurologists), who were attempting to standardize what was then a widely unregulated field; the regulars formed the basis for the American Medical Association, which they started in 1847. The practice of medicine in the nineteenth century was not only full of conflicting theories and sects (the Eclectics being a major dissenting group), but also cliquish and territorial. The Eclectics considered themselves reformers, and challenged the regular profession on what they saw as excessive use of drugs and bleeding. They established their own medical colleges, where they taught their own theories in addition to many precepts of conventional medicine.

The two groups were always looking for a fight, and Tanner, a proclaimed Eclectic, afforded an excellent target. Gray remarked haughtily in his letter to the *Times* that "it would be impossible to get members of the Neurological Society to act conjointly with gentlemen who did not belong to the regular profession." When freethinking members of the Society joined in the Tanner watch, Gray wrote directly to those doctors and demanded to know by what authority they had organized a watch by the Neurological Society. One of them, Edward Harwood, replied that members of the Neurological Society had as much right to watch Dr. Tanner as they had to go to Manhattan Beach or any other place.

One of the greatest of the regular school of doctors was William Hammond, a founder of the Neurological Society and a vocal campaigner for medical standards. That fact made all the more significant a letter that was received in Clarendon Hall on August 5, toward the end of the fast. As Tanner's agony approached its apex in early August, Hammond wrote him what amounted to a document of concession. He indicated that he felt the watch had been conducted honestly (though with some negligence), that he believed Tanner had abstained from food (but not water), that his was the best-authenticated long fast ever accomplished, that he had succeeded far better than Hammond thought he would, and that he had shown "great pluck, determination, and endurance."

As the letter was read aloud to a stony-faced Tanner, who lay curled up in an easy chair, a crowd of doctors proclaimed, "You are at the top! The chief of the aristocratic cabal which has sneered at you now acknowledges that he was wrong and that you were right!" Hammond was, however, unable to resist a few digs. The scientific investigations made by Tanner during the fast—tests of respiration, muscular strength, cardiac function, and so on—had been superficial and restricted; even the weighing had been very imperfectly performed; and therefore the scientific results were not what they should have been. Hammond relayed a clear but unspoken message that the scientific results would of course have been pristine had the Neurological Society run the show.

He included one other unspoken gibe in the letter—directed straight at Mollie Fancher. The most important result of Tanner's trial, Hammond wrote, was that "he has shown that those alleged instances of fasting a month or more without the symptoms of inanition being produced are fraudulent and deceptive." In other words, if Mollie had truly gone even a month without food, she would not have been happily embroidering and chatting with visitors. She would instead have been, as Tanner became in the final two weeks of his allotted time, emaciated, irritable, listless, and vomiting up bits of stomach lining. By the time of Hammond's letter, Tanner was in almost constant distress.

As in the first weeks of the fast, doctors issued frequent warnings of imminent death. On July 29, there was a false report of Tanner's demise, which sent reporters scurrying to the hall, only to find him sitting on the edge of his cot, sick but alive. The physicians of the regular school were especially panicked, a half-dozen of them announcing on July 31 that Tanner had not forty-eight hours more to live. He certainly looked and acted, by then, like a dying man. He was exhausted but could hardly stay asleep for an hour at a time; severe abdominal cramps, along with alternating chills and fevers, would come upon him unexpectedly; his limbs were described as skeletal, his hands nearly transparent.

The most painful symptom was the vomiting that became a frequent occurrence in the last week of the fast. Although Tanner still had moments of rallying, when he would talk with visitors and even smile and joke, his stomach was in complete revolt. Water, which was necessary to his survival, seemed to make it worse. When he retched, his empty stomach sent up horrible stuff, described variously as "thick, glairy, mucous secretion of the gastric lining, tinged with biliary acids," and "mucous slime tinctured with the greenish secretion of the liver, with small fragments of tissue having the appearance of decomposed mucous membrane floating upon the surface, emitting a nauseous and disagreeable odor."

But there was no hope of convincing Tanner to give up so near the finish line, and as the final day approached, the general excitement permeating the hall seemed to buoy him. His keepers began to collect the foods that would end his fast, and greater crowds than ever passed through the hall or collected on the street outside. Tanner had doubled the price, to fifty cents, and still they came. In the last days, daily receipts rose from sixty or seventy dollars to nearly one thousand. On the fortieth day, visitors included a U.S. senator, several generals, and ever more physicians, of every school. The doctors on watch discussed the delicate matter of how Tanner should break the fast, fearing that the wrong foods, or too much food too quickly, could overwhelm his damaged digestive system. For once, even the opposing schools were in almost unanimous agreement that he should begin very slowly, with a little diluted milk, and perhaps a zwieback cracker. Tanner himself was dreaming of beefsteak and watermelons (a shipment of Georgia melons had been delivered, at his request), and would confound all their predictions.

The fast was to terminate at noon on the seventh of August. By ten-thirty in the morning, five hundred people had squeezed into Clarendon Hall, and the street outside was packed from curb to curb. However, as *The New York Times* pointed out the next day as a "curious fact worthy of notice," there were no eminent physicians of the regular school present; "even Dr. Hammond did not condescend to send his congratulations." Tanner was weighed and found to be at 121 pounds; he had lost thirty-six over the forty days, an average of nine-tenths of a pound daily. Within the railed-off enclosure where he had spent so many hours retching and tossing on his cot, a long table had been set up, piled high with delicacies. Among them: a dozen bottles of "Russian milk-wine," a variety of fruit, and of course, the largest watermelons of the season—six of them.

As he waited for the clock to run out, Tanner sat in a window of the hall overlooking the crowded street, lazily paring a peach. Someone fanned him in the heat. When the clock struck twelve, he rose and was escorted to the main hall by two of his keepers. When he appeared in the doorway the spectators gave a great shout and kept up a continuous applause, pressing against the railing as the police held them back from breaking it down. Tanner's first bite was a quarter of the peach he had been paring. A doctor poured out a goblet of fresh milk, and Tanner drained seven ounces at once. "I tell you that tastes good," he said, and the crowd roared. He then demanded that one of the watermelons be split open, and he eagerly devoured a pound of it.

At twelve-ten a carriage pulled up in front of the building, and Tanner and several attendants left the main hall and stood for a while in the doorway, like royalty. Tanner and his entourage then descended the stone steps, and as they drove off in the carriage toward Union Square, people ran after it exuberantly, shouting and waving their hats.

Just as happened with the underfed volunteers at the termination of the Minnesota starvation study, Tanner's first act was to begin to eat, and eat. The day he broke his fast he had two half-pound steaks, four hours apart, in addition to some Hungarian wine and four apples. Then he lay down, saying he felt like a beehive all over, that there was not a grain of tissue in him that was not at work. Over the course of the next day he ate a half-pound of steak every few hours, accompanied by stewed potatoes and milk, wine, or Bass ale. He did not retch, vomit, or seize up, and he gained five pounds in the first twenty-four hours after his fast. Already the deep wrinkles from his nostrils to his mouth were smoothed out, his eyes were bright, his hair was softer and less dry. Tanner said he felt great.

Clarendon Hall was put back in order, the railed-in enclosure and the table of food were dismantled, East Thirteenth Street was cleared of curiosity-seekers—and doctors, scientists, and spectators were left to wonder what, really, had been proven. *The New York Times,* after breathlessly featuring Tanner's adventure every day from July 4 through August 10, ran a biting editorial two days after the fast ended entitled "Tanner's Folly." The fast, the paper held, was invalidated by the fact that little-known doctors had supervised it, and by Tanner's having taken two or three "alcohol vapor baths" toward the end of the forty days (it was believed that nutrition could be absorbed through the skin; hence Mollie Fancher's physicians' insistence on beef-tea baths more than a decade earlier). "Medical science gains nothing from the results of the fast; humanity gains nothing; the public gains nothing," the editors wrote. "[Tanner] has won a victory without fruit and without honor."

The day before, however, the Reverend C. S. Williams, a clergyman at Manhattan's Seventh Street Methodist Episcopal Church, had urged the opposite case: "The fasting of Dr. Tanner in behalf of humanity and science was certainly a great thing." With an argument that re-called the defense of Mollie Fancher nearly two years earlier, the Rev-erend Williams preached that there was more in heaven and on earth than was dreamed of in the doctors' philosophy, and that contempo-rary scientists had failed to recognize the existence of the invisible, spiritual, and eternal. This fast, he proclaimed, taught the superiority of the immaterial over the material.

And yet did it? Or did the Tanner fast simply demonstrate that forty days was just about as far as a human body could run without suste-nance, and that most of those days would be full of a great deal of dis-tress? If anything, Tanner's putatively supportive gesture toward Mollie Fancher accomplished what Hammond hinted at in the letter he sent to Clarendon Hall: that it was unlikely that Mollie could be merrily and painlessly abstaining from food for years; that there were indeed strict physical limits to starvation, limits that fell years short of Mollie's claims. Certainly everything about Tanner's publicity-laden event con-trasted starkly with Mollie's private, sitting room existence.

During his fast, Tanner had received a letter from Mollie, the con-tents of which he refused to divulge. Was she grateful for his public be-lief in her? Did she encourage him to stay the course, or urge him to end his unnecessary agonies? Like so much else about Mollie's case, her words to him will never be known.

In the middle of Tanner's greatest agonies, a *Times* reporter made mention of Miss Mollie Fancher of Brooklyn, whose story was too fa-

miliar to require further description, and whose friends claimed she
had subsisted by then nearly sixteen years (again, an exaggeration)
without food. "No sufficient test of this case has ever been made by
competent persons," the reporter wrote, "and it remains a mystery to
this day." It was a mystery whose solution would ultimately belong to
another era.

CHAPTER TEN

❧

Hysteria's Echo

Hysteria has not died. It has simply been relabeled for a new era.

—Elaine Showalter, *Hystories,* 1997

When *Time* asked in a poll last week whether people believe in miracles, sixty-nine percent said yes.

—*Time,* April 10, 1995

HERE IN THE TWENTY-FIRST CENTURY, no one believes that any person, no matter how unusual, could live for a dozen years without food. Nothing is more certain than the fact that Mollie ate; one has only to examine photographs of her to be convinced of that. But the how and why of her stubborn claims of not eating remain opaque. Aunt Susan did not make note, in her detailed diary of Mollie's contortions and trances, of any midnight suppers devoured on a tray in that fluffy four-poster bed. Mollie never confessed, as did Ann Moore, the Fasting Woman of Tutbury, to receiving secret packets of nourishment, or even to sneaking down to the kitchen at night on legs that were not truly paralyzed.

Beyond the puzzle of how Mollie obtained victuals is the absorbing question of why she created such a fantasy. We would ask today the same thing that doctors and skeptics did more than a century ago: Was she deliberately deceiving people, or did she truly believe what she claimed, through a delusion so powerful that it overrode her reason?

Could someone so seemingly sincere, admired by so many, be so crazy, just below the placid surface?

Nineteenth-century psychology was helpless in the face of questions like these—the tools for understanding the nature of neurotic illnesses simply hadn't been fashioned yet. Mollie was indeed an enigma. The only diagnosis that existed to help explain her state was hysteria, and even that was a hotly debated illness. Was it a physical ailment caused by some kind of lesion, as Hammond's theories had it? Or a combination of "physical states or defects" and "moral causes," as the rest-cure maven Silas Weir Mitchell argued? Or was it just an elaborate form of malingering; was the hysterical woman, in the words of Oliver Wendell Holmes, "a vampire who sucks the blood of the healthy people about her"?

It is clear that the solution to the mysteries of Mollie Fancher's existence will never be found in the past, with its scant historical record of her life and its rudimentary psychological knowledge. The only way to get at Mollie's secrets now, more than a century after they were contained within the four walls of her room, is to drag her into the present. Modern psychiatric treatment is rich in knowledge, therapies, and experience. There are now hundreds of diagnoses in the Bible of the industry, the *Diagnostic and Statistical Manual of Mental Disorders, Fourth Edition* (*DSM-IV*). Millions of patients have been psychoanalyzed or otherwise treated for various mental ills; dozens of psychoactive drugs have been created. It's entirely possible to take Mollie to a modern shrink, to perform a retroactive psychological analysis of her obviously disturbed condition.

To accomplish this, I call a therapist friend, who immediately suggests that the multiple-personality disorder may contain at least part of the answer. "It could well be that one personality ate, and the main Mollie personality didn't," he tells me. "And that the Mollie who didn't eat really believed it, because she wasn't aware of the part that did eat. The mind has the capacity to cut one part off entirely, so that only one section of reality is seen at a time." We all construct our own realities, he adds, to a much greater extent than we realize—and we believe our own stories. Some people's stories, usually for reasons of early trauma or inner conflict, diverge further from the "truth" than others' do.

One incontrovertible truth about Mollie's life is the apparently precipitating event of her invalidism. Could many of the oddities of her story have been due to physical injuries sustained in her horsecar accident? Eliott Mancall, a neurological surgeon at the University of Pennsylvania, doesn't think so. Acknowledging the difficulty of diagnosing a patient without examining her, he has no hesitation in saying that her symptoms "don't sound organic. A spinal cord injury could result in some of those symptoms, but they would be more consistent. You might have muscle spasms along the backbone, your legs might draw up, you might have numbness and tingling. But you wouldn't then be able to lie there doing needlework. And you certainly wouldn't be paralyzed and then not, or have sensory loss that then spontaneously came back."

Equipped with these hints, I approach Charles Ford, a professor in the department of psychiatry and behavioral neurobiology at the University of Alabama at Birmingham School of Medicine. Ford is a psychiatrist with forty years' clinical experience; one of his specialties is treating patients with dissociative disorders. He has written several books on aspects of psychological dysfunction that speak directly to Mollie's condition, among them *The Somatizing Disorders* (about various forms of hysteria, in which psychological distress is expressed physically); *Patient or Pretender: Inside the Strange World of Factitious Disorders*; and *Lies! Lies! Lies!!! The Psychology of Deceit.* If Mollie's family had lived in a psychologically sophisticated age, they might have chosen to send her to someone like Ford.

On the basis of Mollie's history and symptoms, Ford quickly establishes what might have been happening with her—both the formal terms for her condition, and the ways in which she might have acted out her assorted psychiatric disorders. He believes that Mollie almost certainly had what is now called conversion disorder. In the index of the *DSM-IV,* conversion disorder is a fresh name for an old friend: hysteria. Its essential features are neurological symptoms that affect motor or sensory function (paralysis, seizures or convulsions, blindness, deafness, loss of touch or pain sensation) that are precipitated by psychological rather than physical causes, and are not intentionally produced or feigned.

Mollie's other significant psychiatric condition, says Ford, was dissociative disorder. The *DSM-IV* defines dissociation as the disconnection from complete awareness of self, time, and/or external circumstances—something that ranges from "normal dissociation" to "dissociative identity disorder (DID)," the latter the new technical term for multiple-personality disorder. Everyone dissociates at times: daydreaming, "trancing out," becoming so involved in a task or in reading that the rest of the world recedes and one loses sense of time, and even of hearing. This state has been exalted in more recent years as being "in the flow," especially if the task at hand is something creative.

Dissociation becomes a disorder when it interferes with everyday functioning, when it alters the way in which we normally integrate or understand our experiences. We keep a grip on reality by weaving together our sense of identity with memory and consciousness. When we dissociate severely enough to lose the ability to do that, we can become truly lost. The next step away from normality on the dissociation spectrum, for instance, is dissociative amnesia or fugue, in which someone loses a chunk of personal memory, or sometimes even an entire identity. Ford had a patient who came home one day and didn't recognize her husband or children; it was as if she had never seen them before.

At the opposite end from everyday, "normal" dissociation lurks the most bizarre and colorful expression of the disintegration of identity: DID, which the *DSM-IV* describes as "the presence of two or more distinct identities or personality states that recurrently take control of behavior." This is where Mollie lands, with her reported nighttime "alters" Idol, Rosebud, Pearl, and Ruby. Her life with the four "other Mollies," as described in Abram Dailey's biography, fits an impressive number of the criteria outlined in the *DSM-IV*. For example, usually the primary identity is "passive, dependent, guilty, and depressed"; alternate personalities often have a distinct self-image and characteristics that contrast with the primary, namely hostility, control, aggression; alternates often have their own names; alternates often differ in age, vocabulary, and memory; and in general there may be a loss of biographical memory for some extended period of the patient's life.

The last feature recalls Mollie's nine-year "trance," during which she obviously functioned—receiving hundreds of visitors, writing thousands of letters—but of which she had no memory when she emerged in 1875. She didn't recognize her own handwriting from those years, and had to relearn the various needlework skills she had perfected. The psychology professor Anthony Walsh found in this trance period of Mollie's a separate personality, the "isolated X-personality." But Ford characterizes it as a dissociative episode, albeit an especially extended one. "It's as if certain experiences, and the person's awareness of them, are compartmentalized in the brain and not available for conscious retrieval," he explains. His analogy for this "lost" period is a forgotten computer file: it's in the machine somewhere, but you can't remember the name under which you stored it, so you can't open it and read the contents.

The distinction between Walsh's and Ford's takes on the nine-year trance period is greater than it sounds: Ford considers it a state of consciousness rather than a personality as such because he does not believe in the authenticity of multiple-personality disorder. What the *DSM-IV* does not mention in its diagnostic description of DID is that a substantial number of respected psychiatrists don't believe it exists. They might accept, as Ford does, that a person can experience all kinds of dissociated states, can rewrite his own personal history and then believe it, can block out experiences or periods of his life—but not that a person can sit in a shrink's office and legitimately exhibit one personality after another, sometimes as many as one hundred different alters. The *DSM-IV* hints at this controversy only in its comments on the sharp rise in reported cases of DID in recent years. Some doctors feel that the rise is due simply to greater awareness of the disorder and therefore a larger number of diagnosed cases; others, the editors write gingerly, "believe that the syndrome has been overdiagnosed in individuals who are highly suggestible."

Ford's conviction, one that is shared by such prominent physicians as Paul McHugh, Henry Phipps Professor of Psychiatry and director of the Department of Psychiatry and Behavioral Science at the Johns Hopkins Medical Institutions, is that DID is essentially a manufactured idea, encouraged by popular culture and misguided psychiatrists. McHugh has called it an iatrogenic behavioral syndrome, meaning that it is "like hystero-epilepsy [Charcot's *grande hystérie*], created by therapists." The medical historian Edward Shorter agrees, writing that although the diagnosis is still controversial, there is increasing evidence that "the production of multiple personalities is the result of medical shaping by the physician, or by the culture, of inchoate symptoms the patient is unable otherwise to make sense of."

There are, however, believers in DID, and they are a passionate and powerful enough force to convince the American Psychiatric Association to give the disorder legitimacy by including a diagnostic entry for "Multiple Personality Disorder" for the first time in the 1980 *DSM-III* (the name was changed to "Dissociative Identity Disorder" in the 1994 *DSM-IV*). Doctors who feel that DID is real attribute many of the cases to extreme trauma or abuse in early life, which provides a powerful motivation for a child to dissociate himself from the real-life horror of the experiences—to bury them in the memory bank of a separate personality. But that idea too is controversial. Often the abuse is self-reported from "recovered memories" that have been lost for years, and people who claim to have multiple personalities are "highly hypnotizable and especially vulnerable to suggestive influences," says the manual, hinting at the idea of the iatrogenic therapist. The concept of DID appears to be, for now, a toss-up. A recent survey of board-certified psychiatrists published in *The American Journal of Psychiatry* concluded that in the profession itself there is little agreement about the diagnostic status or scientific validity of DID.

Mollie Fancher, of course, had no therapist urging her to describe her other selves or suggesting that she might have buried memories of abuse. There is no evidence of physical or sexual abuse in her childhood. Though it was almost a century before the mass popularization of the idea of multiple personalities through books and films such as *The Three Faces of Eve* (1957) and *Sybil* (1973), multiple personalities were not unheard-of in the middle and late nineteenth century. Mollie may have picked up news about a young woman in Georgia, dubbed "The Lady of Belisle," who reportedly had a double personality (this was written up in *Harper's New Monthly Magazine* in 1858), or about "The Sleeping Preacher" in northern Alabama whose multiple-personality case was written of and discussed avidly in the mid-1870s. There were also the well-known examples of popular Spiritualist mediums, who, while not technically multiple personalities, were said to "channel" various spirits while in a dissociated state.

Although Mollie had no therapist prompting her, she may have had fairly strong encouragement of her self-deception from other sources. Charles Ford, as her posthumous therapist, suggests that one key to understanding a patient as apparently removed from reality as Mollie is to look at the secondary gains she might have been receiving from her symptoms. In Mollie's case, in the days before Social Security and disability insurance, her invalidism and the accompanying fasting and clairvoyance were probably a source of income. Visitors brought gifts, and Mollie's needlework and waxwork were done on commission and sold in the little shop on Gates Avenue. Her work, however artful it may have

been, undoubtedly attained added value from being made by Mollie Fancher, the Brooklyn Enigma. These facts alone may help explain collusion on the part of her caretakers. Aunt Susan may have been content to go along with what everyone, including Mollie, wanted to believe—that she could exist without food, and see without the sense of sight—because it made life more comfortable, both physically and emotionally.

The other benefits Mollie may have accrued from her situation—from the paralysis, the fasting, the dissociation—are more obscure. Ford, like any therapist, examines her personal history through the lens of his professional knowledge and experience, to reconstruct from a century and a quarter away what her deeply buried motivations might have been. He comes up with the following profile.

Mollie suffered a great deal from the early loss of her mother and the emotional insecurity that ensued. As she reached her teens, she began to feel ambivalent about maturing and all that it entailed—adult responsibility, adult sexuality, the prospect of separating from her reconstituted family of aunt and siblings to begin life with a husband. So the symptoms began—intestinal upsets, exhaustion, fainting, and inability to keep food down—that led to her leaving school.

After the horseback-riding accident, Mollie seemed to be recovering from her "nerves" and from what was possibly an early version of anorexia nervosa. Leaving home to recuperate with friends in the Hudson Valley appeared to improve the state of her mind and health. But then she became engaged to John Taylor, a perfectly eligible and proper young man. That, says Ford, may have been a powerful stressor. "Even today, we frequently see conversion disorders—although not as dramatic as the nineteenth-century variety—before a scheduled marriage," he comments. "Engagement brings up responsibility, sexuality, commitment—and it's very difficult to pull out of an engagement by simply saying, 'I don't want to do this.' It feels more socially acceptable to get sick, which necessarily postpones the marriage, and then the issue eventually dies away."

The prospect of marriage may have been highly threatening to Mollie in particular. "In Victorian times there were often enormous conflicts and ambivalence about sexuality," says Ford. "And the fact that two of her 'alters'—if you're going to think about her later dissociation in that way—were very young, one a child and one a teenager, suggests that she may have been very ambivalent about being an adult."

And then a possible escape route opened, in the form of an errant streetcar. Escape through invalidism was a painful solution, and at first Mollie struggled against it. After a few weeks, she got out of bed and hobbled around her room. At that point, though, the advantages started to show themselves to her—all, of course, below a conscious level. There was a model for the symptoms and behavior she began to adopt, a well-known medical phenomenon of female hysteria, of "bed cases." This was how young women who had been injured could respond: with mysterious paralysis, loss of one or more of the senses, inability to rise from their beds, even trances and spasms. And truly, Mollie did not feel well; her broken ribs hurt, her lungs hurt, her head hurt. She got back into bed. People hovered around her, worried half to death, trying to entice her to eat, holding her when she spasmed, speaking in hushed voices, calling in experts. Mollie was finally the injured child she had always felt herself to be.

Over time, the syndrome grew more complicated, taking a course of its own. The myriad symptoms, the violent spasms and twists, the loss of speech and hearing and sight, the vomiting, the contracted limbs, showed Mollie to be clearly beyond health, a permanent invalid. A year into her mysterious illness, the first *Brooklyn Daily Eagle* article showed what everything could add up to in the world beyond her room. Mollie had a life to lead, strange and agonized though it was. And if certain aspects of it became especially fascinating to other people—the fasting, the visits to the spirit world—she was ready to participate fully, and probably sincerely, in keeping to that program.

There was one other deeply meaningful benefit to Mollie from her dissociation. Being like a child again, as well as believing in the other-worldly aspects of her state (seeing her long-lost mother in heaven, for instance, or hearing her voice and being comforted by her), was a way to maintain some contact with her mother—a desire that apparently haunted Mollie for the rest of her life.

"People who are very histrionic—dramatic, emotional—are able to essentially believe the roles they get themselves into," says Ford. "The distinctions between truth-telling and lying and fantasy are not nearly as clear as some philosophers would like to believe. There is a very real phenomenon of knowing and not knowing at the same time—which is basically a dissociative phenomenon, but one that many people who are relatively normal can engage in to some degree." An example is the person who has had a disruptive or traumatic childhood—with an abusive or absent parent, perhaps—who creates the fantasy that it was relatively stable and normal. "They 'know' that's not quite right or true," explains Ford, "but it's much more comfortable for them to live with this reconstructed history." It feels to them both like the truth and, subtly and below the surface, like a fantasy.

In all probability, Mollie knew-and-didn't-know that she ate. Or, if her dissociation was indeed as deep and as fragmented as Abram Dailey described in his vignettes of the five Mollies, perhaps one Mollie knew while the other four—or at least Sunbeam, the daytime Mollie—did not. One witness to the multiple personalities, George Sargent, said about Ruby, the most vivacious of the five: "She has the air of knowing a good deal more than she tells." Perhaps Ruby was the keeper of the secrets, the part of Mollie that could admit the truth: that she ate, she saw, she imagined and yearned for visits to the spirit world, conversations with her departed mother. If so, Ruby kept that knowledge firmly locked away from the Mollie the rest of the world knew.

The primary Mollie doesn't sound like an out-and-out, bald-faced liar. She sounds sincere—and dissociated. Pierre Janet, the influential early-twentieth-century French psychologist who wrote extensively about dissociative states and multiple personalities, felt that hysteria and mental dissociation were two sides of the same coin. Ford agrees, as do many European psychiatrists to this day. "Here in the United States we have split the two apart and put them in different categories," Ford observes, "but it's the same phenomenon—whether it involves your arm, which in hysteria becomes dissociated and is paralyzed, or a part of your memory, which becomes dissociated and is not remembered. They're different manifestations of the same underlying process."

In general, Ford adds, psychiatric diagnoses are never as cut-and-dried as we tend to think, or as the *DSM-IV* would lead one to believe. "In the real world, many of these disorders are not very distinct. The phenomena blur over, the boundaries are fluid." A patient may fit primarily one psychiatric diagnosis at one time and another at another time, depending on a multitude of circumstances—including how much reinforcement there is for a particular symptom or syndrome at any given time. Our understanding of mental illness, and even our experience of it, depends greatly on the beliefs of the world around us. If our neighbors, and doctors, believe in multiple personalities and decade-long fasting and sudden unexplained paralysis, some of us will fall victim to those ailments.

Perhaps the most astonishing aspect of Mollie's story today, long after her claims were discussed with a straight face in the New York press, is the fact that so many people beyond the psychological hotbed of her sickroom appeared to believe such things. We live in an age of technology and skepticism that, at least in our jaded, computer monitor–glazed eyes, seems to tower over the nineteenth century's self-important scientific revolution. From this vantage point, the details of Mollie's existence appear swathed in a mist of Victorian eccentricity and madness—the craziest element of all being not Mollie's powerful dissociations but the gullibility of her audience.

And yet we have our crazy stories too, our dark corners of gullibility. That propensity is one of many similarities—scientific, psychological, and spiritual—between the cultural textures of Mollie's era and of our own. It took a precise mix of influences to create an environment that could support the Brooklyn Enigma: an internalizing of societal pressures and alienation in the form of neurotic illness, a longing for spiritual values in an increasingly scientific and secular world, a questioning of the essential meaning of personality or soul, a struggle with food and eating that was beginning to make the dinner table a symbolic battlefield, a media industry attuned to the Big Story and how to milk it. It is a familiar mix, as well, of some aspects of turn-of-twenty-first-century America.

For instance, is it any less sane to believe in fasting than to believe that practitioners of satanic ritual have managed to conduct secret ceremonies across the country in which babies are sacrificed and their warm blood quaffed by cult members, and in which children are drugged, tortured, and sexually abused? Or than to imprison someone for the rest of his life for murder on the basis of one person's "recovered memory" from childhood (a type of "memory" that some psychiatrists say can be suggested by an overzealous therapist)? Those represent beliefs that have been alive and well in this country within the last decade.

A theory afoot among some philosophers and psychologists posits that these kinds of ideas constitute a modern form of hysteria. Despite the apparently abrupt death of Charcot's *grande hystérie* at the end of the nineteenth century, these thinkers propose that hysteria itself never really went away—that it still occurs as a watered-down conversion disorder in the occasional psychiatric patient, and that it has morphed into other shapes as well to fit the changing cultural landscape. We live in a new era of hysteria, writes the historian Elaine Showalter, characterized not by trances and phantom paralyses but by a panoply of psychogenic ailments. "Psychological plagues at the end of the twentieth century are all too real," she comments, citing multiple-personality disorder, satanic-ritual abuse, alien abduction, recovered memory, and even Gulf War syndrome as examples.

Showalter believes that these contemporary hysterical patients seek external sources on which to blame their problems, pointing to viruses, sexual molestation, chemical warfare, satanic conspiracies, or alien infiltration. These new hysterics strenuously reject psychological explanations for their symptoms, feeling that their pain is trivialized unless both cause and cure are placed outside the self. The central idea of the new hysteria is victimhood. Hysteria is also now more contagious, Showalter feels, because of our vast and instantaneous communication systems. News about the latest psychogenic illness can be spread by self-help books, television talk shows, the Internet, and a newspaper and magazine industry that dwarfs that of a hundred years ago. Showalter and others believe that modern hysteria is reaching a high-water mark, that the United States is becoming a "hot zone of psychogenic diseases."

Others believe that hysteria is an essential part of human experience. The historian Robert Woolsey has called it a "protolanguage" and its symptoms a "code used by a patient to communicate a message which, for various reasons, cannot be verbalized." Another historian who has written widely on hysteria characterizes it as a nonverbal messaging system: it is not a disease, he writes, but rather "an alternative physical, verbal, and gestural language, an iconic social communication."

If the larger message of nineteenth-century hysteria was ambivalence about women's changing role in middle-class society, and frustration on the part of women who had no acceptable outlet for their education and ambitions, today's message may be one of overstimulation. Consider how Beard's five causes of nervousness have expanded exponentially since the 1870s.

"Steam power" has become jet and even rocket travel; "the periodical press" has become a mountain of material appearing at every instant—written, recorded, filmed, transmitted live by satellite, so that the news can never be shut out; "the telegraph" is now not only Bell's telephone but omnipresent cell phones, fax machines, e-mail, instant computer messaging; "the sciences" are uncovering the genetic blueprint of human beings, and can, among other miracles, enable one woman to give birth to another woman's genetic child; and "the mental activity of women," which led to education, employment, and the ubiquity of the working wife and mother, has completely transformed American social and family life. Americans' lives are splintered and transient in ways beyond even Beard's imagining: half of all marriages begun end in divorce, very few children grow up to live in the communities of their childhood, fast food is a way of life, and speed appears to be the quality admired above all others.

Showalter feels that hysteria is a cultural symptom of anxiety and stress, and if ever there was a set of conditions designed to induce stress and overburdened psyches, this twenty-first-century formula would seem to fill the bill. Exhaustion, bad stomachs, headaches, depression, hopelessness, anxiety, heart palpitations, phobias, and many other ingredients in Beard's cauldron of nervousness are everyday experiences for many Americans—and all are typical physical and emotional responses to stress. There is a natural descendant of Beard's neurasthenia among us today, called chronic fatigue syndrome (CFS); it is one of the illnesses Showalter proposes as hysterical. CFS, like multiple-personality disorder, is a controversial diagnosis. Depending on who's talking, it either is nonexistent—merely a vague miscellany of symptoms that are probably psychologically influenced—or is a physical disease, infectious and likely caused by a virus, that in the 1990s was said to be approaching epidemic proportions.

Like neurasthenia, CFS seems, according to some doctors, to include almost every imaginable symptom. David Bell, in his 1994 book *The*

Doctor's Guide to Chronic Fatigue Syndrome, lists forty-three symptoms (in the league of Beard's catalogue of fifty-plus signs of neurasthenia), including: impaired short-term memory or concentration, sore throat, tender lymph nodes, muscle pain, joint pain, headaches, unrefreshing sleep, postexertional malaise, balance disturbance, blurring of vision, diarrhea, dizziness, hair loss, light sensitivity, sexual dysfunction, rashes, numbness and/or tingling in extremities, and chills. Other doctors have included symptoms especially reminiscent of Victorian hysteria: ataxia (failure of muscular coordination), fainting spells, transient focal paresis (weakness or partial paralysis on one side) and transient blindness, both typically lasting six hours to three days. The National Institutes of Health narrowed the official definition in the mid-1990s to include only unexplained, persistent, or relapsing chronic fatigue and at least four of the first eight symptoms on Bell's list.

While Beard attributed neurasthenia to cultural stressors, those who hold that CFS is an actual disease reject the notion of psychological causes. While Beard was forecasting the future of psychiatry by making a connection between mental and emotional states (as well as the social milieu that shaped them) and their effect on a person's overall functioning, CFS sufferers consider a psychological explanation for their ills insulting. Beard, in an era in which medical materialism reigned and every condition was assumed to have a physical basis, was venturing into new terrain by suggesting that social stress could cause malaise. In today's psychologically sophisticated culture, though, many people feel their illness is real only if it is physical in nature. Anything else smacks of malingering or laziness.

In that light, Beard's thinking appears more holistic—more "new age"—than that of modern nonconformist doctors who feel CFS has been given short shrift by mainstream medicine. David Bell, one of the first doctors to view CFS as a physical syndrome, told a reporter in 1994, "If I were to make any suggestions for changes in American medical schools, it would be that they train doctors to be more like doctors in the nineteenth century. They were great clinicians, and I think they would have handled chronic fatigue syndrome quite nicely." But Beard himself probably would have responded to CFS with speculations about the role of social and psychological factors, and wondered whether the patient's "nerve force" was being depleted by the demands of a hurried and technological age. In contrast, Bell, in his *Doctor's Guide,* describes the search for the origins of CFS, stating baldly: "I am among those who do not believe that depression or mental illness is the cause."

Ultimately, whether CFS is considered psychologically based or organic may not matter; symptoms are just as real in psychogenic illnesses as in physical ones. If a patient feels exhausted, he is exhausted; if Mollie Fancher believed she was blind, then she was functionally blind. CFS exists just as nineteenth-century hysteria existed. A Harvard Medical School researcher has suggested that CFS may become "a paradigmatic illness that leads us away from being trapped by the rigidity of the conventional biomedical model and leads us toward a fuller understanding of suffering"—the direction in which Beard seemed headed when his work was cut short by his death in 1883.

In many ways, though, psychiatry has concurrently been moving away from Beard's prophecies and back toward the working model of nineteenth-century materialists such as William Hammond: the notion that biology and chemistry will unlock the secrets of the human mind. The very questions that Leslie Stephen and other Victorian philosophers agonized over as medicine and psychology became more mechanical— Are we simply collections of chemicals? Where is the soul or essence to be found in such a stew, or does it not really exist?—are back in force. Psychiatry in general has made a dramatic turn away from the talking cure and toward the use of Zoloft, Xanax, and other new and effective drugs, in the process seeming to transform elements that once were thought of as simply part of character (pessimism, shyness, reserve, hyperactivity) into neuroses that can be magically shed, or at least softened, with the right chemical. But, as Peter Kramer asks in his 1993 book *Listening to Prozac,* how do we know who the real person is: the shy, depressed wallflower with his inborn formula of brain chemicals, or the happier, friendlier fellow whose level of serotonin has been adjusted?

The eagerness to brand certain behaviors as signs of dysfunctional neuroses rather than signs of personality traits or even of philosophical outlooks—and then to alter those behaviors by redesigning brain chemistry with psychoactive drugs—has become so common that it now invites editorializing and even parody. A commentary on a Broadway revival of Arthur Miller's *Death of a Salesman* subtitled "Get That Man Some Prozac" quoted two psychiatrists diagnosing the tragic hero, Willy Loman, as manic-depressive with hallucinatory aspects. Margaret Talbot, writing for *The New York Times Magazine,* took a jaundiced look at what she called "the latest trait to become a pathology": shyness syndrome. Shyness, renamed social anxiety disorder or social phobia, can now be "treated" by Paxil, an antidepressant.

Even Winnie-the-Pooh and his quirky fellow inhabitants of the Hundred Acre Wood have not escaped the medicalization of personality. A group of pediatricians wrote a parody of a scientific paper, published in the *Canadian Medical Association Journal,* diagnosing Pooh, Piglet, and the rest of Christopher Robin's crowd with *DSM-IV* standards. Their conclusions: Pooh has attention deficit hyperactivity disorder (ADHD) and possibly obsessive-compulsive disorder (OCD) as well, and is a candidate for methylphenidate (brand name Ritalin, a central nervous system stimulant often prescribed for ADHD). Piglet's generalized anxiety disorder would respond to paroxetine (the generic name for Paxil, which counters not only depression but anxiety, panic attacks, and social phobias as well), and the chronically, though mildly, depressed Eeyore would probably benefit from fluoxetine (known the world over as Prozac). Tigger, with his hyperactivity and impulsivity, needs a stimulant medication, perhaps combined with clonidine (prescribed for high blood pressure and Tourette's syndrome). To judge from the letters to the editor received by and later published in the journal, many readers did not get the joke.

Thoughtful doctors have begun to see Prozac and the rest of the new generation of psychoactive drugs as a mixed blessing. Peter Kramer describes how Prozac poses a possible danger of "cosmetic psycho-pharmacology" (using chemicals to modify personality in attractive ways, not just to treat illness), and has changed the way psychiatrists think of various neuroses. When such behaviors as seeking self-destructive personal relationships with the opposite sex or being oversensitive at work respond to a biological treatment, Kramer writes, the suggestion is that these behaviors are "biologically encoded." If they are, how does that affect our notions of responsibility, of free will, of unique and socially determinative individual development: in effect, our notion of our souls, of what makes us who we are? When a patient who has felt unconfident, vulnerable, and depressed for most of her life begins taking Prozac and feels "like herself" for the first time, what does that mean, Kramer wonders. "Who had she been all those years if not herself? Had medication somehow removed a false self and replaced it with a true one?"

Part of the doubt and confusion raised by drugs like Prozac may reside in the fact that we often feel defined by our challenges and our struggles: those are what display our mettle, show the stuff we're made of. If they are resolved by some external power, what does that leave to us? Is our Prozac-inspired happiness just window-dressing, an easy, mindless glide through life? This is where the question of psychoactive drugs begins to intersect with the divine, with our larger ideas of why we're here on earth. Religious belief is rooted in struggle: against evil, against meaninglessness, against the uncaring, unethical part of ourselves. Kramer describes a Walker Percy novel, *The Thanatos Syndrome,* in which a drug called Heavy Sodium is put into the water supply and removes everyone's angst. Writing decades before the introduction of Prozac, Percy might seem to be describing the billion-dollar drug that was to come. But his view of its effects were not happy: "By reducing human self-consciousness," Kramer says of the fictional Heavy Sodium, "the drug robs individuals of their souls. What links men and women to God is precisely their guilt, anxiety, and loneliness."

The magazine *Christianity Today* addressed this matter head-on in 1995 in an article titled "The Gospel According to Prozac: Can a Pill Do What the Holy Spirit Could Not?" Full of anecdotes from religiously devout people who have used Prozac for depression or obsessive-compulsive disorder, the article poses many more questions than we are yet able to answer: What is sin, and what is biology? Are individuals biochemically determined, or are they able to accept the ethical responsibility for their behavior? And for the pious: Are Prozac and similar antidepressants potentially a shortcut for people to feel good without the character-forming discipline of faith and religious belief? (The atheistic may simply replace "faith and religious belief" with "self-examination, possibly through psychotherapy.")

These questions about what makes us who we are could not have risen at a more opportune time. Many Americans are, like their Victorian forebears, in the throes of a spiritual reevaluation. This one is spurred not by shocking new ideas about mankind's origins, or by the threat of a rising scientific hegemony that would replace God and answer all our questions of faith with hard facts, but instead by the realization that science has failed to fulfill certain human needs that refuse to go away. It's as if we've peered over the edge into a world without God, and retreated from the precipice. The soul, wherever it resides, is back in play.

Some of the return to religious belief has taken new and offbeat directions: interest in Eastern religions, miracles, crystals, feminist goddess worship. But mainstream religions are reviving as well; church membership in the United States today stands at more than sixty percent of the population, while in the middle of the nineteenth century it was thirty-four percent. A significant number of people are switching from the religion of their parents to another faith, or "shopping for God," as one such seeker described it in *Vogue*. A cover story in *Newsweek* reported on the yearning for a "sacred dimension to life"— a need to feel connected to something larger than one's own petty concerns. An accompanying article described how for some people the gap between faith and science was closing, how new scientific discoveries in physics, biology, and astronomy are inspiring "a sense of cosmic piety, of serene holism and even a moral code."

Much in the way that Charles Darwin was able to see the work of a Creator in the intricately interwoven laws and essential logic of evolution and natural selection, some scientists have recently begun to perceive divinity in the immutable laws of physics and biology. An astrophysicist at the University of California, Santa Cruz, sees a correlation between the scientific story of the birth of the universe and medieval Jewish texts that describe the universe beginning in a point and then expanding. Stephen Hawking ends his seminal book about the cosmos, *A Brief History of Time,* with a discussion of the role of a deity in the creation of the universe. Even if we ultimately find a complete unified theory that explains the universe, Hawking muses, it will still be just a set of rules and equations. What breathed life into those equations to begin with? he asks. "Why does the universe go to all the bother of existing? Is the unified theory so compelling that it brings about its own existence? Or does it need a creator, and, if so, does he have any other effect on the universe? And who created him?" In the past, Hawking says, science asked *what* the universe was, and philosophers asked *why*. A complete unified theory would unite the two. "Then," he concludes grandly, "we would know the mind of God."

Although *A Brief History of Time* sold more than nine million copies worldwide and was translated into forty languages, it is doubtful that a large percentage of that readership fully understood Hawking's cosmological insights. But esoteric theorizing like his has been echoed in the popular culture—perhaps a truer sign of the penetration of ideas. Angels lurk everywhere from television shows to jewelry designs to greeting cards, medieval and Buddhist chants hit the CD charts, books about near-death experiences and spiritual journeys and advice are fixtures on the bestseller lists. One of these, *Care of the Soul* by Thomas Moore, almost single-handedly brought the word "soul" back into everyday use. Moore, a former Catholic monk who has worked as a professor of religion and psychology as well as a psychotherapist (someone who treats psychiatric disorders through therapy but is not necessarily a medical doctor), suggests in the first sentence of the book that the "great malady of the twentieth century" is "loss of soul." In an echo of the mind-to-soul transition in nineteenth-century psychology, Moore makes the distinction that "psychology is a secular science, while care of the soul is a sacred art." Much as people have welcomed the practical benefits of psychotherapy, he believes that they long for that lost sacred art.

Moore proposes a new definition of psychology that is in some ways a return to the mid-nineteenth-century notion of the inseparability of mind and soul. Our psychology now, he writes, is modern, secular, and ego-centered; it must be "radically re-imagined" so that psychology and spirituality are seen as one. Peter Kramer's *Listening to Prozac* also proposes a rethinking of at least one major aspect of psychology, the definition of neurosis, in a manner that recalls the nineteenth century. "Neurosis of the twenty-first century," he says, "will be a disorder that encompasses the effects of heredity and trauma—risk and stress—on a variety of neuropsychological functions encoded in neuroanatomy and the states of the neurotransmitters." Here he sounds very much like William Hammond in the 1870s, insisting that psychology involved "nervous physiology" above all.

Two psychotherapists, both moving forward by moving back, both forecasting the future of psychiatry in terms that characterized Victorian lines of thought. Mollie Fancher is long forgotten, far more than even William Hammond, George Beard, or neurasthenia. Yet it should not be surprising that her story, and the longings, anxieties, and philosophical controversies that it exposed, have a resonance today. We have moved forward since her heyday in the 1870s into a world increasingly demanding, disorienting, and isolating. We have seen anorexia nervosa and related eating disorders blossom into a scourge of young women; we have found many ways, both cognitive and chemical, to cope with mental illness; we have come close to mapping the chemistry of human life itself through genetic research. And beneath these transformations, we still grapple with the fears and yearnings that characterized the century of upheaval that gave birth to the Fasting Girl.

CHAPTER ELEVEN

The End of the Enigma

Fame had come to the corner of Gates Avenue and Downing Street, and although the outward signs of that fame stole away in the darkness the memory will remain so long as the street corner endures.

—*The Brooklyn Daily Eagle,* February 4, 1916

A S THE 1880S WORE ON, Mollie Fancher maintained her strategic silence. But despite the unresolved ending to her story (or perhaps because of it) she had become an established curiosity, a citizen of note. In the 1890s a friend wrote of Mollie in a letter, "In Brooklyn, not to know about this famous lady is to prove one's self unknowing." In 1883, Mollie was among the prominent city residents to receive a personal invitation to the opening of the Brooklyn Bridge. She did not, of course, attend, but she was so proud of what the offer conveyed that she had the engraved invitation framed.

Mollie was growing a bit stout, and two pictures from 1886 and 1887 show a round face surmounted by tight curls. An official end date to her purported fast was never publicly offered. The time slipped past, and it eventually became common knowledge that this now pudgy woman was eating. A friend who contributed a statement to Abram Dailey's book in 1893 told of eating lunch with Mollie; she ate "very daintily, but she ate something." Mollie's faithful doctor of several decades, R. Fleet Speir, described her 1890s diet as consisting of jellies, fruit, and great quantities of water.

Even as her life descended from the heights of fame to mere prominence and a tamer celebrity, the ripples from her days of controversy wafted gently outward. Thus, for instance, the Mollie Fancher affair later indirectly influenced Franz Kafka, in a six-degrees-of-separation way, with Henry Tanner as the linchpin of the connection. His spectacular forty-day fast in the summer of 1880 may have failed to prove Mollie's integrity, but it did, albeit unintentionally, launch a new age of "hunger artists."

Hunger artists, or "living skeletons," had appeared intermittently as freaks of nature over the centuries: mostly men, who for various reasons had become emaciated to the point of transparency, and who exhibited themselves to the world. Earlier in the nineteenth century, fairs and circuses might count living skeletons among their sideshow artists. Isaac Sprague, who at five-foot-four reportedly weighed all of fifty-two pounds and was billed as "The Original Thin Man," toured with P. T. Barnum at mid-century. The salient point about hunger artists was that they were performing a job: they earned their living by starving.

In the last quarter of the century, hunger artistry took off. Soon no circus or fair was complete without its skeleton man, and prominent fasters from Europe and America toured both continents. Tanner had set the bar high: no hunger artist with any pride at all could fast less than forty days, and several died in the attempt. Spectators were fascinated by the ghoulish spectacle, and came in droves to gape at the starving men.

Hunger artistry declined early in the twentieth century, partly because in the new sophistication of the Freudian age, the living skeletons were now seen as ill or psychologically damaged. It wasn't amusing to gawk at someone who might be self-destructing; it now seemed morally repugnant. By 1930, film and other modern forms of

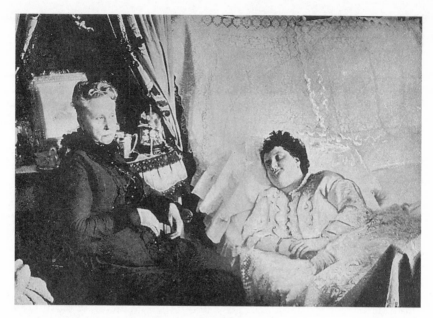

Mollie Fancher in the late 1880s with her long-suffering aunt Susan. Mollie was at her most rotund during this period, and although her fame lingered, no more was spoken of the fast. (FROM *MOLLIE FANCHER, THE BROOKLYN ENIGMA*)

entertainment put an end to many sideshow activities, including the business of human starvation. In 1924, that fading business was immortalized with the publication of Franz Kafka's story "A Hunger Artist" (sometimes translated as "A Fasting Artist"), which chronicled the decline of professional fasting through the life and death of one unnamed practitioner. Not only was Kafka's hunger artist dedicated to "the honor of his profession," he was in love with starving itself. His secret was that for him it was actually the easiest thing in the world to fast. At the end of forty days—the term fixed by his impresario—the hunger artist always wanted to continue, and had to be forced to eat.

Kafka's description of the faster's devotion to hunger is graphic, and many psychiatrists have concluded, from Kafka's life and his writings, that he was anorexic himself. Always extremely thin, he has been described as ascetic in his lifestyle, frightened by sexuality, perfectionis-

302

tic, compulsive, and highly preoccupied with food while at the same time almost phobic about eating. Whether or not he fit the clinical diagnosis of anorexia nervosa, Kafka was clearly a disturbed eater and keenly attuned to the motivations and thought patterns of anorexia. Just as Mollie Fancher provided a bridge between fasting girls' anorexia mirabilis and the pathology of anorexia nervosa, Kafka, the medical historians Walter Vandereycken and Ron Van Deth have theorized, was a "connecting link" to modern anorexia from a different direction—from the nineteenth-century art of fasting, rather than the tradition of religious fasting.

Mollie's case flared briefly back to life more directly in the 1890s, in a smaller recapitulation of the events of 1878. Abram Dailey, who had been a friend of Mollie's for more than a decade, became possessed of the need to establish her credibility once and for all—especially the truth of her clairvoyance, which spoke to his devout Spiritualist beliefs. In August 1892, he read a paper on Mollie before a meeting of the Psychical Congress at the Columbian Exposition World's Fair Auxiliary in Chicago, and described the second sight and fasting that had caused an uproar fourteen years earlier. Dailey's descriptions of her wonders were remarkable enough to raise the ire of a new generation of scientists. His tales, proclaimed members of the Medico-Legal Society of New York, were at such odds with generally held medical beliefs that they should be investigated by a committee of physicians "whose statements would be accepted by the scientific world." As, it was implied, the statements of a nonmedical person, a surrogate court judge who was a member of Mollie's inner circle, would not be.

Abram Dailey wanted to have it both ways: to be Mollie Fancher's chronicler—essentially, her publicist—but without having to present any proof or credentials. He advised Mollie to turn this new crew of doctors away, and when their leader, George Chaffee, knocked on her door, she would not admit him. Dailey later reported to the Medico-Legal Society that Mollie's condition had changed since 1878, so that it would not be fair or accurate to test her when her clairvoyance was less reliable. The Society came down hard. This refusal, its journal proclaimed, would "add to the reserve with which the medical profession receive the details of her case."

Now Dailey had the bit between his teeth. The result was, in 1894, the 262-page *Mollie Fancher, the Brooklyn Enigma* (subtitled *An Authentic Statement of Facts in the Life of Mary J. Fancher, the Psychological Marvel of the Nineteenth Century,* and featuring the "unimpeachable testimony of many witnesses"), the only book written about Mollie. The work is a hodgepodge of anecdotes, newspaper article texts, entries from Aunt Susan's diary, letters of testimony from friends and witnesses, and interviews with the 1890s Mollie. She was then apparently in the process of regaining her sight (cogent evidence that her blindness was hysterical), was regularly "partaking of the juices and strength of food," and had broad fleshy shoulders and a large face.

The small impact that the book registered with the public passed quickly. Mollie, free of further challenges, spent her days making wax flowers and fancy embroideries to sell in the little ground-floor shop at 160 Gates Avenue; the curious came to gaze and buy trinkets fashioned by the "psychological marvel" of a waning age.

But the marvel, as it happened, was due one more visit to the front page.

At the beginning of 1916, Mollie Fancher would have looked out on a much-changed Brooklyn from her window at the corner of Gates and Downing. Motorcar engines rattled down the street—trucks making deliveries; sleek open-air roadsters carrying travelers, and even a few commuters. The worlds of commerce and fashion were accommodating themselves to the ascendance of the car. Women favored motor coats specially made to protect them from the cold, since most cars still were open vehicles. Lectures were held to discuss highway construction and maintenance; road tests were conducted to determine gaso-

Mollie Fancher's home in 1915, the year before she died. She was still living in the second-floor back bedroom, from which she had not stirred for fifty years. Mollie offered her needlework and waxwork for sale in the storefront facing Gates Avenue. (BROOKLYN PUBLIC LIBRARY, BROOKLYN COLLECTION)

line and oil consumption over various distances; Columbia University in New York established a department of highway engineering.

The automobile, proclaimed the president of the Willys-Overland car company to reporters and other manufacturers at the sixteenth annual National Automobile Show in 1916, was a magic carpet of modern civilization, annihilating distance, "converting our wishes to come and go into realities." Little more than a decade previously, the automobile had been the object of sneers and derision; as K. P. Drysdale of Cadillac put it, "The owner of an automobile was the butt of the jester. Today he is the envy of his friends and neighbors." In Drysdale's view, the motorcar had been transformed from the rich man's plaything to the world's necessity.

The accident-prone horsecars of Mollie's girlhood disaster were long gone, replaced by trolleys. Telephones, photographs, phonographs, and electric lamps were appliances of everyday life. Newspapers, once consisting of long columns of type, were now illustrated tabloids full of photos. A picture that poignantly captured the last remnants of nineteenth-century life amid the new tools of the twentieth century was published in *The Brooklyn Daily Eagle* in February 1916. It showed Mountain Chief, a Blackfoot Indian, in full dress—long-fringed leather jacket and pants decorated with a diamond pattern, headdress lined with feathers—sitting on a little upholstered chair with ramrod-straight back and folded hands. His face was impassive, turned slightly to the side, eyes shadowed by the edge of the headdress, mouth set in a straight line. In front of him was the hornlike mouthpiece of a phonograph recorder; a woman in a shirtwaist, a representative of the Smithsonian Institution, sat beside him operating the machine. The U.S. government had commissioned a project to make phonographic records of songs and conversation of the rapidly vanishing Native Americans.

An ordinary Victrola phonograph could be purchased for one's living room for fifteen dollars, and table lamps for a few dollars. Saturday evenings could now be spent at a movie house, where the best seats cost one dollar and the cheapest twenty-five cents. D. W. Griffith's stupendous *Birth of a Nation* had wowed the public the year before. In Brooklyn it had been shown at the Montauk theater with an accompanying thirty-piece orchestra. Brooklyn itself was the home of several "moving picture plants," in the Flushing and Flatbush areas.

In January 1916, dress hems were inching up, often to above the ankle and even sometimes to mid-calf, exposing buttoned-up boots. Long Island train commuters were complaining, as they would for most of the century, about deficiencies of service between Manhattan and the island. Aviation entrepreneurs were contemplating forming a company that would fly summer visitors from New York City to the Jersey shore. And people worried about military preparedness on the

East Coast in case of an attack by the Germans, who the year before had sunk the British passenger liner *Lusitania,* killing 128 Americans.

In Mollie Fancher's bedroom, she and her friends were planning a somewhat macabre celebration. Realizing that she was approaching the fiftieth anniversary of her invalidism, which she calculated as having commenced in earnest on February 3, 1866, someone had conceived the idea of celebrating her "golden anniversary" with a grand reception—a concept enthusiastically embraced by its honoree.

This was no longer the publicity-shy and sensory-deprived young woman of the 1870s. The sixty-nine-year-old Mollie Fancher appeared an ordinary old lady, with perhaps a touch more irony or wit than other old ladies of the era. No longer blind or fasting, and rarely clairvoyant, Mollie had lost some of her middle-aged pudginess; she was moderately thin and had a drawn face appropriate for her age. Most striking was her open enjoyment of the attentions that her moments of fame had brought her. When she planned her reception, she sent an invitation to President Woodrow Wilson—and to her joy received a personal response from his secretary, sending, however, his regrets. She now welcomed reporters, no longer turning them away as she had steadfastly done at the height of her celebrity.

In 1915, when a friend informed the *Daily Eagle* of her approaching anniversary and the newspaper dispatched a reporter to her home, Mollie received him cordially. Ushered into her room, he found something like Miss Havisham's untouched boudoir—but without the bitterness or the cobwebs. Almost nothing in Mollie's room had been altered in half a century. She lay in the same rosewood four-poster bed she had taken to after her accident, which had been in her family for 150 years now. The rosewood dresser had not been moved; the upholstered chairs were the same as they had been when Aunt Susan, who had died in the late 1880s, used to sit in them. (Mollie had since been cared for by paid housekeepers and attendants.) The special curtained bureau-

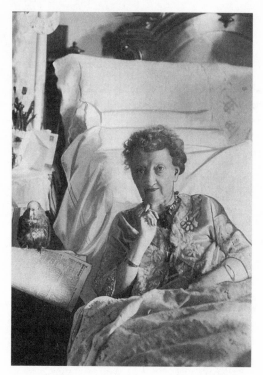

Mollie Fancher in December 1915, with her parrot Joe, on the bed she was carried to after her horsecar accident in 1865. The Brooklyn Daily Eagle *now termed her "Brooklyn's famous invalid, known all over the world."* (BROOKLYN PUBLIC LIBRARY, BROOKLYN COLLECTION)

and-cabinet was next to the bed, its surface covered with framed pictures and ornaments. The bed linens remained snowy white, embroidered and fringed with lace in high Victorian style.

The only difference in the room was the sunlight; gone were the days of drawn curtains and twenty-four-hour gloom. Mollie now sat up against a pile of pillows, with light streaming in through the windows and her parrot Joe hopping around the bed. When the *Eagle* photographer set up his camera, Mollie insisted that Joe be included in the picture (he perched next to her). She rested her chin on her hand, leaned toward the bird, and looked directly into the lens with eyes that unmistakably saw—her straight, unwavering gaze recalls the sixteen-year-old Mollie, still at school, and touched by emotional upheaval but not yet by physical pain.

The bright room and the clear eyes signaled a deeper change in Mollie. Every description of her during the fiftieth-anniversary celebration emphasized her cheerfulness and sunny disposition. She had apparently come to a happier place, psychically, than the one she inhabited in the 1870s. One has the feeling that, in this new century and with her new sense of self, the hysteria that almost surely put her in her bed fifty years before would have found no permanent home. As it was, her body was withered and atrophied from a half-century of immobility, her joints damaged by spasms and extended contracture; she was an invalid by virtue of having long *been* an invalid. But most of the other symptoms of hysteria had vanished: she could hear, see, feel, eat, move her upper body at will, and there was no more mention of trances, spasms, or the "five Mollies."

The 1915 Mollie was eager to talk to the *Eagle* reporter about her party plans. "I shall send out five hundred gold cards," she told him. "There is nothing cheap about Mollie Fancher. When my anniversary comes around, everything that I have will be gold. I shall have yellow flowers and there will be refreshments." Evening approached, and the reporter expressed worry of overstaying his welcome. Mollie told him he need not go so soon; she had no engagements.

As she spoke, her parrot, now in his cage, hung upside down and croaked out, "Hello, Mollie Fancher! Pretty Mollie Fancher!" She explained to the reporter that "the world knows me as Mollie Fancher, and so does Joe. I am not Miss Fancher, for then people would think I am an old maid, and that I don't want to be." Joe had been with Mollie twelve years by then, and she chattered with him often, sometimes revealingly. "I ask him whether life is a burden and if marriage is a failure," she said, "and he sits up to scratch his ear as if he meant to say 'Yes.' Don't you, Joe?"

When the reporter wondered at her cheerfulness, she described it as deriving from her trust in God. "If I should lose faith in God I would have to throw up the sponge," she said, and then laughed at her use of trendy slang. It is not hard to imagine, at such a moment, a Mollie born at the turn of the century, free of hysteria and paralysis, who would be an outspoken flapper in the Roaring Twenties. If her accident had happened in a different era—if she had been a schoolgirl born in 1900 and injured in 1915—there might have been no Enigma, no Fasting Girl, no Psychological Marvel. Mollie would perhaps have been neurotic, maybe even anorexic, but she would not have taken to her bed for fifty years.

The golden anniversary was to be Mollie's payback, recompense for all those lost years. But the buildup to the big day was becoming so fraught that Mollie's friends worried that it might be too much for her to handle. On the day before, February 2, Mollie became uncharacteristically gloomy. As a winter storm blew outside, she compared the dark weather to her trials. "If I have a stormy day for my reception," she said, "it will be a fitting illustration of my life. Many storms and shadows and just a little sunshine."

But the next morning bright skies had returned, and Mollie was ready to enjoy what the *Eagle* grandiosely called "a reception such as the world has never before known" for Brooklyn's famous invalid. Mollie attracted three hundred visitors—an impressive measure of fame for a withered lady whose most public moments had come thirty-eight years before. She and her attendants held two open houses, one in the afternoon and one stretching through the evening until midnight. Her modest house had been transformed, with Japanese lanterns (lit by electric bulbs) strung across the façade and along the hall ceiling inside, while every banister and post was twined with smilax, an evergreen vine, and golden ribbons. The entry hall was a bower of flowers, with huge vases of roses on every table and stand. Mollie's friends had even engaged a doorman to announce to every visitor that she was receiving upstairs.

Mollie's room was another garden, with smilax, decorated with hundreds of tiny electric bulbs, climbing on all four bedposts. Mollie

Mollie Fancher on February 2, 1916, the day before her "golden jubilee" celebration, with parrot Joe looking on. The party, which commemorated the fiftieth anniversary of her invalidism, was a glittering success. Within nine days, the Brooklyn Enigma was dead. (BROOKLYN PUBLIC LIBRARY, BROOKLYN COLLECTION)

sat against a mountain of white pillows, dressed in a pale-blue silk mat-inée dress that she had sewn herself. She had stitched hundreds of tiny white roses onto it, each filled with seed pearls. Beside her on the bed sat her beloved Joe, confined to his cage, as the social swirl made him nervous. Along one side of the room, a long table brought in for the occasion was piled high with gifts.

One by one the guests approached Mollie's bedside from the adjacent parlor. At first she seemed nervous, as though the strain of entertaining was too much. But soon she was happily chattering and greeting her friends, some of whom she hadn't seen in years. The *Eagle* documented the event, relating several especially dramatic moments. One woman approached the invalid and said she had begged for an invitation because she had wanted to meet Mollie all her life. "I live close by," she told Mollie. "This is the first time I have had the courage to come in, although I have hesitated before your door hundreds of times." When Mollie asked how long she had been hesitating, the woman replied, "Since you were first injured." Mollie was astounded. "Think of it—all these years," she said. "Well, dear, you have paid your first visit. Come in every single time you pass and please pass often."

Another guest—an older man, but still alert and firm of step—was recognized by no one but Mollie. "Why, it's Winfield Pettit!" she cried. "It has been forty years at least. I am happy to make you welcome." Pettit had owned the horse that threw Mollie onto the pavement so many decades before, in the first and lesser of her two accidents.

As the evening wore on, Mollie appeared to gain strength from the excitement around her. At midnight, when the reception ended, she had the exhilaration of a hostess who has thrown the party of her life— much anticipated, then almost dreaded, finally enjoyed with a proprietary sense of pride. "Was it not wonderful?" she exclaimed to a few close friends who remained. "I think I should be the proudest woman in the world. Think of it! All these people came to see Mollie Fancher, and I have not left this bed for fifty years." Then she added, "What pleases me most is that everyone who called seemed to love me. . . . I saw people today who have not been here in years. They had to come—the influence of Mollie Fancher again."

When asked if she was tired, she replied, "I am a bit weary now, but think of my wonderful reception." Her friends agreed that she had weathered the event beautifully. Four days later, though, she felt ill— just a slight cold in the head, she said. Her lungs had always been easily congested, and this cold settled in them quickly. By the next day, Tuesday, her doctor was at her side, and on Wednesday relatives were called in and a nurse stayed with her day and night. On Thursday, February 10, one week after the reception, *The Brooklyn Daily Eagle* published a letter Mollie had written three days earlier thanking everyone who had helped with the celebration.

That evening, in accordance with her doctor's orders, a tank of oxygen was carried into 160 Gates Avenue. Late that night, Mollie sank deeper into her pillows, her breathing labored. At twelve fifty-five, her breaths stopped forever. The very day after Mollie's letter of thanks was published, the front page of the *Eagle* announced her demise: "Mollie Fancher at Rest at Last / Death Ends Famous Invalid's Half Century of Suffering." Although the paper reported that she had apparently experienced no ill effects from her "jubilee" reception, it characterized her ailment as the grippe (another term for influenza or a viral infection), and it is likely that her exposure to hundreds of visitors that day may have introduced the virus or bacteria that killed her. One wonders whether, having reached a milestone that she had anticipated for years—and a fame that was vindication rather than burden—she finally felt free to let go.

Mollie's death, like her fiftieth-anniversary celebration, demonstrated the breadth of her fame. For several days mourners streamed through her house to pay their respects; even the mailman, who had delivered letters to Mollie for twenty-three years, requested a private moment with the body. On Sunday, when a memorial open house was held, at least two hundred people visited Mollie's room, where her corpse was laid out on the rosewood bed, the pile of pillows replaced by a single lace-covered one, a solitary white lily lying on her breast. The next day Mollie lay in a casket decorated with four thousand sprays of lily-of-the-valley, and funeral services were conducted in the room she had occupied for so long. Mourners filled every room, upstairs and down; latecomers packed the stairs and hallways. *The New York Times* later estimated that 150 people were in attendance.

Throughout the proceedings, Mollie's characteristic flair for the dramatic was on display. Just as she had stage-managed her life within that small bedroom, she had looked ahead to arrange the decorative details of her death. She had drawn up explicit instructions more than a year before: who the pallbearers were to be, and what accessories they should wear (pearl-gray gloves and ties); which clergymen should officiate at her funeral; which hymns should be sung, and by whom (her favorite, "Lead, Kindly Light," should be sung first); how her body should be dressed (in the pale blue matinée she had worn on her anniversary, with a silver bead necklace). Right before the funeral service began, her physician was to place a bouquet of lilies-of-the-valley in her hand. She even instructed her friends about expressing their emotions: there were to be no outward signs of sorrow, no tears. She was happy finally to be with her lost mother, and the friends who had gone before her, and to be free of the pain and immobility that had marked her life. Her funeral should not be an occasion of sadness.

Mollie was buried on February 15, 1916, a snowy day not quite two weeks after her golden jubilee. Her grave in the Fancher family plot at Green-Wood Cemetery in Brooklyn lay between that of the mother she had so often missed, and that of her aunt Susan, who became her second mother, presiding over her permanent childhood. Nearby were the graves of two prominent nineteenth-century figures, Horace Greeley, longtime editor of the *New-York Tribune,* and Samuel F. B. Morse, of Morse code and telegraph fame.

When Mollie died, the psychoanalytic movement, with its theories of neurosis and repression, was sufficiently established for Freud to have written a history of it. William Hammond, dead only a decade and a half, was well on his way to being forgotten. George Beard's name was fading too, but not his ideas. Within the next decade, the novelist Sinclair Lewis would create, in George Babbitt, one of the first of many striving "nervous Americans" to appear in twentieth-century popular culture.

Spiritualism had long declined, shamed by the exposure of its progenitors, the Fox sisters, as frauds. And fasting girls were no more— although soon a new incentive for self-denial and food refusal would arise, when flappers popularized a thin, boyish figure for women. Fifty years later, the increasingly urgent desire for thinness would lead to a virtual epidemic of anorexia nervosa. This time no one would imagine, even for a moment, that these starving girls were wise or divine or in touch with the spirit world.

Mollie Fancher herself would soon be forgotten. The age of neurosis had begun.

Notes

Complete citations for works cited only partially may be found in the Bibliography.

PREFACE

Most of the details about Henry Tanner's fast come from articles in *The New York Times*, which wrote about the spectacle every day between July 4 and August 12, 1880. Many other New York dailies reported regularly on Tanner's experiment as well.

CHAPTER ONE

Much of Mollie Fancher's early life as described here—her appearance, family history, accidents, and so on—derives from chapters 3 through 5 of Abram Dailey's 1894 biography *Mollie Fancher, the Brooklyn Enigma.* Various newspapers—among them *The New York Times, The Sun,* the *New York Herald, The Brooklyn Daily Eagle, The Buffalo Daily Courier*—published details of her story in November and December 1878, the period of her greatest fame. Descriptions of daily life in Brooklyn in the latter half of the nineteenth century can be found in Margaret Latimer's *Two Cities;* local newspapers from the period also serve as a rich source. The mortality information for the week of June 5–11, 1865, is from *The Brooklyn Daily Eagle* of June 12, 1865.

Rollo May's comments are from page 32 of *The Meaning of Anxiety,* and

Stephen Ambrose's from page 357 of *Nothing Like It in the World*. Descriptions of railway neurosis and lawsuits are from George Frederick Drinka's *The Birth of Neurosis,* pages 109–122. The Greenwood horsecar accident is described in the June 30, 1866, *Brooklyn Daily Times,* and the Catherine Powers incident in *The Brooklyn Daily Union* of October 23, 1866. "The Infelicities of Local Travel" also ran in the June 30, 1866, *Brooklyn Daily Times.* "Rapid Transit: Serio-Comic Aspect of Elevated Railroad Traveling" was published in the *New York Herald* on December 21, 1878. The characterization of railway spine as a classical Victorian neurosis derives from Drinka's *The Birth of Neurosis.*

Sylvester Graham's words are quoted in Hillel Schwartz's *Never Satisfied: A Cultural History of Diets, Fantasies & Fat,* page 25; John Harvey Kellogg's remarks are from his *Rules for "Right Living."* George Beard's "Evolution of Nervousness" tree appears on the frontispiece of his *American Nervousness.* He lays out his theories of the causes of nervousness in the preface to that book, pages iii–v. The 1873 quotation about young misses' appetites is from *The Ways of Women in Their Physical, Moral and Intellectual Relations,* pages 114–115; the observations about dyspepsia are on page 168. The *Daily Eagle* article on the Brooklyn Heights Seminary graduation appeared on June 22, 1866. Beard's comments on girls' schooling are from *American Nervousness,* pages 314–315. The *Daily Eagle* article on Mollie and her schoolgirl days ran on June 7, 1866.

Genealogical information on Mollie's family comes from William Hoyt Fancher's *The Fancher Family,* page 71; the U.S. Census; and nineteenth-century street directories. Background and quotations about infant mortality and mother-child relationships are from Nancy Schrom Dye and Daniel Blake Smith's "Mother Love and Infant Death, 1750–1920." Hope Edelman's observations about losing a mother are from page xxiii of *Motherless Daughters.*

The details about Elizabeth Barrett Browning are from Julia Markus's *Dared and Done: The Marriage of Elizabeth Barrett and Robert Browning* and Drinka's *The Birth of Neurosis,* pages 297–300. Silas Weir Mitchell's rest cure is also described in Drinka, pages 200–201. Beard's antidotes are presented in *American Nervousness,* pages 201–202 and 313–314. The *Brooklyn Daily Union* article on physical education is dated November 16, 1866. Alice James's physical tribulations are described in Drinka, pages 315–318; in Howard Feinstein's "The Use and Abuse of Illness in the James Family Circle"; and throughout *Alice James: A Biography,* by Jean Strouse. The quotations from Charles Fayette Taylor appear in Strouse, pages 107–108. Abram Dailey recounts Mollie's accidents and injuries in chapters 3 and 4 of his biography. Edward Shorter's observations are from his *From Paralysis to Fatigue,* page x.

CHAPTER TWO

Historical details about Brooklyn in the nineteenth century and earlier come from *Francis's New Hand-Book for the Cities of New-York and Brooklyn and the Vicinity*; Jeremiah Johnson Jr.'s *Recollections of Old Roads, Residents and Their Occupations*; Margaret Latimer's *Two Cities, New York and Brooklyn the Year the Great Bridge Opened*; Henry Stiles's *A History of the City of Brooklyn*; and *Brooklyn Daily Eagle* articles from the period. Genealogical information is from Fancher's *The Fancher Family,* pages 7–8, 71; the U.S. Census; and Brooklyn street directories. An account of the first few months after Mollie's accident can be found in chapter 4 of Dailey's biography.

"The great neurosis" is mentioned in Mark Micale's *Approaching Hysteria: Disease and Its Interpretations,* as are the historical details about hysteria through the seventeenth century (pages 3, 19–21). All of the citations from Austin's *Perils of American Women* in this chapter are from pages 188–189; citations of Dixon are from *Woman and Her Diseases,* pages 132–134 and 138. The Pierre Briquet data is from Shorter's *From Paralysis to Fatigue,* pages 97–98. Pierre Janet's descriptions of hysterical symptoms are found throughout his *Major Symptoms of Hysteria* (each chapter is devoted to a group of symptoms); his mention of Mollie Fancher occurs on pages 84–85. The various symptoms during the first year of Mollie's illness are described in Dailey's biography, chapters 4 through 7.

Silas Weir Mitchell discusses the gastrointestinal symptoms of hysteria in his *Lectures on Diseases of the Nervous System, Especially in Women,* pages 201–216. Information given here on Jean-Martin Charcot can be found in Drinka, *The Birth of Neurosis,* pages 74–114, and in Shorter, *From Paralysis to Fatigue,* pages 172–194. The two examples of bed cases, aged twenty and seventeen, are also in Shorter, pages 106 and 114; descriptions of various paralyses are on pages 108–115. Carroll Smith-Rosenberg is quoted from pages 655–656, 659, and 672 of her article "The Hysterical Woman: Sex Roles and Role Conflict in 19th-Century America." Shorter's ideas on family dynamics appear on pages 120–125 of *From Paralysis to Fatigue.* Feinstein is cited from "The Use and Abuse of Illness in the James Family Circle," page 236.

Mitchell's comment on "bed-cases" is from page 218 of his *Lectures on Diseases of the Nervous System.* The narrative of Mollie's treatments is in chapter 4 of

Dailey's biography. William James's description of blistering appears in Feinstein's article cited above, as does Alice James's letter about electrotherapy (both on page 241). Mesmerism is described in Shorter, *From Paralysis to Fatigue*, pages 134–135.

Dailey details Mollie's nine-year trance and her multiple personalities in chapters 9 through 13 of his biography. Shorter writes of the *London Medical Gazette* case in *From Paralysis to Fatigue* on page 130, and of multiple-personality disorder on pages 159–164. Anthony Walsh's remarks are from "Mollie Fancher . . . The Brooklyn Enigma." Smith-Rosenberg's comment about psychoanalysis can be found on page 652 of her article cited above. Discussion of the Anna O. case appears in Drinka, *The Birth of Neurosis*, pages 326–328; in Ronald W. Clark, *Freud: The Man and the Cause*, pages 100–107; and in Ilza Veith, *Hysteria: The History of a Disease*, pages 257–261. The decline of florid hysteria and Charcot's theories are discussed in Drinka, page 150; in Shorter, pages 98 and 196–200; and in Micale's *Approaching Hysteria*, pages 169–175.

CHAPTER THREE

Both "Neighborly Amenities" and "Tragedy in St. Louis" appeared in the May 11, 1864, *Brooklyn Daily Eagle*. Mollie's eye problems and second sight are described in chapters 4, 15, 21, and 22 of Dailey's biography. Examples of hysterical transposition of the senses are found in Shorter's *From Paralysis to Fatigue*, pages 137–139 and 160. Anecdotes of Mollie's clairvoyance appear throughout Dailey; in chapter 9 she speaks of her visits to "heavenly places" and of her refusal to be a medium.

The first *Buffalo Daily Courier* article about the art loan exhibition, which mentioned Mollie's work, is dated October 2, 1878; other notable stories about her ran in the paper on October 22 and November 10. The long *New York Herald* article about Mollie's case appeared on October 20, and its editorial "Hysteria" on November 17. Reaction to *The Sun*'s front-page story ran in the Brooklyn *Daily Eagle* and *Union-Argus,* and the New York *Evening Post, World, Tribune,* and *Times* on November 25, the same day *The Sun* featured its interview of Hammond.

CHAPTER FOUR

Much of the biographical material about Hammond, as well as important perspective on the changing nature of neurology in the late nineteenth century, comes from Bonnie Ellen Blustein's Ph.D. thesis, "A New York Medical Man: William Alexander Hammond, M.D. (1828–1900), Neurologist." "One of the best known medical men" is from Blustein (page 1), as are Hammond's comments about his arrival in New York (page 12). Jack Key's *William Alexander Hammond, M.D.* offers biographical details and describes Hammond's personality.

The story of Hammond's dismissal from the Army is told by Blustein, pages 75–111, and Key, pages 22–25, and by Hammond himself in his self-published *Statement of the Causes Which Led to the Dismissal of Surgeon-General William A. Hammond from the Army*. Information on the changing nature of neurology can be found in Walter Bromberg's *Man Above Humanity: A History of Psychotherapy,* pages 146–160. Hammond's role in the shift is particularly illuminated in Blustein, pages 2, 15–16, 122–130, 168, 185, and 254. Key supplies many examples of Hammond's personal manner and habits, and recounts the Grissom incident (mentioned also in Blustein and in *The Buffalo Daily Courier,* November 9, 1878). Dr. Roosa's comments at Hammond's memorial are from a New York Post-Graduate Medical School publication of 1900.

The comments about Hammond's challenge quoted from daily newspapers—the New York *Tribune, Sun,* and *Herald; The Brooklyn Daily Eagle*—were published between November 26 and December 19, 1878.

CHAPTER FIVE

Hammond's "joining the theologians" remark is in Blustein's "A New York Medical Man," page 248. Most of the biographical information on George Beard comes from A. D. Rockwell's *The Late Dr. George M. Beard: A Sketch* and *Rambling Recollections: An Autobiography,* and Charles L. Dana's *Dr. George M. Beard: A Sketch of His Life and Character.*

The handwritten letter from Rockwell to Dana about Beard's moral and religious ideas is found between the pages of the New York Academy of Medicine Library's copy of Rockwell's *Sketch,* which is filed in the Academy's Rare Book Room. Rockwell describes Beard's character on pages 182–190 of *Rambling Recollections*; anecdotes about his sense of humor appear on pages 197 and 209–210. Dana's comment about "a continual undercurrent of humor" is on page 3 of his own *Sketch,* as is his description of Beard's placid personality.

Rockwell relates his work with Beard on electrotherapy and their professional breakup in *Rambling Recollections,* pages 192–193 and 210–214. Beard's description of electrotherapy appears in his 1869 article "Neurasthenia, or Nervous Exhaustion," in *The Boston Medical and Surgical Journal.*

Beard wrote about the scientific process in his 1880 booklet *What Constitutes a Discovery in Science.* His article on Mollie, "The Scientific Lessons of the Mollie Fancher Case," was published in the November 30, 1878, issue of *The Medical*

Record. Beard's interview with *The Sun* appeared on the front page of the newspaper on November 26, 1878, under the headline "The Case of Miss Fancher: 'If She Can Do All This, Then All Science Goes for Naught.'" Professor West's rebuttal of Beard was printed in *The Sun* on November 27, 1878, in the article "Miss Fancher's Friends: Unshaken in Their Belief by the Skeptical New York Doctors."

The unsigned *Brooklyn Daily Union-Argus* item appeared in the November 27, 1878, issue; the paper's comments about a "woefully deceived" party were made on December 24 of that year. Edwin Carr's letter to the editor was published in the December 29, 1878, issue of *The Brooklyn Daily Eagle.* Speculum's first letter to the editor was printed in the *New York Herald* on December 21, 1878, and M.H.'s questions about the Bible, Moses and the prophets, and so on were raised in the paper's January 5, 1879, edition.

Beard wrote about trance states in his *Nature and Phenomena of Trance*; the passages quoted here are on pages 10 and 11. His descriptions of neurasthenia are from the 1869 article cited above, as are his contentions that the condition is caused by underlying molecular disturbances and that all insanity is based on physical morbidity. In *American Nervousness,* a much more complete work, he presented his major theories in the preface and in chapter 1. "Civil and religious liberty" appears on page 123; "The eyes are good barometers" on page 44; "The excessive nervousness . . . gout and rheumatism" on page 57; "Relation of Nervousness to Beauty" on pages 65–66. Perspectives past and present on Beard's work are discussed in Charles Rosenberg's "The Place of George M. Beard in Nineteenth-Century Psychiatry."

CHAPTER SIX

The passages from Marion Harland's *Eve's Daughters* are from pages 147–148 and 153. Details on dinner-table etiquette are from Susan Williams, *Savory Suppers and Fashionable Feasts: Dining in Victorian America,* chapters 1 and 2. "How to Make Formal Calls" ran in the *Brooklyn Daily Union-Argus* on December 30, 1878. The *Woman's Home Companion* anecdote is cited in Laura Shapiro, *Perfection Salad,* as is "Foods That Tickle the Feminine Palate" (pages 73, 101). Joan Jacobs Brumberg writes about Victorians and meat on pages 176–177 of *Fasting Girls,* and Walter Vandereycken and Ron Van Deth discuss Victorian sexuality on pages 203–204 of *From Fasting Saints to Anorexic Girls.* The female health specialist who wrote of low appetites and perverted passions was Elizabeth Blackwell, M.D., in *The Laws of Life, with Special Reference to the Physical Education of Girls,* page 17.

Brumberg, pages 172–174, and Vandereycken and Van Deth, pages 140–142 and 243–244, provide background on chlorosis. Dixon presented his case of chlorosis in *Woman and Her Diseases*, pages 129–130, and the symptoms are listed on pages 71–72. Harland's comments on plumpness appear on page 124 of *Eve's Daughters*. "Horror of Fat" is found on page 115 of *The Ways of Women*. Nancy Theriot wrote about chlorosis in "Psychosomatic Illness in History: The 'Green Sickness' Among Nineteenth-Century Adolescent Girls" (citations are from pages 465 and 467). Vandereycken and Van Deth's discussion of Victorian womanhood is on pages 196–197 of *From Fasting Saints to Anorexic Girls*. Harland writes about boarding school food on page 142 of *Eve's Daughters*, and the quotation about schoolgirls' underfeeding is from Anna Brackett's *The Education of American Girls*, page 28. Blackwell describes a schoolgirl's regimen in *The Laws of Life*, pages 132–134. Theriot discusses Victorian mothers and daughters in "Psychosomatic Illness in History," pages 468–473.

The quotations from William Chipley are from his article "Sitomania: Its Causes and Treatment," pages 8–10 and 19–22. The texts of William Gull's two articles about anorexia nervosa (1868 and 1873) are reprinted in Kaufman and Heiman, *Evolution of Psychosomatic Concepts*, pages 107–131 and 132–138, respectively. Charles-Ernest Lasègue's descriptions of anorexia can be found in his article "On Hysterical Anorexia." Vandereycken and Van Deth discuss Gull's and Lasègue's backgrounds, and their competition over anorexia nervosa, on pages 154–161 of *From Fasting Saints to Anorexic Girls*. The *Diagnostic and Statistical Manual of Mental Disorders, Fourth Edition* (*DSM-IV*) describes anorexia nervosa on pages 583–589. The quotation from Frank Bruno's *Family Mental Health Encyclopedia* is from page 18.

CHAPTER SEVEN

Background on starvation is from Raymond Battegay, *Hunger Diseases,* and most of the physiological details are from an interview with C. Wayne Callaway, M.D., an endocrinologist and weight-disorders specialist at George Washington University. Information about the Warsaw ghetto studies is from Myron Winick, ed., *Hunger Disease: Studies by the Jewish Physicians in the Warsaw Ghetto* (pages vii–viii, ix–x, 3–5, 9, 14–19, 23, 25, 27, 36, 43). Details from Ancel Keys's research are cited in Frances Berg, *Health Risks of Weight Loss,* pages 140–143.

Case histories and quotations from L. S. Forbes Winslow's *Fasting and Feeding* can be found on pages 10–13, 18–19, and 22–25. The story of Hattie Duell's death was recounted in *The New York Times* on April 13, 1881. Information about Saint Catherine of Siena is from David Rampling, "Ascetic Ideals and Anorexia Nervosa," pages 89–92, and Jules Bemporad, "Self-Starvation Through the Ages," page 222. Mollie's statements about her eating are from Dailey's *Mollie Fancher, the Brooklyn Enigma*, page 22. Hilde Bruch describes the thought processes of the modern anorexic in *The Golden Cage*, pages 3–19. Rudolph Bell presents his central ideas about the similarities between holy and nervous anorexia on pages 20–21 of *Holy Anorexia*, while Joan Jacobs Brumberg discusses the distinction between the two on pages 42–46 of *Fasting Girls*.

Richard Morton's description of "nervous consumption" from his *Phthisiologia* is cited in Joseph Silverman, "Richard Morton, 1637–1698, Limner of Anorexia Nervosa," pages 83–84. Information on "miraculous fasting maids" can be found in Bemporad, "Self-Starvation Through the Ages," pages 223–225; in Brumberg's *Fasting Girls*, chapter 2; and in Vandereycken and Van Deth's *From Fasting Saints to Anorexic Girls*, chapter 4. The Ann Moore story is told in *A Full Exposure of Ann Moore*. The Jacob case is covered in Brumberg, pages 64–73; in Vandereycken and Van Deth, pages 65–73: and in Hammond, *Fasting Girls: Their Physiology and Pathology*, pages 13–31. William Davis's comments are from pages 181–182 of Bell, *Holy Anorexia*.

CHAPTER EIGHT

The Reverend Dr. Hugh S. Carpenter was quoted in the December 2, 1878, issues of *The Sun*, the *Brooklyn Daily Union-Argus*, and *The New York Times*; "A Husband for Miss Fancher" was an item in *The World* on November 29, 1878. The *Daily Union-Argus* reported on December 21, 1878, that admission was being charged to see Mollie Fancher. *The Sun's* interview with Professor Buchanan was published on December 8, 1878; Buchanan described his philosophy of psychometry in *Outlines of Lectures on the Neurological System of Anthropology*, pages 3–5. *The New York Times* and *The Sun* reported on Buchanan's December 28 lecture on December 29, 1878; the *New-York Tribune* and *Brooklyn Daily Union-Argus* on December 30.

R. Laurence Moore describes the birth of Spiritualism in *In Search of White Crows*, pages 7–8, and Elizabeth Stuart Phelps (Ward) writes of its popularity in "The Psychical Wave," pages 377–378 and 384–386. The *Herald* piece on spirit communications was published on June 11, 1866, and the *Brooklyn Daily Times* review of the Spiritualist Society publication ran on June 28, 1866.

Edward Brown presents an insightful account of Beard's and Hammond's battles with Spiritualism in "Neurology and Spiritualism in the 1870s," pages 566–568 and 572–575. Hammond's comment on "fetish-worshipping" is from *The Physics and Physiology of Spiritualism,* page 9. Beard defines trance in *Nature and Phenomena of Trance,* pages 5, 10, and 18.

Ernst Mayr is quoted from his introduction to a facsimile edition of *On the Origin of Species,* page vii. Biographical information on Darwin is from Maitland Edey and Donald Johanson, *Blueprints,* pages 62–63, 70–73, and 84–85. Leslie Stephen's observations are found on pages 190, 192, 199, 200, and 202 of "Darwinism and Divinity"; Stuart Phelps's on page 381 of "The Psychical Wave." A. N. Wilson's remarks about Hume and the Victorian spiritual crisis are from *God's Funeral,* pages 24–25. Edward Reed writes about nineteenth-century science and psychology in *From Soul to Mind*; the passages quoted are from pages 1–3. The characterization of Beard as a pioneer in the study of neuroses is from Rosenberg, "The Place of George M. Beard in Nineteenth-Century Psychiatry."

CHAPTER NINE

Details of Mollie Fancher's bedchamber and social encounters occur throughout Dailey's biography, with the anecdotes cited here mentioned on pages 112, 240–242, and 247. Thomas Townsend's story about the "'ologies" appeared in *The Sun* on November 28, 1878. Descriptions of New Year's Eve 1878, as well as talk of the winter storm, current fashions, and rapid transit, can be found in the Brooklyn *Daily Eagle* and *Daily Times* of January 2 through 8, 1879. Information about Edison's lights is from Robert Friedel and Paul Israel, *Edison's Electric Light,* introduction and pages 1–8; *The Brooklyn Daily Eagle,* January 5 and 14, 1879; and *The Sun,* January 27, 1879. The St. Benoit Twins story ran in the *Daily Eagle* on January 5, 1879. Accounts of the Cobb–Bishop murder trial are from the *Daily Eagle,* January 2 and 5, 1879, and *The Sun,* January 8, 12, 15, 17, and 18.

The Tanner story derives largely from coverage in *The New York Times,* December 31, 1879, and July 4 through August 12, 1880; some information is from the *New York Herald,* July 12 and August 5 through 8, 1880. Background on the Regulars and the Eclectics is from Paul Starr, *The Social Transformation of American Medicine,* pages 90–99.

CHAPTER TEN

Citations from the *DSM-IV* on conversion disorder and dissociative disorders are from pages 492–498 and 519–529. Walsh describes the isolated X-personality in his paper "Mollie Fancher . . . The Brooklyn Enigma." Paul McHugh's remarks are from the article "Multiple Personality Disorder"; Shorter is quoted from pages 159–160 of *From Paralysis to Fatigue*. The survey about DID appeared under the title "Attitudes Toward DSM-IV Dissociative Disorders Diagnoses Among Board-Certified American Psychiatrists" in the February 1999 issue of *The American Journal of Psychiatry* (vol. 156, no. 2, pages 321–323). Walsh refers to the Lady of Belisle and the Sleeping Preacher in his article on Mollie Fancher, cited above.

Elaine Showalter is quoted from *Hystories*, pages 4–9; she cites Robert Woolsey and Mark Micale (hysteria as an iconic social communication) on page 7. Beard gives his five causes of nervousness in the preface to *American Nervousness*. David Bell lists the symptoms of CFS on pages 10–11 of his *Doctor's Guide to Chronic Fatigue Syndrome*; other symptoms are mentioned in Hillary Johnson, *Osler's Web*, pages 359 and 718–719. Showalter discusses CFS in chapter 8 of *Hystories*, and quotes the Harvard Medical School researcher (Anthony Komaroff) on "paradigmatic illness" on page 117.

The commentary about *Death of a Salesman* appeared in *The New York Times* on February 28, 1999. Margaret Talbot's piece in the *Times Magazine* was published on June 24, 2001. A report on the Winnie-the-Pooh parody ran in *The New York Times* on February 4, 2001. Peter Kramer is quoted from *Listening to Prozac*, pages xvi, 18–19, and 250. "The Gospel According to Prozac" ran in the August 14, 1995, issue of *Christianity Today*. The "shopping for God" piece was published in *Vogue* in March 1995, and *Newsweek*'s cover story on yearning for the sacred was in the November 28, 1994, issue. Stephen Hawking poses his cosmic questions on pages 232–233 of *The Illustrated A Brief History of Time*. The quotations from Thomas Moore's *Care of the Soul* are found on pages xi and xv of his introduction. Kramer's predictions of the neurosis of the future are made on page 289 of *Listening to Prozac*.

CHAPTER ELEVEN

The descriptions of Mollie's eating habits and her prominence in the 1890s are from Dailey's biography, pages 119, 215–216, and 253. Background on hunger artists, as well as perspective on Kafka, can be found in chapter 5 of Vandereycken and Van Deth, *From Fasting Saints to Anorexic Girls*. Dailey's efforts on Mollie's behalf in the 1890s are described on pages 256–262 of his biography, and in two articles from *The Medico-Legal Journal*, both titled "The Case of Mollie Fancher" (the first in vol. 11, no. 1, 1893; the second in vol. 12, no. 1, 1894). His discussion of her physical state in 1894 is on pages 257–258 of his book.

Details of daily life in 1916 are derived from newspapers of the time. The quotations about the automobile are from *The Brooklyn Daily Eagle,* January 2 and 3, 1916; the photo of Mountain Chief is in the *Eagle,* February 12, 1916. The long article on Mollie's life and personality ran in the same paper on December 5, 1915. The story of her jubilee and her subsequent death and burial can be found in the *Eagle,* January 26 and February 3, 4, 10–12, and 14–15, 1916; and in *The New York Times,* November 13, 1915, and January 26 and February 4 and 12, 1916.

Bibliography

Ambrose, Stephen E. *Nothing Like It in the World: The Men Who Built the Transcontinental Railroad 1863–1869*. New York: Simon & Schuster, 2000.

Austin, G. L. *Perils of American Women, or A Doctor's Talk with Maiden, Wife, and Mother.* Boston: Lee and Shepard, 1883.

Battegay, Raymond. *Hunger Diseases*. Toronto: Hogrefe and Huber, 1991.

Beard, George. *American Nervousness, Its Causes and Consequences: A Supplement to Nervous Exhaustion*. New York: G. P. Putnam's Sons, 1881.

———. "Current Delusions Relating to Hypnotism (Artificial Trance)." Reprinted from *The Alienist and Neurologist*. St. Louis, January 1882.

———. *Nature and Phenomena of Trance*. New York: G. P. Putnam's Sons, 1881.

———. "Neurasthenia, or Nervous Exhaustion." *The Boston Medical and Surgical Journal,* vol. 3, no. 13 (April 29, 1869), p. 217.

———. *A Practical Treatise on Nervous Exhaustion (Neurasthenia), Its Symptoms, Nature, Sequences, Treatment*. New York: W. Wood, 1880.

———. "The Scientific Lessons of the Mollie Fancher Case." *The Medical Record,* vol. 14 (November 30, 1878), pp. 446–448.

———. *What Constitutes a Discovery in Science*. New York, 1880.

Bell, David S. *The Doctor's Guide to Chronic Fatigue Syndrome: Understanding, Treating, and Living with CFIDS*. Reading, MA: Addison-Wesley, 1995.

Bell, Rudolph. *Holy Anorexia*. Chicago: University of Chicago Press, 1985.

Bemporad, Jules R. "Self-Starvation Through the Ages: Reflections on the Pre-History of Anorexia Nervosa." *International Journal of Eating Disorders,* vol. 19, no. 3 (1996), pp. 217–237.

Berg, Frances M. *Health Risks of Weight Loss,* 3rd ed. Hettinger, ND: Healthy Weight Journal/Healthy Living Institute, 1992.

Blackwell, Elizabeth. *The Laws of Life, with Special Reference to the Physical Education of Girls.* New York: G. P. Putnam, 1852.

Blustein, Bonnie Ellen. "A New York Medical Man: William Alexander Hammond, M.D. (1828–1900), Neurologist." Ph.D. diss., University of Pennsylvania, 1979.

Brackett, Anna. *The Education of American Girls.* New York: G. P. Putnam's Sons, 1874.

Bromberg, Walter. *Man Above Humanity: A History of Psychotherapy.* Philadelphia: J. B. Lippincott, 1954.

Brown, Edward M. "Neurology and Spiritualism in the 1870s." *Bulletin of the History of Medicine,* vol. 57 (Winter 1983), pp. 562–577.

Bruch, Hilde. *The Golden Cage: The Enigma of Anorexia Nervosa.* New York: Vintage, 1979.

Brumberg, Joan Jacobs. *Fasting Girls: The History of Anorexia Nervosa.* New York: Plume, 1989.

Bruno, Frank. *The Family Mental Health Encyclopedia.* New York: John Wiley & Sons, 1989.

Buchanan, Joseph Rodes. *Outlines of Lectures on the Neurological System of Anthropology, as Discovered, Demonstrated and Taught in 1841 and 1842.* Cincinnati: Buchanan's Journal of Man, 1854.

Bunker, Henry Alden, Jr. "Symposium on Neurasthenia: From Beard to Freud, a Brief History of the Concept of Neurasthenia." *Medical Review of Reviews,* vol. 36 (1930), pp. 109–114.

Burnet, James B. "Cases of Chlorosis." *Medical and Surgical Reporter,* vol. 17 (July 27, 1867), pp. 71–72.

Carter, Paul A. *The Spiritual Crisis of the Gilded Age.* DeKalb: Northern Illinois University Press, 1971.

Chipley, William S. "Sitomania: Its Causes and Treatment." *American Journal of Insanity,* vol. 16, no. 1 (July 1859), pp. 1–42.

Clark, Ronald W. *Freud: The Man and the Cause, A Biography.* New York: Random House, 1980.

Clarke, James Freeman. "Have Animals Souls?" *The Atlantic Monthly,* vol. 34 (October 1874), p. 421.

Dailey, Abram H. *Mollie Fancher, the Brooklyn Enigma: An Authentic Statement of Facts in the Life of Mary J. Fancher, the Psychological Marvel of the Nineteenth Century.* Brooklyn, NY: Eagle Book Printing, 1894.

Dana, Charles L. *Dr. George M. Beard: A Sketch of his Life and Character, with Some Personal Reminiscences.* Chicago: American Medical Association, 1923.

Darwin, Charles. *On the Origin of Species.* Cambridge, MA: Harvard University Press, 1964 (facsimile of 1st ed.).

Diagnostic and Statistical Manual of Mental Disorders, Fourth Edition. Washington, DC: American Psychiatric Association, 2000.

Dixon, Edward H. *Woman and Her Diseases, from the Cradle to the Grave.* New York: A. Ranney, 1857.

Drinka, George Frederick. *The Birth of Neurosis: Myth, Malady, and the Victorians.* New York: Simon & Schuster, 1984.

Dye, Nancy Schrom, and Daniel Blake Smith. "Mother Love and Infant Death, 1750–1920." *The Journal of American History,* vol. 73 (September 1986), pp. 329–353.

Edelman, Hope. *Motherless Daughters.* New York: Addison-Wesley, 1994.

Edey, Maitland A., and Donald C. Johanson. *Blueprints: Solving the Mystery of Evolution.* Boston: Little, Brown, 1989.

Fancher, William Hoyt. *The Fancher Family.* Milford, NH: Cabinet Press, 1947.

"Fasting and Feeding." *Spectator,* vol. 64 (May 1890), pp. 618–619.

Feinstein, Howard M. "The Use and Abuse of Illness in the James Family Circle: A View of Neurasthenia as a Social Phenomenon." In Robert J. Brugger, ed., *Our Selves/Our Past: Psychological Approaches to American History,* pp. 228–243. Baltimore: Johns Hopkins University Press, 1981.

Francis's New Hand-Book for the Cities of New-York and Brooklyn and the Vicinity. New York: C. S. Francis, 1859.

Friedel, Robert, and Paul Israel. *Edison's Electric Light: Biography of an Invention.* New Brunswick, NJ: Rutgers University Press, 1986.

A Full Exposure of Ann Moore, the Pretended Fasting Woman of Tutbury, 3rd ed. London: Robert Baldwin and T. Wayte, 1813.

Hale, Nathan. *Freud and the Americans: The Beginning of Psychoanalysis in the U.S., 1876–1917.* New York: Oxford University Press, 1971.

Hammond, William A. *Fasting Girls: Their Physiology and Pathology.* New York: G. P. Putnam's Sons, 1879.

———. "The Physics and Physiology of Spiritualism." *North American Review,* vol. 110, no. 227 (April 1870), pp. 233–260.

———. *The Physics and Physiology of Spiritualism.* New York: D. Appleton, 1871.

———. *A Statement of the Causes Which Led to the Dismissal of Surgeon-General William A. Hammond from the Army; with a Review of the Evidence Adduced Before the Court.* New York, 1864.

———. *A Treatise on the Diseases of the Nervous System,* 9th ed. New York: D. Appleton, 1891.

Harland, Marion. *Eve's Daughters; or, Common Sense for Maid, Wife, and Mother.* New York: J. R. Anderson & H. S. Allen, 1882.

Hawking, Stephen. *The Illustrated A Brief History of Time.* New York: Bantam, 1996.

Janet, Pierre. *The Major Symptoms of Hysteria.* New York: Hafner, 1965 (facsimile of 1929 ed.).

Johnson, Hillary. *Osler's Web: Inside the Labyrinth of the Chronic Fatigue Syndrome Epidemic.* New York: Crown, 1996.

Johnson, Jeremiah, Jr. *Recollections of Old Roads, Residents and Their Occupations: The Past Contrasted with the Present.* Brooklyn, NY, 1894.

Kaufman, M. Ralph, and Marcel Heiman, eds. *Evolution of Psychosomatic Concepts; Anorexia Nervosa, a Paradigm.* New York: International Universities Press, 1964.

Kellogg, John Harvey. *Rules for "Right Living."* Battle Creek, MI: Health Extension Department, Battle Creek Sanitarium, 1935.

Key, Jack D. *William Alexander Hammond, M.D.* Rochester, MN: Davies, 1979.

Kramer, Peter D., *Listening to Prozac: A Psychiatrist Explores Antidepressant Drugs and the Remaking of the Self.* New York: Penguin, 1993.

Lasègue, Dr. [Charles-Ernest]. "On Hysterical Anorexia." *Archives Générales de Médecine,* April 1873.

Latimer, Margaret. *Two Cities, New York and Brooklyn the Year the Great Bridge Opened.* Brooklyn, NY: Brooklyn Educational and Cultural Alliance, 1983.

Lewis, C. R. "Elizabeth Barrett Browning's 'Family Disease': Anorexia Nervosa." *Journal of Marital and Family Therapy,* vol. 8 (1982), pp. 129–134.

McHugh, Paul R. "Multiple Personality Disorder." On Internet, at www.psycom.net/mchugh.html.

MacLeod, Sheila. *The Art of Starvation: A Story of Anorexia and Survival.* New York: Schocken, 1981.

Markus, Julia. *Dared and Done: The Marriage of Elizabeth Barrett and Robert Browning.* New York: Alfred A. Knopf, 1995.

May, Rollo. *The Meaning of Anxiety.* New York: W. W. Norton, 1977 (originally published 1950).

Micale, Mark S. *Approaching Hysteria: Disease and Its Interpretations.* Princeton, NJ: Princeton University Press, 1995.

Mitchell, Silas Weir. *Lectures on Diseases of the Nervous System, Especially in Women.* Philadelphia: Henry C. Lea's Son, 1881.

Moore, R. Laurence. *In Search of White Crows: Spiritualism, Parapsychology, and American Culture.* New York: Oxford University Press, 1977.

New York Post-Graduate Medical School and Hospital. *Record of a Memorial Meeting in Honor of the Late Surgeon General W. A. Hammond, Held Feb. 23, 1900.* Reprinted from *The Post-Graduate,* May 1900.

Noyes, J. C. "Prolonged Abstinence from Food." *The Boston Medical and Surgical Journal,* vol. 103 (August 5, 1880).

Phelps, Elizabeth Stuart. "The Psychical Wave." *The Forum,* vol. 1 (June 1886), pp. 377–388.

Playfair, W. S. *Systematic Treatment of Nerve Prostration and Hysteria.* London: Smith and Elder, 1883.

Rampling, David. "Ascetic Ideals and Anorexia Nervosa." *Journal of Psychiatric Research,* vol. 19, no. 2/3 (1985), pp. 89–94.

Reed, Edward S. *From Soul to Mind: The Emergence of Psychology from Erasmus Darwin to William James.* New Haven, CT: Yale University Press, 1997.

Richmond, Legh. *A Statement of Facts, Relative to the Supposed Abstinence of Ann Moore, of Tutbury, Staffordshire.* Burton-on-Trent, England: J. Croft, 1813.

Rockwell, A. D. *The Late Dr. George M. Beard: A Sketch.* New York, 1883.

————. *Rambling Recollections: An Autobiography.* New York: Paul B. Hoeber, 1920.

Rosenberg, Charles E. "The Place of George M. Beard in Nineteenth-Century Psychiatry." *Bulletin of the History of Medicine,* vol. 36 (1962), pp. 245–259.

Schwartz, Hillel. *Never Satisfied: A Cultural History of Diets, Fantasies & Fat.* New York: Anchor/Doubleday, 1986.

Shapiro, Laura. *Perfection Salad: Women and Cooking at the Turn of the Century.* New York: Farrar, Straus & Giroux, 1986.

Shorter, Edward. *From Paralysis to Fatigue: A History of Psychosomatic Illness in the Modern Era.* New York: The Free Press, 1992.

Showalter, Elaine. *Hystories: Hysterical Epidemics and Modern Media.* New York: Columbia University Press, 1997.

Silverman, Joseph A. "Richard Morton, 1637–1698, Limner of Anorexia Nervosa: His Life and Times." *Journal of Psychiatric Research,* vol. 19, no. 2/3 (1985), pp. 83–88.

Smith-Rosenberg, Carroll. "The Hysterical Woman: Sex Roles and Role Conflict in 19th-Century America." *Social Research,* vol. 39, no. 4 (Winter 1972), pp. 652–678.

Starr, Paul. *The Social Transformation of American Medicine.* New York: Basic Books, 1982.

Stephen, Leslie. "Darwinism and Divinity." *The Popular Science Monthly,* June 1872, pp. 188–202.

Stiles, Henry R. *A History of the City of Brooklyn.* Bowie, MD: Heritage Books, 1993 (facsimile of 1867 ed.).

Strouse, Jean. *Alice James: A Biography.* Boston: Houghton Mifflin, 1980.

Theriot, Nancy. "Psychosomatic Illness in History: The 'Green Sickness' Among Nineteenth-Century Adolescent Girls." *The Journal of Psychohistory,* vol. 15, no. 4 (Spring 1988), pp. 461–480.

Vandereycken, Walter, and Ron Van Deth. *From Fasting Saints to Anorexic Girls: The History of Self-Starvation.* New York: New York University Press, 1994.

Veith, Ilza. *Hysteria: The History of a Disease.* Chicago: University of Chicago Press, 1965.

Walsh, Anthony A. "Mollie Fancher . . . The Brooklyn Enigma." *Newport, The Magazine of Newport College—Salve Regina,* vol. 1, no. 2 (1978). Reprinted on Internet, at http://inside.salve.edu/walsh/mollie.html.

The Ways of Women in Their Physical, Moral and Intellectual Relations. By a Medical Man. New York: John P. Jewett, 1873.

Williams, Susan. *Savory Suppers and Fashionable Feasts: Dining in Victorian America.* New York: Pantheon, 1985.

Wilson, A. N. *God's Funeral.* New York: W. W. Norton, 1999.

Winick, Myron, ed. *Hunger Disease: Studies by the Jewish Physicians in the Warsaw Ghetto.* New York: John Wiley & Sons, 1979.

Winslow, Lyttelton Stewart Forbes. *Fasting and Feeding Psychologically Considered.* London: Bailliere, Tindall & Cox, 1881.

Acknowledgments

I first came across an account of Mollie Fancher a decade ago, while researching my previous book, *Consumed.* I have wanted to tell her story ever since.

From the start, two people were as convinced as I was that the Brooklyn Enigma was a page of history that deserved to be a volume: my agent, Elizabeth Kaplan, and my husband (and excellent editor), David Schonauer. They remained convinced through several intermittent Mollie Fancher scenarios—even a short-lived concept of *The Fasting Girl* as a novel—and through proposals to editors who just didn't get it. I will always be grateful to both of them for getting it right away, and for encouraging me to try one more time.

The final time I pitched *The Fasting Girl,* I was galvanized by Susan Chumsky, among the most clever and insightful magazine editors I have ever worked with. Susan too got it, and urged me to float the idea once more. When I did, I had the good luck, through Elizabeth Kaplan's efforts, to meet Wendy Hubbert, the best book editor one could dream up, who not only got it but also cajoled me, in the nicest possible way, to write a far clearer and more seamless narrative than I could have accomplished on my own (aided by the sensitive and thorough copyediting of Anna Jardine).

Researching and writing *The Fasting Girl* has been one of the most pleasurable, yet also one of the most solitary, endeavors I have undertaken. Despite that solitude, I have been supported throughout by the efforts and ideas of others. My thanks go to archival researcher Sybil Brabner for her detailed canvassing of the Fancher family and the assorted characters in Mollie's life; to William Dubin for his enlightenment on psychology and dissociation; to C. Wayne Callaway for his expert descriptions of metabolism and starvation; to Joan Jacobs Brumberg for her examination of fasting girls, and for introducing me to Mollie in her book *Fasting Girls;* and to the many patient and helpful staff members at the libraries I haunted for months: the New York Public Library (particularly the newspaper archive/microform room, the genealogy collection, and the map room), the Brooklyn Public Library (its local collection), the New York Academy of Medicine Library (especially the Rare Book Room, where I enjoyed the thrill of discovering A. D. Rockwell's handwritten letter tucked into a more-than-century-old book), the New-York Historical Library, and my own local Larchmont Public Library, where patient staff routinely had to roust me from my study carrel at closing time.

This book would also not have been written without my reliance on steadfast personal resources: friends in the writing business who offered perspective in the face of my numerous frustrations and fears (in particular, Cathy Cavender, Kathy Rich, and Kathy Samon), friends at Aroma who endured my daily updates on pages written and midnight oil burned, and most of all, my family. I am unendingly grateful to my husband for his painstaking and perceptive reading of the entire manuscript, as well as his tolerance of my deadline-induced frenzy, and to my children, Anna and Henry, for their continuing enthusiasm for the project despite the fact that it sometimes forced the absence—not to mention the absentmindedness—of their mother.

To my parents I owe special thanks, and thus I dedicate this book to them. I could never have dreamed of *The Fasting Girl* had I not grown up in a home crowded with books of literature and history, in a milieu where ideas mattered, and most important, among people who believed I could do anything I set out to do.

About the Author

Michelle Stacey, the author of *Consumed: Why Americans Love, Hate, and Fear Food,* is a journalist who has written for *The New Yorker, The New York Times Magazine, Elle,* and many other publications. She lives in Larchmont, New York.